# D I S C L A I M E R

The information and ideas in this book are for educational and instructional purposes, and are not intended as prescriptive advice.

*For Paul, Jenny and James*

# ACKNOWLEDGMENTS

I would like to thank VeloPress and all its editors who contributed expertise to this book. Thank you, as well, to all the athletes who took the time to provide their insightful comments regarding sports nutrition. And thanks to all the photographers and to Saturn Cycling, GT Bicycles and Trek Bicycles for their great photographs.

# TABLE OF CONTENTS

# INTRODUCTION

## A guide to using this book

It's true! Sports nutrition can benefit any active person pursuing a healthy, energized lifestyle. Whether you are moderately active, regularly attending a health club, cross-training, strength-training, training for endurance events, or preparing seriously for any type of competition, you can benefit from the sports nutrition guidelines provided in this book.

Proper nutrition will help you complete your first 10km race, maintain energy during a soccer match or volleyball game, power your efforts at jumping and grace in figure skating, and provide fuel for achieving a personal best in an International distance triathlon. The recommendations in this book are for anyone at any fitness level. They can be used by the avid high school athlete, young adults who train seriously, devoted master's athletes, and elite athletes who desire to fine-tune their diets for top performance.

You may train for sheer enjoyment, team spirit, camaraderie, optimal health, or to simply bring out and perform your best. Whether your program is more relaxed and spontaneous, or highly structured, the sports nutrition guidelines that fuel your desired level of performance also promote good health.

Diverse types of sports and athletic goals have their own unique nutrition requirements. If you understand the body

*Lunch break on cross-country ski tour.*

fuel sources used for workouts of various intensities and duration in any sport, you can determine what foods and amounts are appropriate for you. Combined with a good training program, proper equipment, hard work, a good attitude, and making the most of your genes (which you can't change), food and sports nutrition supplements play an important role in making you a winner-in your own eyes and on your own terms, and perhaps even at the highest level.

To help you develop your personal nutrition requirements and goals based on accurate and up-to-date science, and take practical steps in embracing these nutrition guidelines, this book has been organized into several sections.

### PART I: ENERGY FOR ATHLETIC PERFORMANCE

Very basic exercise physiology is covered, along with the body energy systems used at varying intensities and duration of exercise. A brief outline of the optimal sports diet then introduces the more in-depth information presented in the remainder of the book.

## Part II: your optimal training diet

This section describes, clarifies, and translates the latest research on carbohydrate, fat, and protein requirements for training. Vitamin and mineral needs are also covered, as are antioxidants and phytochemicals, because of their growing role in maintaining good health and preventing disease. Supplementation suggestions are provided.

## Part III: creating the optimal training diet

Being familiar with the most current and valid sports nutrition guidelines based on sound research is only the beginning. You need to know how to put these guidelines into action. This section is filled with practical advice regarding food choices, food groups, meal planning, shopping, and eating away from home. It is designed to take you beyond theory and into the real world of devising, preparing and consuming your optimal training diet.

## Part IV: pre-exercise and competition nutrition

Exercise and serious training requires specific nutritional strategies, which take place before and during exercise. Requirements may vary depending on exercise intensity and duration.

Special considerations for competition day are also covered.

## Part V: body weight, body fat, and your diet

Weight management issues, whether they involve muscle gain, or losing body fat, are relevant to most active individuals and athletes. Body composition testing and levels are discussed. Most importantly, healthy weight loss techniques that do not compromise energy for training and overall good health are provided. The dangers of inappropriate dieting, disordered eating and becoming too lean are also addressed.

### PART VI: NUTRITIONAL ERGOGENIC AIDS

Sifting through the information behind the marketing of nutritional ergogenic aids can be complex and bewildering. This section provides guidelines on becoming a better-informed consumer. Popular ergogenic aids are reviewed in view of supportive research and safety issues.

### PART VII: SPECIAL NUTRIENT NEEDS

Topics pertinent to exercise, training and good health are covered in this section. For instance, some athletes may be interested in the unique nutritional needs of training at altitude. Others may want to adopt or currently follow a vegetarian diet. Some additional concerns may be recovering from an injury, muscle cramping, and the specific nutritional needs of pregnancy and exercise.

— *Monique Ryan*

# PART I

# ENERGY
# FOR
# PERFORMANCE

# CHAPTER ONE

# Fueling Your Fire:
## *The Body's Energy Systems*

> "There are many training, ergogenic, and diet strategies that will enhance performance. But nothing will overcome the need to train well."
>
> — *Norman Alvis, Saturn Cycling Team,*
> *1995 U.S. professional road champion*

It's your first triathlon. The swim is over, and you are confidently riding your bike. You decide to test your limits and finish the cycling leg ahead of schedule. Encouraged by your performance thus far, you begin the run. But about halfway through, your muscles are burning. You need to slow down in order to both minimize the pain and finish the triathlon.

For the athlete, energy is everything. At times, training and competing in your sport requires tremendous amounts of effort. That's why one important, performance-determining factor is optimal energy production-or power output-either over a designated distance or when performing a specific skill. An athlete who completes a triathlon in the shortest amount

3

of time finishes first. The pole-vaulter who jumps highest wins. A figure skater with the greatest amount of power and grace receives the highest marks. A soccer player who can repeatedly perform short bursts of high-intensity efforts will contribute to a winning match.

Questions that athletes may frequently ask regarding energy and their training programs are:

- *How does my body produce energy for exercise?*
- *How does the type of training session effect energy use?*
- *Where does my body obtain fuel to produce this energy?*

## YOUR FITNESS LEVEL
### MAXIMAL OXYGEN CONSUMPTION

Without oxygen, the exercise and training you participate in is not possible. The harder you exercise, the more oxygen your body requires to function. Eventually, you and all other athletes reach a level beyond which you cannot increase your oxygen use. This point, where your oxygen consumption plateaus, is called maximal oxygen consumption, or $VO_2$ max. An athlete with a high $VO_2$ max is considered to have a greater endurance capacity than an athlete with a lower $VO_2$ max.

$VO_2$ max is as scientific as it sounds. It is actually a measurement of your aerobic capacity, or the amount of oxygen your muscles can extract from the bloodstream. Remember, oxygen is what makes exercise possible. Unfortunately, your ultimate aerobic capacity or $VO_2$ max is determined by genetics. And while none of you chose your parents, you can follow a training program that will enable you to reach your full oxy-

CASEY B. GIBSON

*Being race-ready for Saturn Cycling team member Norman Alvis means proper training, nutrition, and mental preparation.*

gen capacity potential, and subsequently perform your best.

Highly trained athletes can maintain maximal aerobic capacity for only several minutes. Most of the time, you are exercising at a percentage of your maximal aerobic capacity, often called percentage of VO$_2$ max. Because many athletes have not undergone the scientific testing available to determine VO$_2$ max, exercise intensity is often expressed as a percentage of maximal heart rate. Many athletes are familiar with their maximal heart rate because they train with a heart rate monitor.

## LACTATE THRESHOLD

Lactate threshold is another scientific measurement. It refers to a specific percentage of VO$_2$ max. Like VO$_2$ max, the level at which lactate threshold occurs varies among athletes. During exercise of increasing intensity, a byproduct called lactic acid is produced. The point at which *excess* lactic acid begins to accumulate in your blood is referred to as the lactate threshold. The lactate threshold is usually expressed as a percentage of VO$_2$ max, but can also be expressed as a percentage of maximal heart rate. Every athlete has his or her own lactate threshold. For example, your lactate threshold may be at 80 percent of your maximal heart rate.

Lactic acid has been labeled as a bad guy. This is due to the fact that excess lactic acid accumulation is associated with muscular fatigue. The athlete in our introductory story had increased her race pace and quickly reached her lactate threshold. Because of this increased pace, lactic acid began to accumulate and the result was muscle fatigue. The pace needed to be slowed in order for exercise to be tolerated and to continue.

Lactate threshold is an important indicator of athletic performance. Basically, it measures an athlete's ability to sustain a high rate of energy expenditure without being limited by fatigue. An athlete with a lactate threshold at 75 percent of their $VO_2$ max should have better endurance potential than an athlete with the same $VO_2$ max and lactate threshold at 70 percent. This is because the higher lactate threshold allows the athlete to work closer to their aerobic capacity. In fact, lactate threshold is often a better predictor of endurance performance ability than $VO_2$ max.

Genetics influences your lactate threshold, but so does training. Good training programs are designed to increase your lactate tolerance. Both your $VO_2$ max and lactate threshold can be measured from a graded exercise test on a bicycle or treadmill. Follow-up testing can determine how these performance measurements have responded to your current training program.

## BODY FUEL

Any athlete can benefit from a basic review and understanding of energy production. That's because specific nutritional strategies can enhance your body's energy systems and affect your athletic performance. This chapter provides a brief overview of these energy systems and how they each contribute to meet fuel demands for the different types of exercise or training sessions that you complete. Basically you obtain fuel from three energy systems:

- *The ATP-CP or phosphagen system.*
- *The anaerobic glycolysis or lactic acid system.*
- *The aerobic system, both glycolytic (carbohydrate) and lipolytic (fat).*

*"I have been lifting weights, running, and cross-country skiing, and that has changed my muscles. It has helped my cycling."*
*– Chantal Daucourt, Trek Mountain-Bike Team, World Cup race winner*

All of these energy systems utilize different biochemical pathways. How significantly each system will contribute to the energy required for exercise depends on the type of activity performed, which is determined by exercise intensity (speed) and duration. There are four defined types of physical activity. These categories are classified according to the duration of an all-out effort and the energy system which predominately fuels the activity. The four physical activity classifications are:

- *Power-strength events (ATP): power lift, high jump, shot put, javelin throw.*
- *Sustained power events (ATP-PC system): sprints, football line play, gymnastics routine.*
- *Speed events (ATP-PC + lactic acid systems): 200-meter run, 100-meter swim, and 500-meter speed skate.*
- *Endurance and ultra-endurance events (Aerobic glycolysis and lipolysis systems): 800-meter run to bicycle criterium to ultra-distance marathon.*

As indicated in the parenthesis above, each of these types of physical activities favors one of the three energy systems. Competition in a particular sport can be one classification of activity or even a mix. But well-designed training programs are not so uncomplicated. They generally incorporate many types of physical activity, being even more diverse than the actual competitive event for which they prepare an athlete.

TOM MORAN

*A training program may incorporate many tpes of activities and utilize more than one energy system. Chantal Daucourt, Trek Mountain Bike Team.*

By incorporating several types of training sessions, these structured programs selectively stress and develop the various energy systems required for peak performance in a particular sport.

Each sport, and individuals within a sport, have their own optimal training program that builds on their strengths and works on their weaknesses. For example, a cyclist will train both their endurance and sprinting (power) systems, because this supports successful competition in cycling road races and criteriums. In turn, duration of a competitive event may not reflect the volume of training required to prepare for that event. Collegiate swimmers may train around twenty hours weekly, while most competitive swimming events can last anywhere from twenty-one seconds to sixteen minutes.

## YOUR BODY'S ENERGY SYSTEMS
### ATP—THE ULTIMATE ENERGY SOURCE

Your muscles contain three different energy systems. But ultimately, they all use only one form of energy which produces muscle contraction. This is adenosine triphosphate, or ATP, a high-energy chemical compound found in all muscle cells. When ATP is broken down, the chemical energy released is used by the muscle fiber for contraction. Your muscles cannot contract without ATP, because it is an immediate and essential source of energy. Unfortunately, your muscles contain only very small amounts of ATP, about enough for an all-out effort of several seconds. For muscle contraction to continue, ATP must be steadily supplied. The faster your muscles contract during exercise, the more a rapid supply of ATP is imperative. The purpose of the three energy systems is to supply this required ATP at the needed rate. What energy system predominates during exercise depends on how quickly this ATP is required, which in turn is mainly determined by the intensity of the exercise.

### EXERCISE WITH OXYGEN OR WITHOUT OXYGEN

Your body produces ATP in two ways: without oxygen or anaerobically, and with oxygen or aerobically. When you begin to exercise, your body's demand for energy increases, as does its demand for oxygen. For brief exercise bouts, when you are exceeding your ability to deliver oxygen to your muscles, you can rely on the anaerobic system. However, when exercise lasts longer than one minute, your body requires more oxygen. Aerobic metabolism then begins to provide about half of your energy needs during this short exercise duration.

It's also important for you to realize that although you may specifically train a selected energy system, neither aerobic nor anaerobic metabolism works exclusively to provide energy during exercise. While one system may predominate during a training session, these two metabolic pathways usually work together and complement one another to meet the body's energy demands. For example, during exercise lasting about two minutes, about 65 percent of your energy needs are fueled by aerobic glycolysis and 35 percent from anaerobic glycolysis.

When you understand the conditions under which either the aerobic or anaerobic energy system predominately fuel your exercise, you can fully appreciate the body fuel stores required to energize your training program. This in turn will allow you to develop an appreciation of how the foods and portions you consume directly affect, negatively or positively, these body fuel reserves.

## ANAEROBIC PATHWAYS

### The ATP-CP (phosphagen) system

As its name indicates, the ATP-CP system consists of both ATP and another high-energy compound, called creatine phosphate, or CP. Because ATP is in such short supply, it must be continuously and rapidly resynthesized to provide

RICH CRUSE

*Nutritional intake should be balanced with training.*
*Heather Fuhr, Hawaiian Ironman winner.*

energy. Like ATP, CP is an energy-rich compound. When it is broken down, it too supplies energy. However, CP's released energy does not directly fuel muscle contraction. Rather, the energy released by CP resynthesizes ATP. Like ATP and the energy released from it, CP is in short supply. Energy from

12

the ATP-CP system can fuel high-intensity efforts for only six to ten seconds. Even at six seconds duration, only half of your energy needs come from ATP-CP. Fast-twitch muscle fibers use the ATP-PC system rapidly. This system fuels the initial seconds of sprint events, and other events where maximal force is required. The ATP-CP system does not require oxygen to function and is therefore anaerobic.

### Anaerobic glycolysis energy (lactic acid) system

Anaerobic glycolysis is the second metabolic pathway within your muscle cells which is capable of rapidly producing ATP. As its name indicates, this occurs through the breakdown of glycogen or carbohydrate, without oxygen being present. In anaerobic glycolysis, a single glucose molecule is broken down from muscle glycogen to produce ATP. Anaerobic glycolysis provides energy for short-duration, high-intensity exercise, lasting ten seconds to several minutes. As exercise continues beyond one to two minutes, this system provides less than half of your energy needs. Anaerobic glycolysis fuels activities such as sprinting down a basketball court or interval training sessions. At the onset of intense exercise, when oxygen cannot be delivered to your muscles quickly enough, this energy system is rapidly ignited to supply ATP.

*"If I know that I am doing a long training day and will be within my aerobic limits, I try and ingest some protein along with carbs in my pre-training meal. If I am doing a shorter, harder effort, above my aerobic threshold, my pre-training meal consists of mainly carbohydrates."*
*—Heather Fuhr, professional triathlete, winner, Hawaiian Ironman*

Besides being a limited source of energy, anaerobic glycolysis has another drawback-the production of lactic acid. When heavy demands are placed on this energy pathway, levels of lactic acid increase quickly. Though accumulation of

## TABLE 1.1 DESCRIPTION OF THE BODY'S ENERGY SYSTEMS*

| PREDOMINANT FUEL SYSTEM | EXERCISE DURATION | BODY FUELS UTILIZED | OBJECTIVE AND WORKOUT |
|---|---|---|---|
| **ATP-CP SYSTEM (ANAEROBIC)** <br><br>Highest rate ATP production<br>Very limited supply ATP<br>Highest power output<br>Highest intensity level | 6-10 seconds or less | ATP-CP | Development explosive power<br><br>Sprints<br>Football line play<br>Gymnastics routines |
| **ANAEROBIC GLYCOLYTIC** <br><br>High rate ATP production<br>Limited supply ATP<br>High power output<br>High intensity level | 2 minutes or less | ATP-CP<br><br>Carbohydrate:<br>Muscle Glycogen | Development lactate tolerance<br><br>Basketball<br>200-meter run<br>100-meter swim<br>500-meter speed skate |
| **AEROBIC GLYCOLYTIC** <br><br>Lower rate ATP production<br>High supply ATP<br>Lower power production<br>Lower intensity | 15 minutes or less | Carbohydrate:<br>Muscle glycogen<br>blood glucose | Develop maximal aerobic power<br>Develop anaerobic glycolytic system<br><br>3km steeplechase |
| | 15 to 60 minutes | Carbohydrate:<br>Muscle glycogen<br>blood glucose | Lactate threshold training<br>Steady state repetitions<br>Maximal aerobic pace<br><br>10,000-meter run<br>10-kilometer road race |
| | 60 to 90 minutes | Carbohydrate:<br>Muscle glycogen<br>blood glucose<br><br>Fat:<br>Intramuscular fat | Development of fatigue resistance<br>Sustained moderate to high intensity exercise<br><br>Sprint distance triathlon<br>Cycling criterium |
| **AEROBIC: GLYCOLYTIC AND LIPOLYTIC** <br><br>Lowest rate of ATP production<br>High supply ATP<br>Lowest power output<br>Lowest intensity level | Longer than 90 minutes | Carbohydrate:<br>Muscle glycogen<br>Blood glucose<br><br>Fat:<br>Intra-muscular fat<br>Adipose tissue fat | Development of endurance<br>Prolonged low- to moderate- intensity exercise<br>Both carbohydrate and fat burned<br>Fat burning predominates after 4 hours<br><br>Cycling road race<br>Marathon<br>Ironman triathlon |

*Adapted with permission from "Peak Performance," by John Hawley and Louise Burke, Allen & Unwin, NSW, Australia.

lactic acid itself has been associated with fatigue, most likel̲y, it is the subsequent increase in muscle acidity which contributes to fatigue and inhibits further high-intensity exercise. Anaerobic glycolysis, therefore, can produce energy at a rapid rate, but not for very long.

## The Aerobic Energy System

The aerobic pathway is the primary energy source for lower- intensity, prolonged exercise. This system is glycolytic (aerobic glycolysis) and lipolytic, as it derives energy from both carbohydrates and fat respectively. This pathway provides half of the energy for exercise lasting longer than one minute and the majority of the energy for exercise lasting longer than two minutes. When you begin exercise, you initially use the anaerobic pathways for energy, but then switch to a predominately aerobic pathway.

An adequate supply of oxygen must be delivered to the muscles in order for the oxygen system to release the energy stored in carbohydrates and fats. Protein is not normally used for energy production, but under certain conditions may become a significant source of energy for the oxygen system.

While the aerobic system cannot produce ATP as rapidly as the two anaerobic systems, it can produce much greater quantities at a slower rate. The rate at which the oxygen system produces ATP also depends on whether aerobic glycolysis (carbohydrate) or aerobic lipolysis (fat) takes place. Carbohydrate is a more efficient fuel than fat, and is the predominant fuel for exercise lasting over two minutes and up to three hours.

But your storage capacity for carbohydrates in the muscles and liver is inadequate for certain endurance events, whereas fat stores are extensive. For longer, and less intense ultra-endurance events, lasting four to six hours, fat is primarily burned for energy. Table 1.1 summarizes various characteristics of the three energy systems.

### ENERGY SYSTEMS: HOW THE BODY STORES ENERGY

Because your body stores ATP and CP in small amounts that last only several seconds, it requires plenty of stored energy as a back up. Body stores of carbohydrate, protein, and fat, which are obtained from the food you eat, can provide ample amounts of ATP.

ATP may be formed and energy released when either carbohydrate, fat, or protein is burned inside your cells. When you consume food sources of these nutrients, they are first digested in your stomach. Carbohydrate is broken down to glucose, protein to amino acids, and fat into fatty acids. These smaller particles are absorbed from your intestine into your bloodstream, and then transported to your muscle cells. In the muscle, they are then available to produce ATP.

Carbohydrate is stored in limited amounts in your blood as glucose and in your muscles and liver as glycogen. The largest amount of energy is stored as fat or triglycerides in the adipose tissue, with smaller amounts of fat stored in the muscles. Triglycerides and free fatty acids in the blood are in even shorter supply. Protein which makes up body tissue, particularly muscle, is a relatively large reservoir of energy, though not highly utilized.

Table 1.2 describes how energy is stored in the human

| TABLE 1.2 BODY FUEL STORES | | |
|---|---|---|
| **ENERGY SOURCE** | **MAJOR STORAGE FORM** | **TOTAL CALORIES STORED** |
| ATP | MUSCLE TISSUES | 1 |
| CP | MUSCLE TISSUES | 4 |
| CARBOHYDRATE | SERUM GLUCOSE | 80 |
| | LIVER GLYCOGEN | 400 |
| | MUSCLE GLYCOGEN | 1400 - 1800 |
| FAT | SERUM FREE FATTY ACIDS | 7 |
| | SERUM TRIGLYCERIDES | 75 |
| | MUSCLE TRIGLYCERIDES | 2700 |
| | ADIPOSE TISSUE TRIGLYCERIDES | 80,000 |
| PROTEIN | MUSCLE PROTEIN | 30,000 |

body as carbohydrate, fat, and protein. The amount is expressed in total calories of stored energy. These calorie levels are just an estimation and can vary among individuals depending on their body size, training level, and diet.

## BODY FUEL: HOW THE BODY DETERMINES USAGE

Training will enhance both your aerobic and anaerobic systems. Anaerobic training improves your body's ability to remove lactic acid and builds your muscle size and strength. Endurance training builds your aerobic system and enhances your muscular oxygen uptake. A number of factors determine whether your muscles use a particular energy system, and consequently the relative amounts of carbohydrates, fats, and proteins used for energy during exercise.

Four factors that influence energy system and fuel usage, are:
- *exercise intensity*
- *exercise duration*

- *your fitness level*
- *your diet composition*

### Exercise intensity

Exercise intensity, which can be measured as a percentage of your maximum heart rate or maximum oxygen capacity, is particularly important in determining the fuel your body utilizes. Let's review how progressive exercise utilizes body fuel stores.

During shorter, high-intensity sprint events, there is a rapid activation of both the ATP-CP and anaerobic glycolysis systems. ATP and CP last up to ten seconds, then only glucose, derived mainly from muscle glycogen, is used for fuel. The rate of muscle glycogen breakdown is rapid and eventually the demand of ATP exceeds the body's readily available supply. Performance is also limited by excess production of lactic acid. There is a gradual increase in muscle acidity that causes a decrease in the force of muscle contraction.

These anaerobic energy systems are also utilized when high intensity exercise bouts are part of aerobic events, such as all-out efforts during a bike race or

CASEY B. GIBSON

*Proper eating is part of being a successful athlete. Karen Bliss Livingston, Saturn Cycling Team.*

marathon. Intermittent exercise, as seen in team sports like soccer and basketball and interval training, use an extended combination of aerobic and anaerobic exercise-also resulting in a
rapid breakdown of muscle glycogen. High-intensity, repeated
resistance training also depletes these muscle glycogen stores.

Aerobic exercise does not cause fuel
depletion as quickly, and therefore can be
sustained longer. Exercise at low to moderate
intensity-at less than 60 percent maximum
heart rate-is fueled mainly from fat stores.
Training results in changes in hormone levels, which cause your fat tissue to release
fatty acids in the bloodstream. These fatty
acids, and fat stores in your muscles, fuel
your low-intensity efforts.

*"There are too many things that go into training and racing to be concentrating solely on what I am eating or not eating. But, if I am aware of meals and foods as one part of the bigger picture and make sound nutritional choices, I usually perform better."*

*– Karen Bliss Livingston, Saturn Cycling Team*

During low to moderate-intensity exercise, at about to 60
to 80 percent of your maximum heart rate, muscle glycogen
and blood glucose stores supply about half of your energy
needs. The other half comes from fat, and a very small
amount from protein. When exercise exceeds 80 percent of
your maximum heart rate, fat cannot be utilized effectively
as a fuel, providing less than 25 percent of your energy needs.
This is because fat cannot be broken down quickly enough
to produce ATP at the rate required. To meet these energy
demands, fuel is provided mainly by your carbohydrate
stores because ATP can be rapidly supplied. As would be
expected, there is an increased production of lactic acid at
this higher intensity. Lactic acid also impedes the release of
fat as an energy source.

### Exercise duration and fuel usage

The duration of your exercise also affects fuel usage. The longer you train, the more fat fuels your exercise. As exercise duration increases, intensity must decrease due to limited muscle glycogen stores. When muscle glycogen stores run low, fat must supply most of the needed additional energy. But fat can only be used effectively as a fuel source at up to 60 to 70 percent of your aerobic capacity. A certain level of carbohydrate is also needed for fat to be burned as energy. For longer-duration exercise of four to six hours, which requires lower intensities to be sustained, fat can supply as much as 60 to 70 percent of your total energy needs.

But, overall, muscle glycogen is a significant fuel for most types of exercise. Even in longer events, where the slower pace accommodates fat burning, muscle glycogen stores can eventually become depleted.

### Fitness level and fuel usage

What fuel your body will burn is also determined by your fitness level. Training has many benefits in terms of fuel usage. When you are fit, your body becomes more efficient at producing energy aerobically at a given intensity. This allows you to maintain this intensity at a lower percentage of your maximum heart rate. Consequently, you burn more fat and less glycogen than previously, saving your limited glycogen stores.

For example, untrained individuals could begin to accumulate lactic acid in the blood at 50 to 60 percent of their maximal aerobic capacity. Training can bump this lactate threshold up to 70 to 75 percent, or even higher in elite athletes. Because lactic acid interferes with fat burning and

| TABLE 1.3 : NUTRITIONALLY RELATED CAUSES OF FATIGUE |
|---|
| DECREASED CREATINE PHOSPHATE LEVELS<br>DEPLETION OF MUSCLE GLYCOGEN<br>DECREASE IN BLOOD GLUCOSE LEVELS<br>DECREASED BLOOD BRANCH CHAIN AMINO ACIDS<br>INCREASED MUSCLE ACIDITY DUE TO LACTIC ACID ACCUMULATION<br>DECREASED BLOOD VOLUME DUE TO DEHYDRATION<br>INCREASED BODY TEMPERATURE DUE TO DEHYDRATION<br>ELECTROLYTE IMBALANCES SUCH AS HYPONATREMIA |

speeds up muscle glycogen use, having a higher lactate threshold allows you to use more fat and less glycogen at the same exercise intensity.

Endurance training has another benefit. It increases your muscle storage capacity of glycogen. Your muscle glycogen is not only used at a slower rate when you are trained, but you also begin exercise with higher glycogen stores. Table 1.5 summarizes some of the benefits of training.

**Diet and fuel usage**

Finally, your diet influences the fuels burned during exercise. A high carbohydrate diet not only maximizes your muscle glycogen stores, but also increases your use of glycogen as a fuel. Full glycogen stores are needed during high-intensity exercise and during low- to moderate-intensity exercise of longer duration.

If your diet is high in fat, you will use more fat as a fuel. But this does not support consuming a high-fat diet. Even very lean athletes have enough fat stores to fuel an endurance event. The goal is to increase your utilization of fat at a given

| TABLE 1.4: NUTRITIONAL PROFILES OF CATEGORIES OF SPORTS* | | |
|---|---|---|
| RESISTANCE TRAINING | INTERMITTENT EXERCISE/TEAM SPORTS | ENDURANCE SPORTS |
| Power athlete | Power and middle-distance athletes | Uses all three energy systems |
| Uses ATP-CP system | Potential use all three energy systems | Relies heavily on glycolytic and lipolytic energy systems |
| Uses glycolytic system | | High calorie needs |
| High carbohydrate training diet | ATP-CP and glycolytic used repeatedly | High carbohydrate training diet |
| Adequate pre-training carbohydrate with careful timing | What predominates varies with position and style play | High carbohydrate pre-event Carbohydrate-loading |
| Fluid replacement daily and during event | Moderate to high carbohydrate training diet | Fluid replacement daily and during event |
| Carbohydrate replacement during event | Adequate pre-event carbohydrate | Carbohydrate replacement during event |
| Moderate protein for repair and recovery | Fluid replacement daily and during event | Replace electrolytes for ultraendurance |
| Avoid excess fat intake | Carbohydrate replacement during event | Recovery carbohydrates |
| Meet energy needs | Moderate protein for repair and recovery | Moderate to high protein for recovery and repair |
| | Avoid excess fat intake | Avoid excess fat intake |
| | Meet moderate to high energy needs | Meet moderate to high energy needs |

*Adapted with permission from "Peak Performance," by John Hawley and Louise Burke, Allen & Unwin, NSW, Australia.

intensity. Endurance training is the most effective way to achieve this benefit. Also, fat can only be burned in the presence of carbohydrate.

High-fat diets also have been shown to lower muscle glyco-

| TABLE 1.5: BENEFITS OF TRAINING |
|---|
| INCREASED USE OF FAT AS A FUEL<br>INCREASED MUSCLE GLYCOGEN STORAGE<br>GREATER GLYCOGEN SPARING<br>HIGH LACTATE THRESHOLD<br>INCREASED CALORIE NEEDS OR IMPROVED WEIGHT CONTROL |

gen stores, which makes it more difficult to maintain high-intensity exercise. In addition, as stated previously, fat cannot meet energy needs quickly enough during high-intensity exercise, especially above 80 percent of your maximum heart rate.

It is clear that carbohydrate, as described in Table 1.4, is an important dietary component for any sport. Since prevention of fatigue and adequate energy is a main goal of optimal sports nutrition, sports scientists recommend a diet that is adequate in calories to fuel your training, with at least 60 percent of the calories coming from carbohydrates.

Besides adequate carbohydrate, your training diet also requires a balance of all nutrients that is optimal for maintaining energy and replacing losses. Table 1.3 lists some nutritionally related causes of fatigue.

Athletes participating in any sport require the following:

• *Adequate water and fluid intake.*

• *Adequate calories to maintain or reach appropriate and healthy body weight.*

• *Adequate carbohydrate based on training hours and intensity.*

• *Protein requirements for tissue building, repair, and to replace losses.*

• *Fat to provide essential fatty acids and contribute to energy needs.*

• *Adequate vitamin and mineral intake.*

Section One describes these nutrients and their requirements for activity, training, good health.

**FINAL THOUGHTS**

Your body produces energy anaerobically, through the ATP-CP and glycolysis (lactic acid) energy systems, and aerobically through aerobic glycolysis and lipolysis. Most exercise is supplied by a combination of aerobic and anaerobic exercise. But what fuel system predominates depends mainly on the exercise intensity and duration. While competitive events are often one category of physical activity, most training programs are a mix of various types of exercise.

Endurance workouts, repetitive sprint training, and long sessions of interval training, as well as intense resistance training sessions, all can significantly deplete stored glycogen. That's why most athletes require a diet that is around 60 percent carbohydrate or more. In addition, they also require a balance of protein and fat, and optimal amounts of vitamins, minerals, and fluids.

# PART II

# YOUR
# TRAINING
# DIET

# CHAPTER TWO

# Fluid First

> "Sometimes when I feel sluggish, I will drink a liter of water
> and immediately feel better. Before consciously drinking
> more, I was often dehydrated and would get headaches."
> — Sarah Tueting, goalie
> 1998 Olympic ice hockey gold medalist

Does this scenario sound familiar? You feel tired, sluggish, your eyes feel dry, and you have a slight headache. Your energy levels are low, but you are not certain of the cause. You make an effort to drink more water throughout the day, and soon you start to feel better.

When you are feeling fatigued, the cause could be as simple as dehydration. Water and adequate hydration is crucial for both general well-being and top performance, no matter what level you are training at. In fact, even though it is a nutrient that deserves top priority from any athlete, water is often minimized and even ignored. But water is so simple-and can still be found with no packaging and no gimmicks. Don't take water for granted.

Some questions that athletes may have regarding water, fluid intake, and their performance are:

- *What are the functions of water?*
- *What are the signs of dehydration?*
- *How much water does my body require for good health and training?*

## FLUID FACTS

About 60 percent of your total body weight is water. Water is an essential building material, as it gives body cells their shape and form. Because water cannot be compressed, it provides structure to the body parts, consequently protect-

*"Almost all athletes could stand to drink more water."*
*—Craig Virgin, long-distance runner, three-time U.S. Olympian in 10,000 meter event, 1976, '80, '84*
*Two-time world cross country champion, '80, '81*

ing important body tissues such as your spinal cord and brain. It helps lubricate joints. Water is the main component of blood, which carries oxygen, hormones, and nutri-ents such as glucose to your cells. It is involved in digestion and eliminates waste products through urine and sweat. Water is also essential for all your senses, such as hearing sight, and smell, to function properly.

Clearly the roles water plays in maintaining overall health are extremely important. That's why you can live without water for only a few days.

Besides all the functions listed above, there is one addi-tional role of water, one that is of great importance to the ath-lete. Water plays a major part in body temperature regulation. Humans are able to maintain a constant body temperature under various environmental temperatures. The body does this by constantly making adjustments to either lose or gain heat. Heat may be lost through the body in several ways:

- *Radiation: Heat is transferred from the body to cooler objects or surrounding air.*
- *Conduction: Heat is transferred from the body by direct physical contact.*
- *Convection: Heat is transferred by the movement of air or water over the body.*
- *Evaporation: Heat is lost when sweat is converted to a vapor. The lungs also evaporate heat.*

Fluid balance is a result of output versus intake. At rest, body heat is lost through water loss from urine output, exhaled air, and through insensible perspiration. Water intake comes from the fluids we consume, water in some of the foods we eat, and from metabolic water produced by the body. Urine output represents our greatest water loss, and fluid intake our greatest water input. Fluid loss is increased by warm or humid weather, living in a dry climate, breathing air from an air conditioner, or living at altitude. Traveling, especially in airplanes, can also boost water loss. In general, your body loses about 10 cups of water daily.

## SWEATING

During exercise, heat is a major by-product of the working muscles. Body temperature rises as heat builds up. Water then acts as a coolant to keep the body from overheating. During

BRUCE BENNET

*Optimal hydration is essential for any type of exercise. U.S. women's Olympic gold medal hockey team.*

exercise, sweating is the body's primary mechanism for getting rid of excess heat.

Water maintains adequate blood supply to the skin. This blood transfers heat to the environment through sweating. When sweat evaporates, it cools the skin, blood, and your body's inner core. Athletes who are in top shape actually sweat even more during exercise than their sedentary counterparts, subsequently increasing their fluid needs.

While sweating does the important job of keeping your body cool, the resultant minor to large fluid losses can impair athletic performance. That's because the blood that was sending oxygen to your working muscles needs to go to your skin in order to eliminate heat. Eventually your blood volume decreases due to fluid loss from these sweat losses.

With this decreased blood volume, exercise begins to seem harder because of the increased demand placed on the cardiovascular system. Losing even only one quart of fluid causes your heart rate to increase by about eight beats per minute to compensate. Your body core temperature also increases by three degrees Celsius. In an effort to conserve body fluid and protect cardiovascular function, skin blood flow and sweat rate decrease. Body temperature rises further, and exercise becomes harder.

> *"I am always carrying a water bottle with me. I have three, regular-size water bottles daily, in addition to other fluids such as juice."*
> *– Chad Hedrick,*
> *In-line skater*
> *Rollerblade Racing Team*
> *Overall world champion,*
> *'94, '95, '96*

## SIGNS AND SYMPTOMS OF DEHYDRATION

Depending on your body weight, exercise intensity, and environmental conditions, you may sweat from one to two quarts of fluid per hour. Large amounts of fluid can evaporate via sweating in hot, dry weather. You may not feel sweaty in these conditions, and be unaware of how much water you've actually lost. Humidity also affects fluid loss. As the moisture in the air increases and humidity goes up, sweat cannot be evaporated as effectively. Instead, sweat drips off your skin, and you don't benefit from the cooling effect of evaporation.

Thirst occurs with a 1-percent loss in body weight. When water losses reach about 2 to 4 percent of body weight, physical performance can become impaired. Symptoms of greater thirst, such as irritability, nausea and lethargy occur. Losing 5 to 6 percent of your body weight will result in impaired temperature regulation and increased heart and breathing rates. Table 2.1 describes some physiological effects of dehydration.

| TABLE 2.1: PHYSIOLOGICAL EFFECTS OF DEHYDRATION |
| --- |
| DECREASED BLOOD VOLUME |
| DECREASED URINE OUTPUT |
| DECREASED CARDIAC OUTPUT |
| DECREASED SKIN BLOOD FLOW |
| DECREASED SWEAT RATE |
| INCREASED BODY TEMPERATURE |

## DAILY HYDRATION ESSENTIALS

Because it can be difficult to keep up with water losses during exercise, you want to begin training sessions as well-hydrated as possible. Optimal daily hydration takes planning and practice. Begin each day with 8 to 16 ounces of water. Caffeine slightly increases your fluid needs. If your caffeine intake is excessive, cut back. Routine water breaks are also important. Drinking 4 to 8 ounces of fluid every hour is ideal.

Casey FitzRandolph, Olympic Speedskater

TOM MORAN

Keep fluids like juice, noncaffeinated beverages and water accessible in your car, at work and at home. Sip throughout the day. Foods like fruits and vegetables and soups can have a hydrating effect. Salty foods increase your need for water.

Sedentary people need a minimum of eight to ten, 8-ounce glasses of fluid every day. Athletes

| TABLE 2.2: SIGNS AND SYMPTOMS OF DEHYDRATION | |
|---|---|
| **MILD DEHYDRATION** | **SEVERE DEHYDRATION** |
| THIRST | DIFFICULTY SWALLOWING |
| FATIGUE | SHRIVELED, DRY SKIN |
| DECREASED APPETITE | STUMBLING |
| HEAT INTOLERANCE | SUNKEN EYES AND POOR VISION |
| LIGHT HEADINESS | DELIRIUM |
| SMALL AMOUNT DARK URINE | MUSCLE SPASMS |

also require this amount, plus the amount lost during training. Don't depend on thirst to trigger drinking. Typically, this signal will cause you to replace only one-third to two-thirds of your water losses.

Monitor your hydration status by the color and quantity of your urine. Clear urine reflects adequate fluids, while darker urine means that you require more fluid. You should have at least four full bladders of urine everyday. Certain vitamin supplements can darken urine, so volume, rather than color, will be a better indicator of hydration if you take supplements.

*"Through a number of measures, I have become conscious of how hydrated I am, from checking my complexion, weight, and the color of my urine."*
*— Casey FitzRandolph, 1998 Olympic speedskating team*

Besides meeting your daily hydration needs, several steps can help you stay hydrated before and during exercise. Food and fluid needs before and during exercise, and the use of sports drinks, are covered in greater detail in Section Three. But some basic exercise fluid guidelines to be followed are:

**Daily**

8 to 12, 8-ounce servings of fluid.

**BEFORE EXERCISE**

Two hours beforehand, have up to 24 ounces of fluid. Drink 8 to 16 ounces fifteen minutes before to offset early exercise fluid losses.

### DURING EXERCISE

Hot and adverse conditions can cause dehydration in as little as fifteen minutes. Drink 4 to 8 ounces of fluid every fifteen to twenty minutes during exercise. Meeting these fluids requirements during exercise takes practice.

### AFTER EXERCISE

Try to replace any lost fluid as quickly as possible. For every pound of weight lost during exercise, drink 2, preferably 3 cups of fluid. Keep drinking throughout the day.

## FINAL THOUGHTS

Adequate hydration is essential for optimal well-being and peak performance. Keeping up with normal daily fluid losses is required in order to begin exercise well-hydrated. Fluid losses during exercise can reach more than 2 liters per hour. These losses should be replaced as closely as possible during exercise. After exercise, fluid intake should replace net losses to restore adequate hydration.

# CHAPTER THREE

# Carbohydrates
## to Fuel *Your*
## *Fire*

*"When it comes to recovery, I also try to take in some type of carbohydrate drink right after a race or training session. The thing about trying to perform day after day, is that you have to keep your body on an even keel. Carbohydrates help me sustain my performance throughout a stage race or long training period."*
                                                    —Bliss Livingston

Your training session was long and intense. Despite completing a fairly routine workout, you didn't feel like your usual self. Your normal drive just wasn't there, and you arrive home especially fatigued. You ponder the possibilities of what went wrong. You have successfully been building your training program, especially the intensity. Because you appreciate the demands this places on your body's fuel supplies, you have increased your dietary carbohydrate intake. Yet, something isn't quite right. But for now, you are hungry and need to refuel. You open the refrigerator door and reach for some leftovers. A good meal should help.

While proper eating cannot compensate for a poorly designed training program, eating poorly can seriously diminish your energy reserves and recovery. This is especially true of inadequate carbohydrate intake. Carbohydrate body stores—muscle and liver glycogen, and blood glucose—fuel the diverse types of physical activity that make up your training program. These exercise sessions may rely moderately to exclusively on carbohydrate stores to produce ATP for energy. That's why low muscle glycogen stores can compromise training at intensities anywhere from 65 to 90 percent of $VO_2$ max. To maintain and replenish these stores, you need to meet your dietary carbohydrate requirements.

Questions athletes may have concerning their carbohydrate requirements are:
- *Where does my body store carbohydrate?*
- *How do my carbohydrate body stores become depleted?*
- *What does the current research on carbohydrate demonstrate?*
- *What are my daily carbohydrate requirements?*
- *How should I time my carbohydrate intake?*
- *What types of carbohydrates are best?*
- *Do I need carbohydrate supplements?*

## WHERE YOU STORE CARBOHYDRATE

As was discussed previously (see Chapter 1), with a high fitness level and optimal diet, athletes can store around 1800 calories worth of carbohydrate. The majority of these calories are stored as muscle glycogen. These supplies, directly and specifically, fuel the muscle in which they are located. Training produces biochemical changes that increase the amount of glycogen stored in muscles. Trained endurance athletes can increase muscle glycogen levels with a high carbohydrate diet that in one study were affected as follows:

- *Moderate carbohydrate diet: baseline levels*
- *High carbohydrate diet: 27-percent increase above baseline*
- *Carbohydrate loading diet: 30-percent increase above baseline*

More limited amounts of glycogen are stored in the liver. This organ does its small share to supply fuel by releasing glucose directly into the bloodstream. In addition, blood glucose contributes a very small amount of carbohydrate. Blood glucose is your brain's sole source of energy. Besides drawing from liver stores, blood glucose can also be maintained from absorption of glucose through the intestine.

*Muscle glycogen: 1400-1800 calories*
*Liver glycogen: 400 calories*
*Blood glucose: 80 calories*

## HOW YOU DEPLETE GLYCOGEN STORES

Early on during exercise, the major source of carbohydrate fuel is muscle glycogen, though some blood glucose is also used. As exercise continues, muscle glycogen stores begin to run low. Depending on your exercise intensity and diet, muscle glycogen stores usually last anywhere from seventy-five to ninety minutes. When your muscle glycogen stores get too low you "hit the wall." Your legs feel heavy, you are fatigued, and want to quit. Complete depletion of muscle glycogen may not be necessary to impair performance. But rather, glycogen depletion of the muscle fibers which predominately fuel that particular training session, may be the limiting factor.

As these muscle glycogen stores run low, blood glucose plays a larger role in meeting energy needs. With this high rate of blood glucose utilization, liver glycogen stores, which help maintain blood glucose, can become rapidly depleted. Over half of your liver glycogen stores can be used up in one hour of aerobic exercise. Eventually, blood glucose levels fall, resulting in hypoglycemia or low blood sugar, also referred to as "bonking." Symptoms of hypoglycemia include dizziness, poor concentration, and lack of coordination. Prevention of hypoglycemia is one of the major strategies of fueling your body during exercise (Chapter 10).

## THE SCIENCE BEHIND CARBOHYDRATES
## AND PERFORMANCE

There is plenty of scientific support to demonstrate that for a single training session, higher body carbohydrate stores promote improved endurance and performance. You may have even experienced the intense symptoms of depleting muscle glycogen stores in one training session.

But as described in the introductory paragraph to this chapter, the symptoms of gradual glycogen depletion related to successive days of heavy training are much more subtle.

These symptoms can creep up over a week or longer, producing feelings of sluggishness and heaviness often associated with "staleness" or overtraining. Besides feeling lethargic, you may be putting out an increased effort during training and find it difficult to maintain a given intensity. Workouts which you previously accomplished may become difficult.

Numerous studies have found that a carbohydrate-rich diet is superior in building, maintaining, and replenishing muscle glycogen stores. A diet only moderately high in carbohydrate leads to partial replenishment of carbohydrate stores. If this incomplete replenishment occurs from one day to the next, stores are gradually depleted over a week's or more time, and performance may suffer.

Unfortunately, most studies testing the effects of carbohydrate on performance occurred over a one week's time or less. Further studies are needed to verify that high-carbohydrate diets promote superior performance over the long-term. But it does make sense that maintaining high glycogen stores is prudent and consuming a high carbohydrate diet a wise nutrition strategy. Lack of long-term research cannot be interpreted to support a low-carbohydrate diet for athletes. Simply consider glycogen's role in fueling various types of activity. Then consider that adequate glycogen stores are dependent upon carbohydrate in the diet.

*"Carbohydrates provide the most readily available energy source for an athlete in any sport, but especially for vigorous endurance competition."*
—*Virgin*

In addition, recovery can also be facilitated by incorporating "rest days" into a structured training program. Even a good diet may not keep up with training demands and fully

## TABLE 3.1: DAILY CARBOHYDRATE REQUIREMENTS

| Daily carbohydrate requirements gms/lb body wt. | Training regimen | Goals | 125-pound athlete | 165-pound athlete |
|---|---|---|---|---|
| 4.5 to 5.5 gms/lb | Very prolonged<br><br>Moderate-high intensity<br><br>Daily<br><br>greater 5 to 6 hours | Daily muscle glycogen recovery<br><br>Refueling during exercise<br><br>Meet high energy needs | 563 to 690 grams | 742 to 907 grams |
| 3.0 to 4.5 gms/lb | Prolonged<br><br>Moderate-high intensity<br><br>Daily<br><br>greater 90 minutes | Daily muscle glycogen recovery<br><br>"Load muscle" prior exercise<br><br>Refuelling during exercise | 375 to 562 grams | 495 to 742 grams |
| 2.25 to 3.0 gms/lb | Moderate duration<br><br>Moderate-intensity under one hour<br><br>Low-intensity several hours | Daily muscle glycogen recovery | 280 to 375 grams | 370 to 495 grams |

replenish muscle glycogen stores on a daily basis. This is because the rate of glycogen storage may be slowed by muscle damage and other factors related to heavy training. Muscle fuel stores need to "catch-up" on these rest days.

## DAILY CARBOHYDRATE REQUIREMENTS FOR TRAINING

Clearly, eating carbohydrates is all about refueling and optimal recovery. Adequate recuperation allows you to start the next training session, whether it is six, twelve, or twenty-four hours away, with enough fuel to perform your best.

Your total daily carbohydrate needs depend upon both the duration and intensity of your training program and particular training sessions. Let's look at some individualized carbohydrate requirements.

Carbohydrate recommendations are often provided in percentages. However, this may not be the most accurate and appropriate way to express carbohydrate needs for the athlete. Rather, absolute amounts, expressed as grams per pound of weight, define best how much carbohydrate an athlete requires to recover before the next training session.

Carbohydrate requirements per pound of weight are based on the intensity and duration of training, with ultra-endurance, intense exercise, such as the Tour de France cycling race, requiring the greatest amount of carbohydrate.

Most athletes should average around 60 percent carbohydrate. But, depending on whether an athlete is interested in restricting calories, or has exceptionally high calorie needs, meeting total carbohydrate requirements could result in consuming anywhere from 50 to 70 percent of total calories from carbohydrate.

Your carbohydrate needs can also be fine-tuned and adjusted according to your current training load and ability to recover. Clearly, successive days of heavy training requires you to reach the high end of your recommended carbohydrate intake. Also keep in mind that rest days are "catch-up" recovery days during which you should eat enough carbohydrates to allow for adequate replenishment, without the concern of burning additional carbohydrate stores with exercise.

| TABLE 3.2: DAILY CARBOHYDRATE REQUIREMENTS BASED ON WEIGHT | | |
|---|---|---|
| BODY WEIGHT IN POUNDS | POST-EXERCISE CARBOHYDRATE REQUIREMENTS | DAILY CARBOHYDRATE REQUIREMENTS |
| | 0.5 TO 0.7 GMS/LB DAILY | 2.25 TO 5.0 GMS/LB |
| 100 | 50 TO 70 GMS | 225 TO 500 GMS |
| 110 | 55 TO 77 GMS | 248 TO 550 GMS |
| 120 | 60 TO 84 GMS | 270 TO 600 GMS |
| 130 | 65 TO 91 GMS | 292 TO 650 GMS |
| 140 | 70 TO 98 GMS | 315 TO 700 GMS |
| 150 | 75 TO 105 GMS | 338 TO 750 GMS |
| 160 | 80 TO 112 GMS | 360 TO 800 GMS |
| 170 | 85 TO 119 GMS | 380 TO 850 GMS |
| 180 | 90 TO 126 GMS | 405 TO 900 GMS |
| 190 | 95 TO 133 GMS | 428 TO 950 GMS |

## RECOVERY CARBOHYDRATE EATING

Generally, the amount of carbohydrate you consume over twenty-four hours is crucial. The more carbohydrates you take in, the greater amount of glycogen you will store post-exercise, until your muscle storage capacity is reached.

How you time the amounts of these daily totals, and the types of carbohydrates you choose, can also enhance your synthesis of glycogen. You should especially focus on the three keys to carbohydrate fueling—timing, amount, and type—after endurance training of moderate to high intensity.

### Timing

Research has demonstrated that the initial 30 minutes after longer, more intense training sessions are a window of opportunity through which you should feed your starving muscles carbohydrate. Muscle glycogen storage appears to be

# Do you need protein post-exercise for recovery?

In the early 1990s, one study added protein to the post-exercise carbohydrate intake consumed by research subjects. What researchers discovered was an enhanced rate of muscle glycogen resynthesis after endurance exercise. However, the study protocol resulted in the protein-carbohydrate intake actually providing more calories than the carbohydrate supplement alone.

To determine if this increase in muscle glycogen resynthesis was actually due to higher calories or the addition of protein, another group of researchers more recently compared two feedings equal in calories. One group received all carbohydrates after resistance training, while another received the caloric equivalent of carbohydrate (66 percent), protein (23 percent), and fat (11 percent). Both formulas resulted in similar rates of muscle glycogen resynthesis. Researchers concluded that 0.45 grams carbohydrate per pound weight or the caloric equivalent of carbohydrate-protein-fat are both effective. A comparison was also made between carbohydrate alone versus a mix of carbohydrate, protein and fat, when they were consumed within one hour after endurance exercise. Both supplement trials resulted in increased glycogen resynthesis. In other words, the addition of protein is fine, but not necessary. Just make sure you consume enough!

enhanced the first two hours after exercise, as the muscle has a greater ability to take up blood glucose. One study demonstrated that subjects fed carbohydrate a full two hours after exercise synthesized the carbohydrate into muscle glycogen 45 percent more slowly than subjects fed carbohydrate immediately after exercise.

Immediate post-exercise carbohydrate consumption is especially important if your training session significantly depleted muscle glycogen stores, and if you need to train again in four to twelve hours. Athletes requiring 500 to 700 grams of carbohydrate daily should also focus on post-exercise carbohydrate consumption. Meeting these high daily carbohydrates totals requires you to consume carbohydrate at most of your meals and snacks.

*"Our team became conscious of eating after playing and replenishing quickly. A lot of us tried to get food in right after a hard practice, such as fruit."*
*—Tueting*

Your carbohydrate allotment can be spread throughout the day, with more emphasis on consuming carbohydrates the four to six hours after exercise. After you consume carbohydrates within thirty minutes of exercise, and again in about two hours, the rest of your carbohydrate intake can come from several small snacks or large meals-according to your lifestyle and preferences. The key is to have adequate daily intake of the total grams of carbohydrate required.

## Amount of carbohydrates

While your total daily carbohydrate intake significantly affects your recovery, so does the amount of carbohydrate you consume within thirty minutes of exercise. You should have 0.5 to 0.7 grams of carbohydrate for every pound you weigh as outlined in table 3.3. If these amounts sound awkward refer to table 3.2 for your post- exercise carbohydrate prescription. Most athletes will require anywhere from 50 to 150 grams of carbohydrate. Consuming carbohydrate above

| TABLE 3.3: POST-EXERCISE RECOVERY GUIDELINES | | | | |
|---|---|---|---|---|
| CARBOHYDRATE REQUIREMENTS GRAMS PER POUND WEIGHT | GOALS AND GUIDELINES OF CARBOHYDRATE INTAKE | CARBOHYDRATE FOR 125 LBS ATHLETE | CARBOHYDRATE FOR 165 LBS ATHLETE | FOOD CHOICES |
| 0.5 TO 0.7 grams per pound | Within 30 minutes post-exercise | 63 to 88 grams | 88 to 115 grams | Concentrated carbohydrate drinks |
| | Two hours post-exercise | | | |
| | | | | Energy bars |
| | Emphasize fluids | | | |
| | | | | Cereals |
| | Emphasize high glycemic index foods | | | Bagels |

these amounts at one particular meal should not significantly enhance muscle glycogen storage further.

### Type of carbohydrates

Chances are you are interested in what form or type of carbohydrate is best for your recovery. From a practical standpoint, liquid carbohydrate may be the most appealing post-exercise choice. You likely will need to rehydrate after training anyway. A post-exercise snack consisting of liquids and easily digested solids could also work. While large meals and solids may be unappealing, they do replenish muscle glycogen stores. Research has shown no difference in the rate of glycogen synthesis whether carbohydrate was in solid or liquid form.

You may be confused regarding the classifications of simple and complex carbohydrates, or have heard of an alternative carbohydrate classification system referred to as the glycemic index. Chances are, that as both a consumer and athlete, you will encounter this terminology. Let's take a brief overview of these carbohydrate classifications.

### Classifying carbohydrates — making it simple

One general carbohydrate classification is simple or complex— which refers to the molecular structure of the carbohydrate. Simple carbohydrates are both single sugar molecules or monosaccharides or double sugar molecules or disaccharides. Single sugar molecules include glucose, fructose, and galactose. Fructose, found mainly in fruits and honey, is the sweetest simple sugar. Glucose is found naturally in foods and produced in the body through digestion.

Double molecule simple sugars which you may encounter on labels are sucrose or table sugar, lactose or milk sugar, and corn syrups. Sucrose is half fructose and half glucose, whereas high-fructose corn syrup is about 56 percent fructose and 43 percent glucose. Both sucrose and high-fructose corn syrup are eventually broken down to glucose in the bloodstream.

Simple sugars are packaged under a variety of marketing guises. Despite popular claims, honey, brown sugar, molasses, and date sugar supply only small amounts of nutrients and are not much better nutritionally than table sugar. Like some manufactured products, fruits and vegetables naturally contain different mixtures of glucose, sucrose, and fructose. All these sugars are converted to glucose before being used for energy.

Glucose polymers are a third type of sugar which have been on the sports market for several years. Polymers are

| TABLE 3.4: TRADITIONAL CLASSIFICATION OF CARBOHDRATES | |
|---|---|
| **CARBOHYDRATE CLASSIFICATION** | **EXAMPLES** |
| Monosaccharides | Glucose<br>Fructose<br>Galactose |
| Dissaccharides | Lactose = glucose + galactose<br>Sucrose = glucose + fructose<br>Corn syrup = glucose + fructose<br>Maltose = glucose + glucose |
| Polysaccharides | Glucose polymers<br>Corn<br>Breads<br>Cereals<br>Pasta<br>Rice |

chains of about five glucose molecules. Also referred to as maltodextrin, glucose polymers are created by breaking down cornstarch into these small glucose chains.

**Classifying your carbohydrates—making it complex**

When three to thousands of sugar molecules are linked together, they are referred to as polysaccharides, or complex carbohydrates. Starch in plant foods is the most common complex carbohydrate, just like your body stores of the complex carbohydrate, muscle and liver glycogen. Starch in foods is found in corn and various grains from which bread, cereal, and pasta are made. Starch is also present in dried peas and beans, potatoes, and rice. All the starches you eat are digested down to glucose, which fuels your brain or is used for energy. Surplus glucose is stored as glycogen. You store twice as much glycogen from glucose or sucrose, than from fructose which is processed differently by the body.

While both simple sugars and complex starches fuel your exercising muscles, they nourish your body differently. Sugars and polymers found in sports drinks provide only carbohydrate energy. Whole grains, mono- and disaccharides from natural fruits and vegetables, and simple natural sugars from fruit all provide important vitamins, minerals, and phytochemicals.

Various fibers found in whole grains, fruits and vegetables, though they are not starches, are another form of complex carbohydrate. Fibers from these foods can help prevent heart disease and certain types of cancer.

## TABLE 3.5: GLYCEMIC LEVELS IN VARIOUS FOOD SOURCES*

| LOW GLYCEMIC FOODS less than 40 | | MODERATE GLYCEMIC FOODS 40 TO 70 | | HIGH GLYCEMIC FOODS greater than 70 | |
|---|---|---|---|---|---|
| FRUCTOSE | 20 | NAVY BEANS | 40 | CARROTS | 71 |
| SOYBEAN | 20 | ORANGE | 40 | WATERMELON | 72 |
| CHERRIES | 22 | PASTA | 41 | WHEAT BREAD | 78 |
| PLUMS | 24 | GRAPES | 43 | GRAPENUTS FLAKES | 80 |
| GRAPEFRUIT | 25 | PINTO BEANS | 45 | CORNFLAKES | 80 |
| LENTILS | 29 | REGULAR OATMEAL | 49 | RICE CAKES | 82 |
| PEACH | 30 | ORANGE JUICE | 53 | SHREDDED WHEAT | 83 |
| SKIM MILK | 32 | GREEN PEAS | 54 | BAKED POTATO | 85 |
| PEARS | 33 | SUCROSE | 59 | INSTANT RICE | 87 |
| WHOLE MILK | 34 | BANANA | 62 | GLUCOSE | 100 |
| ICE CREAM | 36 | BEETS | 64 | | |
| CHICKPEAS | 36 | RAISINS | 64 | | |
| YOGURT with fruit | 33 | MACARONI | 64 | | |
| APPLES | 39 | GREEN PEAS | 65 | | |
| NAVY BEANS | 40 | MUESLI | 66 | | |

*Numbers are based on reference of glucose at 100.

## CARBOHYDRATES-SWIFT OR SLOW?

It used to be simple—starchy complex carbohydrates were thought to be digested slowly and produce a more flattened and stable blood glucose curve, while simple carbohydrates were believed to quickly raise blood glucose for a short period of time.

Now, thanks to another method of classifying carbohydrates, the glycemic index, predicting blood glucose changes has become much more complex. The glycemic index refers to a food's ability to affect blood glucose levels. Pure glucose has a rating of 100 on the scale; all other foods are ranked against glucose and assigned a corresponding number.

High-glycemic-index foods quickly raise blood glucose, trigger higher insulin levels, and maximize glycogen synthesis. Ideally these foods should be consumed in your early post-exercise meals and snacks. High-glycemic choices include most liquid carbohydrate supplements, breads, cereals, instant rice and potatoes. Your recovery diet over the hours before exercise can also emphasize these high glycemic index foods, particularly if your next training session is in less than twelve hours.

Subsequent chapters will discuss the application of consuming high glycemic index foods during exercise (Chapter 10), and low glycemic index foods before exercise (Chapter 9). Table 3.5 provides a list of the glycemic index of tested foods. Chapter 6, reviews some of the more practical, everyday issues in choosing carbohydrates for a sports diet.

Applying the glycemic index of foods to performance enhancement actually requires more research and development. Many factors, such as the portion consumed, certain fibers, food preparation methods, protein and fat content of the meal, the "ripeness" of foods, and interactions with food factors that block absorption, all influence the glycemic index.

*"I have no doubt on how effective getting enough carbohydrates after a hard race is on refilling the muscles."*

*—Alvis,*

For example, plain sucrose has a higher glycemic index than sucrose combined with fat in products such as ice cream and cookies. Boiled potatoes have a lower glycemic index than a baked potato, while pasta has a lower glycemic index than bread, though both are made from wheat.

Depending on your food choices, there are hundreds of various glycemic responses possible. However, when you consume a large amount of one food by itself after exercise, your recovery may benefit from properly utilizing this ranking system.

## CARBOHYDRATE SUPPLEMENTS

For athletes with high energy and carbohydrate needs, it can be difficult to choose foods that meet your requirements. For this reason, high carbohydrate supplements, which do not replace nutritious foods but simply add them to the diet, may be useful.

You can try high carbohydrate drinks supplying anywhere from 80 to 100 grams of carbohydrate per serving. Sports bars are another convenient food which can provide around 50 grams of carbohydrate. Carbohydrate gels and nutrient-dense liquid meals supplements are also some applicable choices. These supplements can also be less filling than fiber-containing or bulky carbohydrates, and are less likely to cause gastrointestinal discomfort. Liquid choices are also very appealing when you are dehydrated.

## FINAL THOUGHTS

Carbohydrates are an important fuel source for any type of athlete undergoing a variety of training sessions. Total daily carbohydrate requirements depend upon the intensity and total training hours. In consideration of current research, meeting these carbohydrate needs on a daily basis makes sense for optimal recovery. Recovery can also be enhanced by paying close attention to optimal post-exercise carbohydrate intake. High glycemic index choices may work best at this time, though more research on this carbohydrate ranking system is required. Carbohydrate foods higher in vitamin, minerals, and phytochemicals should be emphasized for optimal health.

# That Matter
## of *Fat*

*"Everything in America is fat-free this and fat-free that. I tried a very low fat diet for a couple of years and it didn't work at all. My body fat got too low and I found that I was getting sick all the time."*

—*FitzRandolph*

It's time to pick up training again for the competitive season ahead. As you evaluate this year's goals, you decide that you could stand to lose a few pounds, as loss of body fat would improve your performance. To achieve this, you try to maintain a very low fat diet. Also, in order to burn more fat as a fuel, you focus on low intensity, longer training sessions.

At some point in their career, every athlete evaluates how body fat and dietary fat affect training and performance. Despite an almost national compulsive focus on this dietary nutrient and body tissue, fat does warrant some healthy attention. High-fat diets are clearly associated with increased health risks, while appropriate body fat levels support peak performance and a positive body image. Fat also serves as a significant fuel during endurance exercise and is almost always burned in combination with carbohydrate. Endurance training also improves your ability to burn fat for energy at a given intensity, sparing your glycogen stores. Clearly fat is an important issue for athletes. Questions that athletes may frequently ask regarding fat and their training program are:

- *When do I use fat as a fuel?*
- *How much fat does my training diet require?*
- *What types of dietary fat are appropriate for good health?*
- *What about the current controversy regarding fat and performance?*

## WHERE FAT IS STORED

At nine calories per gram (compared to carbohydrates and protein at 4 calories per gram), fat is a calorically dense and compact storage tissue. Body fat also contains very little water, compared to the 3 to 4 grams of water stored with every gram of carbohydrate or protein.

The average person can store anywhere from 50,000 to 100,000 calories of adipose tissue triglycerides. Fat or triglycerides within or between the muscle cells can provide up to 2800 calories of stored energy, while triglycerides in the blood provide 70 to 80 calories. Your liver also stores triglycerides, contributing to this large total body reservoir of fatty energy.

Every pound of fat on your body supplies 3500 calories of energy, whereas your total body glycogen stores only reach 2000 calories with proper training and diet. Even the leanest athletes store several pounds of body fat. That's why the vast majority of athletes shouldn't attempt to store or load fat as you would carbohydrate. Excess body fat can impair your performance and adversely affect your health.

## USING FAT FOR ENERGY

F at or triglyceride, and carbohydrate (glycogen and glucose,) are the two main sources of energy during exercise. One of the key determiners of which body fuel is predominately used is exercise intensity. Above 65 to 70 percent $VO_2$ max, carbohydrate is the preferred fuel. During very mild exercise, at about 25 percent $VO_2$ max, fat provides about 80 percent of the total fuel. Adipose tissue is the major source of fat at this low intensity. As exercise increases towards 65 percent $VO_2$ max, more of the fat used is supplied by muscle triglycerides.

While there are no advantages to fat-loading, there are clear benefits to increasing your ability to burn fat for energy during exercise. Studies have shown that athletes burn more fat than untrained individuals when performing the same standardized exercise task. This increased ability to utilize fat spares muscle glycogen and improves your endurance capacity. Your ability to burn more fat is related to a number of mechanisms, one of which is changes in muscle enzymes related to fat burning. Increasing your lactate threshold also improves your ability to utilize fat.

*"I have never gotten down to the onion skin look all over my body. But I do know how heavy an extra water bottle can feel on a climb."*

*—Alvis*

### FAT REQUIREMENTS FOR TRAINING

An increased ability to burn fat during exercise is a major training benefit, as greater fat burning conserves your limited supply of muscle glycogen. But it has yet to be proven that dietary fat loading results in greater fat burning. Judging how much total dietary fat you need, without being excessive, depends upon your calorie needs. For most athletes, a diet adequate in calories for their training requirements and weight goals should supply about 20 to 25 percent of the total calories from fat. These moderate amounts supply essential fatty acids, should replenish muscular fat stores, and leave room for enough dietary carbohydrate and protein.

## FAT IN YOUR DIET

Besides fueling your training, fat is an important source of essential fatty acids, and is involved in the transport and absorption of fat-soluble vitamins. Fats also add flavor to foods and keeps you from becoming hungry between meals. But fats come in several chemical forms, some healthier than others. They are divided into two categories: saturated and unsaturated. Unsaturated fats include both polyunsaturated and monounsaturated fats. No matter what types of fat you eat, health experts, particularly those at the American Heart Association, recommend that fat intake not exceed 30 percent of your total calories. For most Americans, who average about 37 percent fat calories, this is a significant decrease in fat. This high national average has been linked to heart disease, strokes and certain cancers. The AHA sets 15 percent as the lower limit for fat intake, because very low fat intakes may not benefit the general population and could cause nutrient deficiencies in some individuals.

*"At one point in everyone's athletic career, you think that fat is bad. But part of being healthy and taking care of yourself is not really obsessing about diet restrictions. Fat is part of a healthy diet."*
*—Tueting*

Besides keeping your total fat intake to about 20 to 25 percent of your calories, for both training and good health, limit

your saturated fat intake. Saturated fats raise blood cholesterol levels, particularly the harmful low density lipoprotein
(LDL) cholesterol, more than any other type of fat in your
diet. Saturated fat comes mainly from animal foods. Sources
include cheese and whole milk products, fatty cuts of meat,
high fat processed lunch meats, butter, lard, shortening and
bacon grease.

Only three plant oils are highly saturated:
palm oil, palm kernel oil, and coconut oil.
Found often in commercial baked goods likes
cookies and crackers, these oils contain no
dietary cholesterol (which is found only in
animal foods), but may be packaged and
marked "contains only plant oil." Ignore this
misleading claim and limit these three tropical
oils. Saturated fats should comprise no more than one-quarter
to one-third of your total fat intake.

*"I think all of us have tried, at one time or another, to cut out fat from our diets. I have in the past fallen victim to this. I have realized that your body needs fat, and so I try to use moderate levels of good fats and try to keep the bad fats down."*
                                                  *—Fuhr*

Unsaturated fats, both polyunsaturated and monounsaturated, may help lower your blood cholesterol when they
replace saturated fat in your diet. But still limit these calorically dense fats. Polyunsaturated fats come mostly from plant
foods such as walnuts, sunflower seeds, and corn, sunflower,
and safflower oils. These oils are liquid at room temperature.
Large amounts of polyunsaturated oils have been linked to the
development of certain cancers in animals. These oils should
make up no more than one-third of your total fat intake.

Monounsaturated fats, of which olive oil is a rich source,
are probably your best choice. Besides lowering your bad
LDL cholesterol, olive oil may keep LDL from being oxidized.

Oxidized LDL increases your risk for developing heart disease. In addition, olive oil may help protect your levels of the good, high-density lipoprotein (HDL) cholesterol. Other sources of monounsaturated fats are canola oil, peanut oil, avocados, almonds, and hazelnuts. Monounsaturated fats should supply one-third to one-half your total fat intake. Table 4.1 outlines the types of fats contained in various oils and fats. As olive oil is 77-percent monounsaturated, it is referred to as a monounsaturated fat.

Fish oils, or "omega-3 fatty acids," are a type of polyunsaturated oil found to reduce risk of heart disease. In one study, men consuming at least seven ounces of fish per week had a 42-percent reduction in heart-attack deaths. Omega-3 fatty acids produce these benefits by reducing serum triglycerides, another harmful type of fat circulating in your blood. These fats also have the benefit of reducing blood-clot formation and stabilizing the heart's muscle cells, possibly preventing life-threatening arrhythmias.

ROLLERBLADE

*Athletes need to eat the correct amounts and types of fat.*

In addition to their heart-health benefits, omega-3 fatty

| TABLE 4.1: PERCENTAGES OF FAT OF VARIOUS OILS | | | |
|---|---|---|---|
| OIL | % SATURATED | % POLY-UNSATURATED | % MONO-UNSATURATED |
| CANOLA OIL | 6 | 32 | 62 |
| SAFFLOWER OIL | 10 | 77 | 13 |
| SUNFLOWER OIL | 11 | 69 | 20 |
| CORN OIL | 13 | 62 | 25 |
| OLIVE OIL | 14 | 9 | 77 |
| SOYBEAN OIL | 15 | 61 | 24 |
| MARGARINE (TUB) | 17 | 34 | 24 |
| PEANUT OIL | 18 | 33 | 49 |
| COTTONSEED OIL | 27 | 54 | 19 |
| LARD | 41 | 12 | 47 |
| PALM KERNEL OIL | 81 | 2 | 11 |
| COCONUT OIL | 92 | 2 | 6 |
| SOURCE: USDA | | | |

acids in fish may mitigate the symptoms of rheumatoid arthritis because of their anti-inflammatory effect. Though the evidence is very preliminary, they may also slow breast-cancer tumor growth. Americans consume relatively low amounts of omega-3 fatty acids. The AHA recommends increasing food sources of these fats. Good sources are salmon, mackerel, tuna and whitefish, while halibut, trout, and bass are also decent sources. However, the AHA cautions against fish oil supplements as they interact with some medications, and their long-term benefits and side effects are unknown.

Another category of fat, hidden in many of the foods you

eat, are trans fatty acids. In the last several years, evidence has continued to mount that trans fat raises bad LDL cholesterol, and may even lower the good HDL.

Trans fats are made from altered fatty acids. They are created when liquid oils are "partially hydrogenated." Hydrogenation turns corn oil into margarine sticks and makes oils more stable, increasing product shelf-life. Besides margarine, cooking oils used at fast food establishments, shortening and commercially baked chips, cooking, crackers, are sources of trans fat.

Even with labels marked "partially hydrogenated," it's hard to know the exact amount of trans fat. On some labels, you can add up the grams of saturated, polyunsaturated and monounsaturated fat, and subtract this from the total grams of fat. The amount left over is trans fat. Foods containing trans fat are allowed by the FDA to be labeled "low cholesterol." Until labeling is clearer, avoid "completely hydrogenated" oils and limit "partially hydrogenated" oils, especially if these oils are one of the first several ingredients listed.

Finally, dietary cholesterol is found only in animal foods such as egg yolks, cheese, meats—especially organ meats—and poultry. If you limit your intake of saturated fat and control portions of animal proteins, you should consume no more than 300 milligrams of cholesterol daily. In addition, limit egg yolks to two to three weekly. And despite advertising, remember, that cholesterol is never found in plant foods, but saturated fats such as palm kernel oil often are found in non-animal products.

For both performance and good health, keep the following dietary fat guidelines. How you respond to these guidelines also depends upon your genetics, but they are the best place to begin. Keep total fat to 20 to 25 percent of calorie intake.

- *Use limited amounts of olive oil and canola oil and cooking sprays instead of margarine, when possible.*
- *Limit margarine intake. Choose soft tub with liquid oil as the first ingredient.*
- *Limit saturated fat from animal fats like butter, cream, whole milk, and whole-fat cheese. Use skim or 1-percent milk products.*
- *Buy products that do not contain hydrogenated oils.*
- *Choose the leanest cuts of red meat possible. Use lean poultry and increase your fish intake.*
- *Read labels to compare the amount of total fat, saturated fat, and trans fat in the product.*

| TABLE 4.2: FAT ALLOWANCE FOR 25-PERCENT CALORIES | | |
|---|---|---|
| **DAILY CALORIE INTAKE** | **CALORIES FROM FAT- 25% TOTAL** | **UPPER LIMIT FAT IN GRAMS** |
| 1400 | 350 | 39 |
| 1500 | 375 | 42 |
| 1600 | 400 | 44 |
| 1800 | 450 | 50 |
| 2000 | 500 | 55 |
| 2200 | 550 | 61 |
| 2400 | 600 | 67 |
| 2600 | 650 | 72 |
| 2800 | 700 | 78 |
| 3000 | 750 | 83 |
| 3200 | 800 | 89 |
| 3400 | 850 | 94 |
| 3600 | 900 | 100 |
| 3800 | 950 | 106 |
| 4000 | 1000 | 111 |
| 4200 | 1050 | 117 |
| 4400 | 1100 | 122 |

Table 4.2 outlines a 25-percent of total calories fat budget for various calorie levels.

## FACTS AND FALLACIES ABOUT HIGH FAT DIETS

One intriguing idea which constantly pervades sports nutrition marketing and research is the concept of increasing the athlete's ability to utilize fat as a fuel during exercise. Even the leanest of athletes have plenty of stored fat, and burning these untapped stores would be beneficial. But burning body fat is not as simple as it sounds. As was previously discussed, fat used for fuel during exercise actually comes from two storage areas. During training, you burn fatty acids released from the fat tissues very slowly. Fat stored in your muscles, or intra-muscular fat, is really the greater fat fuel supply, especially at higher intensities.

As you do with glycogen, you need to replenish this intra-muscular fat after training. Dietary fat can do this, but so can fatty acids released from your stores of body fat. There is a constant cycling of fat from various areas in your body. Most often, adipose tissue or body fat loss is simply the result of the total calories burned, regardless of the type of fuel your body was predominantly burning during training.

Athletes do require fat in their diet, amounts easily met when energy needs are met and fat supplies 20 to 25 percent of the total calories consumed. It is not unusual for endurance athletes with very high energy needs to consume a high amount of total fat daily. But they do this only after meeting higher-than-average demands for carbohydrate and protein. Dietary fat simply helps some athletes meet their very high energy requirements.

Let's take a look at the evidence that fat improves athletic performance. Overall, most arguments and studies have failed to convince scientists and sports nutritionists that athletes should adopt a high-fat eating plan.

Many studies regarding fat and performance have been performed on rats and dogs. While these studies may demonstrate adaptations to a high-fat diet, this information should not necessarily be extrapolated to humans. That's because these animals behave differently than humans in their ability to utilize fat and carbohydrate.

Many current human studies cited to support a higher fat diet contain design flaws or cannot be extrapolated to real-life improvements in performance. One study, conducted in 1983, took an extreme approach and fed a group of male endurance athletes a high-fat diet containing less than 20 grams of carbohydrate for four weeks. Muscle glycogen levels decreased with the high-fat diet, and there was a shift toward higher fat utilization. However, this was found at relatively moderate-intensity exercise of about 64-percent $VO_2$ max.

Most scientists have contested the conclusion that this fat adaptation did not harm athletic performance. Besides using a very small number of subjects—only five—the results were distorted by a large performance improvement in one subject. The other four subjects showed only small changes, both positive and negative, in performance. Study results among subjects were averaged, showing that the high-fat diet did not hurt performance.

But any athlete realizes that what is really desired is an actual improvement in performance. This study showed no evidence of performance benefits. Subjects were not able to increase their intensity and endurance on the high-fat diet. Testing should have occurred above 70-percent $VO_2$ max, the intensity above which glycogen becomes the preferred fuel. This study also did not compare the results of a high-fat diet to a high carbohydrate diet. Another widely quoted study regarding fat loading and performance employed questionable design methods. Runners were assigned three diets—normal, high fat and high carbohydrate—in a designated order, rather than in a randomized fashion during the season. Training also varied during the season, rather than remaining consistent on all three diets. Finally, there was not a great enough difference between the carbohydrate and fat content of the various diet. This means the study did not really test the body's adaptation to a high-fat diet.

Adaptation to a high-fat diet takes up to two weeks. Athletes may find exercise during this time to be difficult, due to low muscle glycogen stores. Even with adaptation, exercise would need to occur below 70-percent $VO_2$ max. Fat adaptation is likely only to be important to the ultra-endurance athlete. More research in the area of fat adaptation and performance benefits is required. The 40-30-30 diet theory, which is actually a very high protein diet, will be covered in Chapter 5.

## FINAL THOUGHTS

Athletes require about 20 to 25 percent of their total calories from fat, though requirements can vary slightly among individuals and sports. Saturated and trans fats should be limited, with monounsaturated fat and then polyunsaturated fat supplying the majority of fat in the diet. Dietary intake of omega-3 fatty acids can also be increased. In addition, high-fat eating should not become a long-term strategy for any athlete. Extremely high-fat (and low carbohydrate) diets have been associated with heart rhythm disturbances and electrolyte losses. Blood cholesterol levels, namely the harmful LDL, can also increase on a high-fat diet. Besides increasing the risk of developing heart disease, high-fat eating has also been linked to certain types of cancer.

Tom Moran

*Endurance athletes have increased protein reauirements.*

# CHAPTER FIVE

# The Power
## *of Protein*

*"It has always been easy to obtain carbohydrates in my diet. But I need to make an effort to take in more protein, because it often requires more preparation time and effort."*
*— Brian Walton, Saturn Cycling Team*
*1996 Olympic silver medalist*

The cyclist had just finished a long stage race. He felt tired and spent. After chugging down a recovery drink providing mainly carbohydrates, he was looking forward to a nice large portion of chicken. After all, the wear and tear of hard racing means increased protein requirements.

For centuries, protein has been associated with powerful athletic performance. The ancient logic was that if muscle mass was made of protein, then increased dietary protein supported muscle building. Most efforts of physical performance involve strenuous muscular activity, so this belief persists now. Strength-training athletes especially support this view, often consuming several times the Recommended Daily Allowances of protein. Endurance athletes, while often aware of their increased requirements for carbohydrates, also question just how much protein they need for their training.

It doesn't clear the confusion when specific amino acid

CASEY B. GIBSON

*Endurance athletes, such as Brian Walton (center) of the Saturn Cycling Team, have increased protein requirements.*

supplements are heavily promoted for improved endurance training and recovery. In addition, sports nutrition marketing heavily encourages whole protein supplements and amino acid products to all types of athletes. One popular diet book even states that good health and peak performance hinges on protein intake.

In reality, researchers who have conducted and evaluated well-designed studies on protein requirements and exercise have made recommendations for increased protein intake, but not to the high levels often promoted. Sports nutritionists support obtaining the correct amounts of low-fat natural food sources of protein.

Questions that athletes may frequently ask regarding protein and training requirements are:

- *What are the functions of protein in the body?*
- *Do I utilize protein as a fuel during exercise and during recovery?*
- *What are my protein requirements?*
- *Do I need protein supplements?*
- *What is the validity regarding high protein diet claims?*

## HOW PROTEIN PROMOTES HEALTH AND PERFORMANCE

Proteins are composed of amino acids, of which twenty have been identified. These amino acids can be combined in various ways to form proteins that provide structure to the human body and perform a variety of functions. When two amino acids are linked, proteins form a dipeptide. Several linked amino acids form polypeptides. Most proteins are polypeptides, and can include combinations of up to three hundred amino acids linked together. We obtain amino acids from both animal and plant foods.

Some amino acids can be synthesized by the body. The nine amino acids which we cannot make ourselves are called essen-

*"Being a sprinter, I make sure I get quite a bit of protein."*
*—FitzRandolph*

tial amino acids, because we must obtain them in our diet. Eleven amino acids that can be formed in the body are called nonessential. Foods that contain an adequate amount of all nine essential amino acids are referred to as complete proteins. Foods that are deficient in one or more amino acids are called incomplete proteins.

Animal protein is complete because it has large amounts of all nine essential amino acids in the proper proportions. The amino acids in plant proteins usually exist in smaller concentrations. While high in several of the essential amino acids, plant proteins may contain insufficient amounts of one or more essential amino acids. Your body can make complete proteins from plant foods, but only if a variety of plant foods and sufficient calories are eaten during the day.

Protein performs many important functions in the body that are essential for good health and quality training. Protein is involved somehow in almost all body functions. It provides structure for body tissues, regulates metabolism, and can be utilized as an energy source. Some protein functions include:

- *A role in tissue growth and repair*
- *A role in formation of almost all body enzymes*
- *Forming various hormones, neurotransmitters, or neuropeptides*
- *Forming key components of the immune system*
- *Maintaining optimal fluid balance in body tissues*
- *Providing energy in aerobic metabolism*

It is protein's function in tissue repair and in energy metabolism which plays a large role in determining the athlete's protein requirements.

## PROTEIN'S ROLE IN EXERCISE AND RECOVERY

Basically there are several categories of exercisers or athletes who may require greater protein than the RDA:

- *Endurance athletes*
- *Athletes performing intense strength-training programs*
- *Teenage athletes with growth as well as exercise requirements*
- *Exercisers and athletes following a calorie-restricted weight loss programs.*

There are a number of reasons why these types of athletes require additional protein. Endurance athletes undergoing heavy training have a significant increase in protein requirements. First, this is required to cover some protein fuel costs incurred when training. As was mentioned previously, the two most important factors determining fuel usage are exercise intensity and the amount of carbohydrate available for energy.

When muscle glycogen stores are low due to longer duration exercise or an inadequate diet, protein, which can eventually be converted to glucose, is needed to supply fuel. In the latter stages of endurance exercise, protein could contribute up to 15 percent of the total energy cost. This is a significant increase, as protein only contributes to about 5 percent of energy needs when glycogen stores are high. Not consuming enough calories will increase your use of protein during exercise. Endurance athletes also require protein for the repair and recovery process after training.

> "A lot of people on our team were very conscious of getting enough protein. Our strength coach really promoted it. Adding more protein definitely improved our diet."
>
> —Tueting

Protein losses may occur in other ways. Elevated levels of protein have been found in the urine after exercise, and protein may also be lost in sweat. But overall, both these losses are relatively minor. Regular training both reduces muscle protein breakdown and improves protein synthesis during recovery.

Strength-training athletes also require additional protein for exercise fuel, repair and recovery, and to build muscle mass. Though strength-training athletes often consume large amounts of protein in hopes of building more muscle mass, the actual requirements for this tissue building are relatively small. Protein consumed in excess of actual requirements will not be used to build more muscle, but rather will be converted and used for energy or stored as fat.

Based on a number of variables, an athlete's protein requirements can range from 0.45 to 0.9 grams of protein per pound of weight (1 to 2 grams per kilogram). Table 5.1 describes the protein requirements of various types of athletes.

## MEETING PROTEIN REQUIREMENTS

These elevated protein requirements for training should be put into perspective. Basically, your increased protein requirements are easily met in a balanced training diet which is adequate in calories. A 150 pound endurance athlete would require anywhere from 82 to 110 grams of protein daily. Currently, the average American consumes 100 grams of protein daily, with about 70 percent coming from animal protein. This easily exceeds the RDA of 0.36 grams per pound of weight. Most consumers as well as athletes meet or even exceed their protein requirements. (See Table 5.2: Protein Requirements Based On Weight.)

For most athletes, increased training often means increased caloric intake and more protein intake. Often diet composition remains constant, with protein continuing to contribute 12 to 20

---

**TABLE 5.1: PROTEIN REQUIREMENTS OF ATHLETES**

**PROTEIN NEEDS PER POUND OF WEIGHT**

CURRENT RDA
Sedentary adult: 0.4 grams

EDURANCE ATHLETES
Moderate training: 0.45 grams
Heavy training: 0.50 to 0.75 grams
Very intense training: 0.8 to 0.9 grams

STRENGTH TRAINING ATHLETES
Experienced: 0.5 to 0.7 grams
Novice: 0.8 grams

GROWING TEENAGE ATHLETE
0.8 to 0.9 grams

ATHLETE RESTRICTING CALORIES
0.8 to 0.9 grams

MAXIMUM RECOMMENDED AMOUNT 1.0 grams

percent of the total calories.

Protein foods are readily available. Lean and low fat sources are best. Sources include:

- *Skim dairy foods: Milk, yogurt, cheese*
- *Lean cuts of meat: Chicken, fish, beef, pork, lamb, veal, eggs*
- *Plant foods: Beans, legumes, soy foods, nuts or seeds*

## PROTEIN SUPPLEMENTATION

Much marketing of whole protein and amino acid supplements is directed to both endurance and strength athletes. Yet clearly, an athlete's elevated protein needs are easily met or exceeded on an adequate calorie diet, rendering protein supplements unnecessary. Generally, protein accounts for about 12 to 20 percent of the calories in the diet. As stated previously, when energy intake increases due to training, the proportion of calories from protein remains constant. These means that the total protein consumed per pound of weight also increases.

Supporters of amino acid supplementation claim that their products are more readily digested and absorbed than protein found in food. This simply isn't true. Your body is well-equipped to handle whole proteins from real foods. Through a number of enzymes that break down the protein in

| TABLE 5.2: PROTEIN REQUIREMENTS BASED ON WEIGHT | |
|---|---|
| **BODY WEIGHT** | **PROTEIN INTAKE RANGE (0.45 TO 0.9 GRAMS)** |
| 110 | 50 TO 99 GRAMS |
| 120 | 54 TO 108 GRAMS |
| 130 | 59 TO 117 GRAMS |
| 140 | 63 TO 126 GRAMS |
| 150 | 68 TO 135 GRAMS |
| 160 | 72 TO 144 GRAMS |
| 170 | 77 TO 153 GRAMS |
| 180 | 81 TO 162 GRAMS |
| 190 | 86 TO 171 GRAMS |
| 200 | 90 TO 180 GRAMS |

food to amino acids, absorption of both plant and animal proteins is more than 90 percent. Amino acids are also marketed as being more rapidly digested and absorbed, and in turn, repairing damaged muscle tissue more quickly. Again, there is no evidence to support this claim. Besides, post-exercise muscle repair takes hours, not minutes, further invalidating claims surrounding these products.

*"Several years ago, I became a little more conscious of having some protein with the carbohydrates, with fat in the meal as well."*
*–Reid*

There are a variety of claims surrounding amino acid supplementation. For example, those marketed to body builders claim that some build muscle and burn fat. Arginine and ornithine are two such promoted amino acids. Supposedly, they stimulate the secretion of growth hormone, which then increases muscle mass. In fact, what seems to occur is that large amounts are needed to promote a temporary rise in growth hormone. In addition, there is no proof that this rise results in increased muscle mass. There is currently no sound scientific data to support that supplementing with these amino acids produces this muscle-building effect.

Endurance athletes may also be sold on three amino acids, leucine, isoleucine and valine, often referred to as branched chain, due to their structure. When protein is required for energy during endurance exercise, branched chain amino acids are the protein utilized because they can be converted to glucose. You can minimize the use of branched chain amino acids as a fuel source by beginning exercise with adequate carbohydrate stores.

Regardless, obtaining branched chain amino acids from foods before and after endurance exercise is fairly simple.

TOM MORAN

*Increased protein needs for sports such as back-country skiing are easily met with a balanced diet.*

Some foods high in branched chain amino acids include many liquid protein-carbohydrate supplements, milk and yogurt, fish, poultry, and lean red meat.

In summary, amino acid metabolism is very complex. It is affected by a variety of factors including amino acid concentration in the blood, competition with other available amino acids, and the presence of other nutrients. Amino acid mixtures could potentially lead to nutritional imbalances, as an excess of one amino acid may negatively affect the absorption of another.

Amino acid supplement dosing may also be misleading. A bottle listing up to 500 milligrams in a capsule actually contains only 0.5 grams or less than 1 gram of amino acids. One ounce of chicken contains 7000 milligrams, or 7 grams of

# The 40-30-30 Diet

A new, high protein diet twist, referred to as the 40-30-30 diet, has been marketed heavily to athletes and received much attention for the past several years. This acronym refers to a recommendation of 40 percent carbohydrate, 30 percent protein, and 30 percent fat. Often touted as a high-fat diet that helps athletes burn fat, it is in reality a diet very high in protein, moderate in fat, and possibly low in carbohydrate, depending on the amount of calories consumed. It is advised that when carbohydrates are consumed, they should be those with a low glycemic index.

Advocates of the diet contend that this lower consumption of carbohydrates, coupled with increased protein, allows the body to use more fat by decreasing the production of insulin and producing a better balance between insulin to glucagon. Let's take a look at this untested theory.

Consumption of carbohydrates does trigger the release of insulin. Insulin aids the body in processing carbohydrates and at the same time inhibits fat burning. Insulin is also said to affect production of eicosanoids, hormone-like substances produced by the body. According to this diet theory, eicosanoids are classified as "good" or "bad." The "bad" eicosanoids are said to impair athletic performance by decreasing the body's utilization of fat as an energy source. They also are said to reduce oxygen transfer to cells and lower blood glucose. "Good" eicosanoids are said to improve performance by having the opposite effects of the "bad" eicosanoids.

Again, carbohydrate and insulin are described as the culprits. Too much carbohydrate, especially those with a high glycemic index, produces too much insulin, which then produces "bad" eicosanoids. Conversely, limiting insulin secretion with an increased protein intake, results in more "good" eicosanoids.

This approach makes some very bold promises. Like any diet that can impact an athlete's health and performance, it deserves close scrutiny and scientific verification.

Insulin has received negative reviews in the popular press for the past several years. But to date, there is very little evidence that excess body weight is caused by an abundance of insulin triggered by a high carbohydrate diet. It is generally accepted that excess body weight is simply the result of too great a consumption of calories when compared to the amount burned by exercise. Those excess calories can come in any form: fat, protein and carbohydrate.

Estimates suggest that about 10 to 25 percent of all Americans can be classified as "insulin-resistant"— a condition that leads to greater storage of body fat. Studies suggest, however, that a regular aerobic training program lowers insulin resistance in susceptible individuals. For most athletes, body weight should come down to a question of calories consumed versus calories burned.

Biochemists involved in eicosanoid research have expressed concern regarding their role in the 40-30-30 theory. Many argue that eicosanoids are not considered to be the most powerful hormonal system in the body, and should not have as great an impact on health and athletic performance as this theory would suggest. Since all eicosanoids are an integral part of the important, but much larger physiological process, classifying them as "good" or "bad" is an oversimplification. It is also important to be aware that many hormones that are not controlled by insulin affect eicosanoid production. The insulin-eicosanoid link is described as weak and indirect at best.

Concerns regarding this diet theory don't stop there. Protein is also known to induce secretion of insulin. In addition, meal plans for this diet are very low in calories. Much of the weight loss that has been reported could simply be the result of calorie restriction. Also, this diet could be excessively high in protein, leading to some of the health concerns already addressed in this chapter. The very low energy intake on this diet could eventually impair athletic performance. Depending on the caloric consumption, this diet could also be very deficient in carbohydrate for the endurance athlete.

Overall, following a 40-30-30 ratio of nutrients at every meal and snack may be difficult. It appears that the manner in which athletes adopt this diet has been varied and open to interpretation. Some athletes have simply increased their protein and fat intake slightly, while others have eliminated excess carbohydrate. Only accurate food records and a computerized analysis could indicate for certain what exact nutrient breakdown is consumed.

| TABLE 5.3: PROTEIN CONTENT OF FOODS | |
|---|---|
| **FOODS** | **GRAMS OF PROTEIN** |
| KIDNEY BEANS, 1 CUP | 15 GRAMS |
| BLACK BEANS, 1 CUP | 15 GRAMS |
| TOFU, FIRM, 1/4 CUP | 10 GRAMS |
| BEEF, 1 OUNCE | 8 GRAMS |
| PORK TENDERLOIN, 1 OUNCE | 8 GRAMS |
| POULTRY, 1 OUNCE | 8 GRAMS |
| SKIM MILK, 8 OUNCES | 8 GRAMS |
| YOGURT, 1 CUP | 8 GRAMS |
| PEANUTS, 1 OUNCE | 7 GRAMS |
| SOY MILK, 1 CUP | 7 GRAMS |
| PASTA, 1 CUP | 6 GRAMS |
| POTATO, BAKED, 1 MEDIUM | 5 GRAMS |
| PEANUT BUTTER, 1 TBSP | 5 GRAMS |
| RICE, 1 CUP | 4 GRAMS |
| OATMEAL, 3/4 CUP | 4 GRAMS |

amino acids, in the form of whole protein. Clearly, amino acid supplements cannot meet the dosing in a compact source of natural protein.

## DANGERS OF EXCESS PROTEIN

A well-balanced diet with adequate calories and up to 20 percent protein calories provides enough grams of protein for growth and repair. Protein which is consumed in excess of your requirements is simply excess calories and is then burned for energy and stored as fat. Converting protein to fuel for exercise is inefficient. Carbohydrates are a much more efficient source of energy.

There are other effects of consuming excess protein. Protein, from both food and supplements, increases your need for fluid. Your kidneys require more water to eliminate the end products of protein metabolism. Individuals with liver or kidney problems may also be susceptible to negative effects of excessive dietary protein. Excess dietary protein also leads to urinary excretion of calcium, and can possibly contribute to development of osteoporosis.

While food sources of protein are best, they can also be substantial sources of fat and cholesterol. As was discussed in an earlier chapter, consuming excess fat and cholesterol can increase your risk of certain health problems. You should be selective in the type of protein foods you eat. Try to emphasize low fat animal proteins, and plenty of plant protein as well. Table 5.3 lists the protein content of various foods.

## FINAL THOUGHTS

Athletes do have elevated protein requirements. However, these increased amounts are easily met on a well-balanced diet. Protein supplements are usually not required and are not better absorbed than natural sources of protein, despite popular claims to the contrary. Excessive protein intake can have negative health side effects. For athletes, enough protein is important, but there is such a thing as too much, beyond which no additional benefits are derived.

SIMON CUDBY

*Optimal vitamin and mineral intake helps maintain goood health, especially when you need it the most. Alison Dunlap, professional mountain bike racer.*

# CHAPTER SIX

# Vitamins and Minerals
## *for an Active Life*

*"I occasionally stressed as an amateur about taking the
right vitamin supplements. However, I never really
noticed a difference between them and came to rely on a
well balanced diet of the freshest foods available."*

*—Alvis*

Nearly every athlete is concerned about the effects
that training and competing have on nutrient
requirements. How do you keep the immune system
healthy? What amounts of vitamins and minerals does your
body require? There are a variety of messages from consumer marketing and various health professionals that are
often conflicting.

Active individuals and athletes have long been advised by
nutritionists to obtain optimal levels of nutrients from the
foods they eat. In addition, active people are heavily targeted
by advertising promoting vitamin and mineral supplementation. Which is correct?

Like many Americans, you may not be filling your diet with enough nutrient-dense foods such as fruits, vegetables, whole grains, and low-fat dairy foods. Busy lifestyles, combined with a demanding training program, can make optimal daily nutrition a challenge. Often, athletes want to find a balance between improving their food choices and utilizing vitamin and mineral supplements without overdoing doses and experiencing negative reactions.

Clearly optimal vitamin and mineral intake is required for both good health and peak athletic performance. Some questions athletes may have concerning vitamins and minerals are:

- *Does training increase my vitamin and mineral requirements?*
- *What are the best food sources of important vitamins and minerals?*
- *Will vitamin and mineral supplements improve my performance?*
- *What are some of the current and safe recommendations regarding vitamin and mineral supplements?*
- *What about phytochemicals?*

## FUNCTIONS OF VITAMINS AND MINERALS
### VITAMINS

Vitamins are thirteen organic compounds found in small amounts in foods. They act as catalysts to facilitate hundreds of biochemical reactions. Vitamins play additional roles in growth, maintenance and repair. Some are antioxidants which protect cells from potentially toxic "free-radicals,"

*Optimal vitamin and mineral intake helps maintain good health.*

which are unstable molecules implicated in contributing to development of a number of diseases. Each vitamin has its own particular function and interacts with other nutrients in the body. Vitamins themselves do not contain or provide energy—only carbohydrates, proteins, and fats can do that— but vitamins play a key role in releasing energy from food.

Vitamins are separated into two classifications. There are four fat-soluble vitamins and nine water-soluble vitamins. Your body may contain large stores of the fat-soluble variety —A, D, E and K. Deficiencies are rare, though excessive intakes may have toxic effects.

The water-soluble vitamins are vitamin C, and the eight B vitamins: thiamin (B1), riboflavin (B2), pyridoxine (B6), niacin, B12, folacin, biotin, and pantothenic acid. These vitamins are not stored in your body in significant amounts. Several of the B vitamins are involved in energy metabolism.

While it's true that inadequate dietary intake of vitamins eventually results in deficiencies that can impair physical performance, actual vitamin deficiencies are rare in the U.S. More likely, some individuals may have marginal intakes due to poor food choices. On the other hand, excessive intakes of these water-soluble vitamins through supplements are usually harmless, though there are exceptions. Table 6.1 list vitamins, their functions, and food sources.

*"I get most of my vitamins and minerals from food. But when I travel, I may take a vitamin and mineral supplement, especially when I am getting on some germ-infested plane."*
*—Walton*

## MINERALS

Minerals are also involved in energy metabolism, and play important roles in building body tissue, muscle contraction, oxygen transport, maintenance of acid-base balance of the blood, and regulation of normal heart rhythm. We obtain minerals from both plant and animal food sources and water. Minerals are excreted daily and must be replaced.

Twenty-five minerals are known to be essential; the major minerals are calcium, phosphorous, magnesium, potassium, sodium, and chloride. Iron, zinc, iodine, copper, manganese, fluoride, chromium, selenium, and molybdenum are some of the known trace minerals. Each mineral has unique functions. Calcium contributes to bone structure, potassium and sodium maintain water balance, while iron plays a crucial role in oxygen transport. Inadequate dietary intake of some minerals can contribute to certain health problems and

# TABLE 6.1: FACTS ABOUT VITAMINS

| VITAMINS | DRI's, | MAJOR SOURCE | MAJOR FUNCTIONS |
|---|---|---|---|
| **WATER SOLUBLE**<br>Thiamin (vitamin B1) | **RDA's for 31 to 50yrs**<br>RDA males: 1.2 mg/day<br>RDA females: 1.1 mg/day | Wheat germ, whole grain breads and cereal, organ meats, lean meats, legumes | Energy production from carbohy-drate, essential for healthy nervous system |
| Riboflavin (vitamin B2) | RDA males: 1.3 mg/day<br>RDA females 1.1 mg/day | Milk and dairy products, green leafy vegetables, lean meats, beans | Energy production from carbohydrates and fats, healthy skin |
| Niacin (nicotinamide, nicotinic acid) | RDA males: 16 mg/day<br>RDA females: 14 mg/day | Lean meats, fish, poultry, whole grains, peanuts | Energy production from carbohydrate, synthesis fat, blocks release FFA |
| Vitamin B6 (pyridoxine) | RDA males: 1.3 mg/day<br>RDA females: 1.3 mg/day<br>males: > 51 yrs: 1.7<br>> 70 yrs: 1.7<br>females: > 51 yrs: 1.5<br>> 70 yrs: 1.5 | Liver, leans meats, fish, poultry, legumes, bran cereal | Role in protein metabolism, necessary for formation hemoglobin and red blood cells, synthesis essential fatty acids, required for glycogen breakdown |
| Vitamin B12 (cobalamin) | RDA males: 2.4 ugs/day<br>RDA females: 2.4 ugs/day | Lean meats, poultry, dairy products, eggs | Formation of red blood cells, metabolism nervous tissue, involved folate metabolism, formation DNA |
| Folic acid (folate) | RDA males: 400 ugs/day<br>RDA females: 400 ugs/day | Green leafy vegetables, legumes | Role in red blood cell and DNA formation |
| Biotin | RDA males: 30 ugs/day<br>RDA females: 30 ugs/day | Meats, legumes, milk, egg yolk, whole grains | Role in metabolism of carbohy-drates, protein, fat |
| Pantothenic acid | RDA males: 5 mg/day<br>RDA females: 5 mg/day | Liver, lean meats, eggs, salmon, all animal and plant foods | Role in metabolism carbohydrate, protein, fat |
| Vitamin C | RDA males: 60 mg<br>RDA females: 60 mg<br>(report due Sept.99) | Citrus fruits, green leafy vegetables, broccoli, peppers, stawberries, potatoes | Essential for connective tissue development, role in iron absorption, antioxidant, role wound healing |
| **FAT SOLUBLE**<br>Vitamin A (retinol, provita-min carotenoids) | **RDA's**<br>RDA males: 1000 RE<br>RDA females: 800 RE<br>(update in 3-4 yrs) | Liver, milk, cheese, fortified margarine, Carotenoids in plant foods orange, red, deep green in color) | Maintains healthy tissue in skin and mucous membranes, essential night vision, role bone development |
| Vitamin D (cholecalciferol) | RDA males: 200 IU/day<br>RDA females: 200 IU/day<br>Males: > 51 yrs: 400 IU<br>> 70 yrs: 600 IU<br>Females:> 51 yrs: 400 IU<br>> 70 yrs: 600 IU | Vitamin D fortified milk and margarine, fish oil, action of sunlight on skin | Increase intestinal absorption of calcium, promotes bone and tooth formation |
| Vitamin E (tocopherol) | Alpha-tocopherol equivalents<br>RDA males: 10 mg<br>RDA females: 8 mg<br>(update Sept. 99) | Vegetable oils, margarine, green leafy vegetables, wheat germ, whole grain products | Formation red blood cells, antioxidant |
| Vitamin K (phylloquinone) | RDA males: 80 ugs<br>RDA females: 65 ugs<br>(Report due 3-4 years) | Liver, soybean oil, spinach, cauliflower, green leafy vegetables | Essential normal blood clotting |

adversely affect performance. Table 6.2 lists minerals, their functions, and food sources.

### EXERCISE REQUIREMENTS OF VITAMINS AND MINERALS

Adequate vitamins and minerals in the diet are necessary to perform optimally, and correcting a nutrient deficiency could improve performance. But most importantly, vitamin and mineral deficiencies probably indicate the need for a full dietary makeover.

Exercise can induce mineral losses from the body, usually through urine, sweat, and gastrointestinal losses. But research has not conclusively proven that "extra" amounts of vitamins and minerals, when no deficiency is present, will improve exercise performance. Improved food choices may easily solve the problem. While all vitamins and minerals are important, athletes simply need to be educated on food choices of specific nutrients especially crucial to top performance.

Clearly, a balanced diet is essential. This means selecting a wide variety of foods from all the food groups and within each group. It's also helpful to eat foods in their natural state, store food properly, and avoid prolonged cooking and excessive heat. Let's take a look at some vitamins and minerals important to the athlete for top performance and good health.

### IMPORTANT VITAMINS
#### B VITAMINS

Due to their role in processing energy, B vitamins have received much attention from athletes. Because requirements of several B vitamins—thiamin, riboflavin, and niacin—are

## TABLE 6.2: FACTS ABOUT MINERALS

| MINERALS | DRI's, | MAJOR SOURCE | MAJOR FUNCTIONS |
|---|---|---|---|
| **MAJOR MINERALS** | **RDA's for 31 to 50yrs** (unless otherwise noted) | | |
| Calcium | RDA males: 1000 mg RDA females: 1000 mg Males:> 50 yrs: 1200 mg > 70 yrs: 1200 mg Females: > 50 yrs: 1200 mg > 70 yrs: 1200 mg | Milk, cheese, yogurt, ice cream, dried peas and beans, dark-green leafy vegetables | Bone formation, enzyme activation, nerve impulse transmission, muscle contraction |
| Phosphorus | RDA males: 700 mg RDA females: 700 mg | Protein foods: meat, poultry, fish, eggs, milk, cheese, dried peas and beans, whole grains | Bone formation, cell membrane structure, B vitamin activation, component of ATP-CP, and other important organic compounds |
| Magnesium | RDA males: 420 mg RDA females: 320 mg | Milk, yogurt, dried beans, nuts, whole grains, tofu, green vegetables, chocolate | Roles in protein synthesis, glucose metabolism, muscle contraction |
| **TRACE MINERALS** Iron | RDA males: 10 mg RDA females: 15 mg (Adults over 25 yrs) | Organ meats, lean meats, poultry, shellfish, dried peas and beans, whole-grain products, green leafy vegetables | Hemoglobin formation, oxygen transport |
| Zinc | RDA males: 15 mg RDA females: 12 mg (Adults over 25 yrs) | Organ meats, meat, fish, poultry, shellfish, nuts, whole-grain products | Part of enzymes involved in energy metabolism, immune function |
| Copper | Estimated safe and adequate daily dietary intake (ESADDI) Males: 1.5 to 3.0 mg Females: 1.5 to 3.0 mg | Organ meats, meat, fish, poultry, shellfish, nuts, bran cereal | Role in use of iron and hemoglobin by body, involved in connective tissue formation and oxidation |
| Fluoride | Adequate intake Males: 4 mg/day Females: 3 mg/day | Milk, egg yolks, drinking water, seafood | Helps form teeth and bones |
| Selenium | RDA males: 70 ugs RDA females: 55 ugs (adults over 25 yrs) | Meat, fish, poultry, organ meats, seafood, whole grains and nuts from selenium-rich soil | Part of antioxidant enzyme |
| Chromium | ESADDI Males: 50 to 200 ugs Females: 50 to 200 ugs (adults over 25 yrs) | Organ meats, meats, oysters, cheese, whole grain products, beer | Enhances insulin function as glucose tolerance factor |
| Iodine | RDA males: 150 ugs RDA females: 150 ugs | Iodized table salt, seafood, water | Part of thyroxin which plays role in reactions involving cellular energy |
| Manganese | ESADDI Males: 2.0 to 5.0 mg Females: 2.0 to 5.0 mg | Beet greens, whole grains, nuts, legumes | Part if essential enzyme systems |
| Molydenum | ESADDI Males: 75 to 250 ugs Females: 75 to 250 ugs | Legumes, cereal grains, dark green leafy vegetables | Part of essential enzymes involved in carbohydrate and fat metabolism |

based on the total calories consumed, active people do require more of them. However, these vitamins are easily obtained from carbohydrate-rich foods such as breads and whole grains—foods which often provide the additional calories required to meet energy needs.

Though these water-soluble vitamins are easily excreted, excesses of these nutrients can present a problem. Pyridoxine (vitamin B6) in doses of more than 1 gram daily over several months may cause numbness and even paralysis. Symptoms have also been experienced with chronic doses as low as 200 milligrams. Excess niacin can block the release of free fatty acids, resulting in greater use of muscle glycogen, and thereby depleting a limited energy source for endurance exercise. In other words, large doses of niacin may actually reduce performance.

## FOLACIN

Folacin is a B vitamin which has deservedly received increased attention over the past several years. Folacin is the collective term for folate, folic acid, and other forms of the vitamin. Folate is the form found naturally in foods, and folic acid is the form of the vitamin found most often in your body and added to foods and supplements. Folic acid is actually absorbed twice as well as the folate that occur naturally in foods.

Since January 1998, manufacturers have been required to add folic acid to all enriched products, including flour, bread, rolls, grits, corn meal, rice, pasta, and noodles. There is good reason for this fortification. Obtaining enough folic acid in the early weeks of pregnancy can significantly reduce the risk of neural tube defects, such as spina bifida, in newborns. Most Americans take in only about 200 micrograms of folic acid daily, falling short of the recommended 400 micrograms. Fortification will prevent half of all neural tube defects. But this fortification may not only benefit pregnant women and newborns.

Evidence is building that folic acid may reduce risk of heart disease, stroke, and certain cancers. Folic acid helps reduce blood levels of the amino acid homocysteine. High levels of homocysteine are a strong predictor for heart disease and stroke, maybe even stronger than blood cholesterol. Keeping homocysteine low also requires adequate intake of the vitamins $B_6$ and $B_{12}$. Thirty percent of all older Americans don't produce enough stomach acid to absorb the $B_{12}$ found in foods. Synthetic $B_{12}$, however, doesn't have this stomach acid dependency. Connections between folic acid and the pre-

*B vitamins play an important role in processing energy.*

| TABLE 6.3: FOLATE CONTENT OF FOOD | |
|---|---|
| LENTILS, cooked, 1 cup | 358 mcg |
| YEAST, brewer's, 1 Tbs. | 312 mcg |
| LIVER, beef, 3 ounces | 285 mcg |
| GARBANZO BEANS, boiled, 1 cup | 282 mcg |
| KIDNEY BEANS, boiled, 1 cup | 229 mcg |
| TURNIP GREENS, cooked, 1 cup | 171 mcg |
| ASPARAGUS, boiled, 6 spears | 131 mcg |
| BEANS, white, baked, 1 cup | 122 mcg |
| ORANGE JUICE, 1 cup | 110 mcg |
| SPINACH, raw, chopped, 1 cup | 108 mcg |
| MUSTARD GREENS, cooked, 1 cup | 103 mcg |
| BROCCOLI, cooked, 1 cup | 78 mcg |
| ROMAINE LETTUCE, 1 cup | 76 mcg |
| ENDIVE, 1 cup | 72 mcg |
| WHEAT GERM, raw, 1/4 cup | 70 mcg |
| CABBAGE, raw, 1 cup | 40 mcg |

vention of cervical cancer and colorectal cancer, through prevention of damage to DNA, have also been suggested.

Many researchers recommend that individuals over age 50 take a supplement providing the RDA's (high doses are not advised) of folic acid, $B_{12}$, and $B_6$. Older individuals are also more likely to take medications which interfere with folic acid absorption. Of course, every active individual should increase their intake of folate-rich foods. See table 6.3 for the best sources of folate.

## ANTIOXIDANT NUTRIENTS

### Vitamin C

Another water-soluble vitamin of interest to and heavily marketed to athletes is vitamin C. Several functions of the vitamin are important to athletes. It is necessary for the formation of connective tissue and scar tissue, and certain hormones and neurotransmitters which are secreted during exercise. Vitamin C plays a role in iron absorption and in the formation of red blood cells. This vitamin is also strongly promoted because

TOM MORAN

*Iron deficiency is the most common nutrient deficiency in the U.S., and is especially felt in high-impact sports.*

of its role as a powerful antioxidant. Symptoms of vitamin C deficiency could impair athletic performance.

Despite being a water-soluble vitamin which is easily excreted, the human body actually has a pool of vitamin C ranging from 1.5 to 3.0 grams. Serious vitamin C deficiencies are rare because fresh or frozen fruits and vegetables are so abundant in our food supply.

Despite being readily available from food, athletes often consume vitamin C supplements. Correcting a deficiency clearly improves performance, but research does not demonstrate performance enhancement when subjects not deficient in vitamin C are provided supplements.

On the other hand, because exercise is a stressor, moderate amounts of vitamin C, above the Recommended Daily

| TABLE 6.4: VITAMIN C CONTENT OF FOOD ||
| --- | --- |
| FOOD | VITAMIN C IN MILLIGRAMS |
| Pepper, green, 1 large | 130 mg |
| Orange juice, 1 cup | 124 mg |
| Cranberry juice, 1 cup | 108 mg |
| Grapefruit juice, 1 cup | 94 mg |
| Broccoli, cooked, 2/3 cup | 90 mg |
| Brussels Sprouts, cooked, 7 | 85 mg |
| Strawberries, raw, 1 cup | 85 mg |
| Orange, navel, 1 | 80 mg |
| Kiwi, 1 medium | 75 mg |
| Cantaloupe, pieces, 1 cup | 70 mg |
| Cauliflower, cooked, 1 cup | 65 mg |

*"I was one of the few U.S. Olympic Team distance runners of my era who ate some red meat, and while I did not have any problems with ferritin and iron deficiency, many of the other runners did."*

*—Virgin*

Allowance of 60 milligrams, may be appropriate for athletes. Some scientists have recommended 200 to 300 milligrams daily. Research has shown that 200 milligrams daily of vitamin C leads to full saturation of plasma and white blood cells, which should contribute to optimal immune function. Vitamin C supplements may also reduce the symptoms of upper respiratory tract infections often seen after strenuous physical efforts. However, most studies have not found it to prevent colds. A diet rich in fruits and vegetables provides ample amounts of vitamin C and other healthful substances found in those foods. See table 6.4 for the best sources of vitamin C.

### Vitamin E

Vitamin E also receives much attention from athletes because of its major role as an antioxidant. This vitamin prevents the oxidation of unsaturated fatty acids in cell membranes and protects the cell from damage.

Vitamin E is widely distributed in foods and stored in the body, so vitamin E deficiencies are rare. The current RDA for males is 15 IU and for females is 12 IU. The DRI (Dietary Reference Intake) is 30 IU. Polyunsaturated oils, such as soybean, corn, and safflower oils, are the most common sources of vitamin E. Other good sources are fortified grain products and wheat germ.

| TABLE 6.5: VITAMIN E CONTENT OF FOODS | | |
|---|---|---|
| FOOD | PORTION | VITAMIN E (IU) |
| WHEAT GERM OIL | 1 Tbs. | 25 |
| SUNFLOWER SEEDS | 1 ounce | 21 |
| ALMONDS | 1 ounce | 11 |
| SUNFLOWER OIL | 1 Tbs. | 10 |
| WHEAT GERM | 1 ounce | 5 |
| MARGARINE, SOFT | 1 Tbs. | 3 |
| MAYONNAISE | 1 Tbs. | 3 |
| BROWN RICE | 1 cup | 3 |
| MANGO | 1 medium | 3 |
| ASPARAGUS | 4 spears | 2 |

Experiments on vitamin E supplementation at altitude have produced some interesting results, such as reduced blood lactic acid levels, but more research is required, especially to determine real performance benefits. Vitamin E may also be beneficial to athletes training in high-pollution areas, due to its antioxidant effects. Though no performance benefits have been established, vitamin E supplements may be recommended for possible prevention of chronic diseases, especially heart disease. Researchers currently feel that a daily supplement dose of 100 to 400 IU is safe and consistent with the scientific data. Persons with a bleeding disorder or on anticoagulant medication should be cautious and first check with their physician before taking the blood-thinning vitamin E. See table 6.5 for good sources of vitamin E.

## Carotenoids

Beta-carotene is just one of 600 carotenoids pigments which give fruits and vegetables their yellow, orange, and red colors. Carotenoids are also abundant in green vegetables. While carotenoids are not vitamins, many act as antioxidants, also protecting cells from free radicals.

Carotenoids most commonly found in blood and tissues are alpha-carotene, beta-carotene, beta-cryptoxanthin, lycopene, lutein, and zeaxanthin. Only Alpha-carotene, beta-carotene and beta-cryptoxanthin can be converted to vitamin A in the body. Research is just beginning to determine how specific carotenoids can boost immunity and protect the heart and eyes from chronic disease.

To obtain a variety of carotenoids in your diet, aim for at least five servings combined of fruits and vegetables daily, focusing mainly on yellow-orange, red, or dark green choices.

---

### TABLE 6.6: SUPER SOURCES OF CAROTENOIDS

**FOODS HIGH IN CAROTENOIDS (Including alpha-carotene, beta-carotene, B-Crypto-xanthin, Lutein/Zeanthin, Lycopene)**

| | |
|---|---|
| APRICOT HALVES, 6 dried | ORANGE, 1 medium |
| BROCCOLI, 1/2 cup cooked | PAPAYA, 1/2 medium |
| CANTALOUPE, 1 cup chunks | PEPPER, red, 1/2 raw |
| CARROT, 1 medium raw | PUMPKIN, 1/2 cup cooked or canned |
| COLLARD GREENS, 1/2 cup cooked | SPINACH, 1/2 cup raw |
| GRAPEFRUIT, 1/2 medium | SWEET POTATO, 1/2 cup mashed |
| KALE, 1/2 cup cooked | TANGERINE, 1 medium |
| MANGO, 1 medium | TOMATO SAUCE, 1/2 cup |
| MUSTARD GREENS, 1/2 cup cooked | |

You can easily obtain ample amounts in your diet. See table 6.6 for good sources of carotenoids.

Supplements may require some caution, especially for beta-carotene supplements, which were found to increase cancer in smokers. In addition, carotenoids interact with one another. Supplementing with one carotenoid may impair the absorption of others. Foods high in carotenoids may provide other health-promoting substances. It is also quite possible that these protective nutrients work best when they are packaged together, as in food.

### Phytochemicals

While vitamin A can be formed from some carotenoids, this group of nutrients is actually one of many which fall under the broader classification of phytochemicals. Many important disease-fighting properties have been attributed to these plant chemicals. Unlike vitamins and minerals, phytochemicals are not nutrients. Most phytochemicals are found in carbohydrate-containing foods, such as fruits, vegetables, and grains. Some of the more well-known phytochemicals include: allylic sulfides found in garlic, flavonoids found in citrus fruits, genistein found in soybeans, indoles in broccoli and cauliflower, and phytoestrogens in soy products, to name a few.

Basically, all these great phytochemicals mean one thing: Eat plenty of fruits and vegetables, dried peas and beans and soy products. In the future, probably even more phytochemicals will be discovered.

# Optimal health and the new RDA's

With the recent and ongoing release of guidelines by the National Academy of Sciences (NAS), the Recommended Daily Allowances (RDA's) are finally reflecting goals consistent with the 21st century. Rather than merely preventing nutrient deficiencies, the new guidelines are set with the goal of optimizing health by reducing risk of chronic diseases, such as heart disease, cancer, and osteoporosis. For the first time, specific recommendations are being made for individuals over the age of 70, reflecting the unique considerations of aging.

The updated RDA's are being issues in stages, with certain nutrients grouped together. A report on calcium and its related nutrients, phosphorous, magnesium, vitamin D, and fluoride, were released in August 1997. In April 1998, a report on folate, the B vitamins, and choline was released. The report on vitamins C and E, beta carotene and other selected compounds is due in September 1999.

At least three additional groups of nutrients and food components are due for review over the next three to four years. Included in these reports will be trace minerals, vitamins A and K, electrolytes and fluid, and other food components such as phytoestrogens, fiber, and phytochemicals. You can

## IMPORTANT MINERALS
### CALCIUM

Calcium is the most abundant mineral in the body. Ninety-eight percent of calcium is found in bones, 1 percent in teeth, and the remaining 1 percent circulates in the bloodstream. This circulating calcium has a significant effect upon metabolism.

Calcium has several physiological functions. It is involved in all types of muscle contraction, including the heart mus-

monitor the NAS Web site at http://www.nas.edu.

The new recommendations are officially known as Dietary Reference Intakes, or DRI's. Each updated nutrient will acquire a number of terms, under the umbrella heading of DRI. The following classifications will now be used:

## RECOMMENDED DAILY ALLOWANCE (RDA)

The amount of a nutrient that should decrease the risk of chronic disease for most healthy individuals in a specified age group and gender. It serves as a goal for individuals only.

## ADEQUATE INTAKE (AI)

Used when there is not enough scientific evidence to set an RDA. It is a recommended daily intake based on observed or experimentally determined approximations of nutrient intake by a group of healthy people.

## ESTIMATED AVERAGE REQUIREMENT (EAR)

A nutrient value estimated to meet the requirements of half the healthy individuals in a group. It is used to develop RDA's and assess adequacy of intakes of and plan diets for population groups.

## TOLERABLE UPPER INTAKE LEVEL (UL)

The highest level of a daily nutrient intake, from both food and supplements, which should not be exceeded or adverse health effects may result to most individuals. This is not a recommended amount.

cle, skeletal muscle, and smooth muscle found in blood vessels. By activating a number of enzymes, calcium also plays a role in both the synthesis and breakdown of muscle and liver glycogen. Calcium is also involved in nerve impulse transmission, blood clotting, and secretion of hormones. These physiological functions of calcium take precedence over formation of bone tissue. If the diet is low in calcium, calcium can be pulled from the bone for these functions.

| TABLE 6.7: CALCIUM CONTENT OF FOODS | | |
|---|---|---|
| **GREAT SOURCES**<br>**300 MG SERVING** | **GOOD SOURCES**<br>**200 MG SERVING** | **FAIR SOURCES**<br>**100 MG SERVING** |
| 1% milk, 8 ounces | Cheddar cheese, 1 ounce | Skim milk, dry, 1 Tbs. |
| Skim milk, 8 ounces | Brick cheese, 1 ounce | Cottage cheese, 1%, 1 cup |
| Yogurt, 6 to 8 ounces | Colby cheese, 1 ounce | Parmesan, grated, 1.5 Tbs. |
| Swiss cheese, 1 ounce | Edam cheese, 1 ounce | Frozen yogurt, 1/2 cup |
| Mackerel, cnd, 3 ounces | Mozzarella cheese, 1 ounce | Pudding, 1/2 cup |
| Sardines, canned, | Instant breakfast, 1 packet | Shrimp, cooked, 6 ounces |
| w/bones, 3 ounces | Broccoli, cooked, 1 cup | Lobster, cooked, 6 ounces |
| Salmon, canned, | Collard greens, cooked, 1 cup | Tofu, 1/2 cup |
| w/bones, 3 ounces | Kale, cooked, 1 cup | Soybeans, cooked, 1/2 cup |
| | Turnip greens, cooked, 1 cup | Navy beans, cooked, 1 cup |
| | Mustard greens, cooked, 1 cup | Pinto beans, 1 cup |
| | Bok Choy, fresh, 1 cup | Orange, 1 large |

Calcium deficiency can develop from inadequate intake or increased calcium excretion. Strenuous exercise increases sweat loss of calcium. Inadequate intake of calcium has been associated with osteoporosis. Adequate calcium ensures optimal bone mass development in adolescence and early adulthood. This is a disorder in which bone mass decreases and susceptibility to bone fracture increases. Inadequate calcium intake has also been linked to colon cancer and high blood pressure.

Estrogen loss also contributes to development of osteoporosis, making women more susceptible to this disease after menopause occurs, though men can also develop osteoporosis (See Chapter 16). Hormonal status in younger female ath-

*"I soundly believe in eating red meat. Look at Mother Nature. The animals that eat red meat are lions and tigers, and the animals that eat vegetables are the bunny rabbits. Who would you rather be like when you ride your mountain bike?"*

*—Dunlap*

letes also plays an important role in bone health. Extra calcium intake is recommended for post-menopausal women and younger female athletes with lower estrogen levels. Weight-bearing exercise such as running and weight training enhances calcium skeletal absorption, increases bone mass, and can help prevent osteoporosis at any age.

Dairy products are a very concentrated source of calcium, and provide about three-fourths of most individuals' total calcium intake. These and other sources are listed in table 6.7. Try to choose low-fat options as much as possible. For adults ages nineteen to fifty, the new calcium recommendation is 1000 milligrams. Adults over fifty-one are advised to obtain 1200 milligrams. Vitamin D is also important for good bone health, as it aids in calcium absorption. Persons fifty-one to seventy are now advised to double their vitamin D intake from 200 IU to 400 IU. After age seventy, the recommendation increases to 600 IU. As we age, our bodies become less efficient at converting sun exposure to vitamin D.

*"About five of the twenty players on the team took a vitamin and mineral supplement regularly, while the rest of us didn't. Everyone on the team ate healthfully and we did eat a high amount of calories, so we didn't all feel that a supplement was needed."*
*—Tueting*

Some dietary factors are harmful to calcium absorption. Excess sodium, protein, and caffeine increase calcium excretion. Alcohol can also be damaging to bone cells. In fact, the high-protein North American diet is considered to be a major contributing factor to development of osteoporosis.

## IRON

Athletes are very aware of the importance of the mineral iron. Iron's major function is in the formation of hemoglobin. Hemoglobin transports oxygen in the blood and myoglobin in the muscle. Many muscle enzymes involved in metabolism require iron. Other iron compounds facilitate oxygen use at the cellular level. The body storage form of iron, ferritin, is used as an indicator of iron stores, as are transferrin and hemoglobin. About 30 percent of iron is stored, and the other 70 percent is involved in oxygen metabolism.

Iron deficiency is the most common nutrient deficiency in the U.S. It is estimated that 22 to 25 percent of female athletes are iron deficient, with 6 percent being anemic. When

*"I am a firm believer in supplements, just because the food we consume is so processed."*

*—Reid*

iron stores are low, total hemoglobin drops, and the muscles do not receive as much oxygen. Normal hemoglobin levels for males are 14 to 16 grams per deciliter (grams per pound), with anemia classified as less than 13 grams per pound. Normal ranges for women are 12 to 14 grams per pound, with anemia below 12 grams per pound. Blood work should then be interpreted to determine if you have early iron deficiency or full iron deficiency anemia.

Inadequate dietary intake of iron is the most common cause of iron deficiency or anemia, with women also experiencing menstrual blood loss. Exercise also increases iron loss from sweat and may decrease iron absorption. Strenuous training may also accelerate red blood cell destruction from mechanical trauma, such as during running.

## TABLE 6.8: IRON CONTENT OF SELECTED FOODS

| Sources of Heme Iron | | Sources of Plant Iron | |
|---|---|---|---|
| Liver, beef, cooked, 3 ounces | 6.0 mg | Cereal, iron-fortified | 2-18 mg |
| Beef, cooked, 3 ounces | 3.5 mg | Cream of wheat, 3/4 cup | 9 mg |
| Pork, cooked, 3 ounces | 3.4 mg | Lentils, 1 cup | 6 mg |
| Shrimp, cooked, 3 ounces | 2.6 mg | Instant breakfast, 1 envelope | 4.5 mg |
| Turkey, dark, cooked, 3 ounces | 2.0 mg | Kidney beans, canned, 1 cup | 3.2 mg |
| Chicken, breast, cooked, 3 ounces | 1.0 mg | Baked potato, with skin, 1 | 3.0 mg |
| Tuna, light, 3 ounces | 1.0 mg | Prune juice, 8 ounces | 3.0 mg |
| Flounder, sole, salmon, 3 ounces | 1.0 mg | Wheat germ, 1/4 cup | 2.6 mg |
| | | Apricots, dried, 10 halves | 1.7 mg |
| | | Spaghetti, enriched, cooked, 1/2 cup | 1.4 mg |
| | | Bread, enriched, 1 slice | 1.0 mg |

Iron is obtained from food in two forms. Heme iron is found in animal foods—good sources are lean meat and dark poultry. About 10 to 30 percent of heme iron is absorbed from the intestines. Non-heme iron is found in plant foods—dried peas and beans, whole grain products, apricots, and raisins are good sources. About 2 to 10 percent of non-heme iron is absorbed. Non-heme iron absorption is compromised by phytates which are found in many vegetables and whole grains.

Consuming meats and plant iron sources together can enhance iron absorption from plant foods. Small amounts of red meat in bean chili, spinach with chicken, and turkey with lentil soup combine heme and non-heme iron. Vitamin C-containing foods also enhance plant iron absorption. Try having orange juice or strawberries with fortified cereal. Table 5.8 lists good sources of iron. (See Chapter 16 for more on anemia).

Increased risk of anemia is associated with:

- *growth spurts*
- *heavy menstrual losses*
- *increased requirements during pregnancy*
- *blood loss from GI bleeding and some anti-inflammatory medications*
- *red blood cell destruction from high-impact exercise*
- *altitude training*
- *low-calorie diets*
- *vegetarian diets (see chapter 17)*
- *very high carbohydrate diets containing only small amounts of animal protein*
- *various fad and unbalanced diets*

To boost iron intake you can:

- *Incorporate meat regularly into your diet. Have small amounts several times weekly.*
- *Try adding small amounts of red meats to your favorite recipes like stir-frys, soups, pasta sauces, and casseroles.*
- *Mix heme-iron foods with non-heme choices, such as a bean chili with dark turkey meat.*
- *Incorporate iron-fortified cereals into you diet.*

## SUPPLEMENT SAFELY

Most athletes are able to eat more than their sedentary counterparts. With the right food choices, this generally results in a greater vitamin and mineral intake. But often, it's the individuals who are least likely to need supplements that take them. A broad-range, reasonable-dose supplement may just be that little extra insurance that active individuals who care about their health often seek.

Active individuals who may want to consider a daily multivitamin mineral or other type of supplement are athletes:

- *On low calorie diets, less than 1500 calories daily.*
- *With food allergies that restrict a significant number of choices from one food group.*
- *Who are lactose intolerant or at risk for developing osteoporosis.*
- *Who are pregnant or planning a pregnancy.*
- *Who are picky eaters with limited food choices.*
- *Who are traveling frequently.*
- *With disordered eating and erratic diets.*
- *In an athletic event that is prolonged and does not allow for regular meals.*
- *Vegans who may need supplemental vitamin D, riboflavin, B12 and minerals.*

If you choose to take a supplement, try to stick to the following guidelines:

- *Choose a broad-range, balanced supplement of vitamins and minerals that provides 100 percent of the Daily Values (DV). These doses are known to be safe.*
- *Avoid supplements that contain an excess of minerals or any one mineral, as these nutrients compete with one another for absorption.*
- *Choose a supplement with the USP stamp of approval on the label, to guarantee it dissolves properly in your body.*

- *Choose a supplement in which the majority of vitamin A is actually beta-carotene, the precursor to vitamin A.*
- *A blend of natural and synthetic supplements is fine.*
- *Calcium and magnesium may need to be purchased separately as they are too bulky for a regular multivitamin pill.*
- *Keep antioxidant supplements to 400 IU vitamin E and 250 milligrams vitamin C.*
- *Take your multivitamin with a meal or snack and plenty of water.*

Antioxidant supplements are strongly marketed to athletes. But it is actually diets high in foods that contain antioxidant nutrients that have been shown to prevent cancer. So don't discount the importance of increasing food sources of these nutrients. You may wonder if training increases the effects of free radicals. Or do athletes learn to cope with these negative by-products? Probably both. It is impossible to directly measure free-radical production in humans. Free-radical byproducts do increase with exercise, but trained athletes may dispose of them more effectively.

It is very easy to obtain moderate doses of vitamin C, beta-carotene, and other carotenoids with food choices. However, one nutrient which may be difficult to obtain in a low-fat diet is vitamin E. Good sources are high in fat, and you would need to consume large amounts of them to reach even the low antioxidant dose of 100 IU. Researchers still need to determine the optimal doses of antioxidant supplements needed for preventing heart disease and cancer.

If you do supplement, do so wisely. A multivitamin and mineral supplement providing 100 percent of the DVs should be safe, though not always necessary. But remember, the hazards of vitamin and mineral overdosing are real, and can be subtle. If you take a supplement, understand the good reasons for taking it, consume appropriate doses, and discontinue its use when it is no longer needed.

## FINAL THOUGHTS

Athletes require optimum vitamin and mineral intakes for peak performance. Foods sources provide these nutrients, as well as the growing list of phytochemicals. While a balanced diet should always be the first step in obtaining these nutrients, some athletes may consider supplementation. Supplementation should be done safely, with avoidance of excessive doses.

*A healthy sports diet takes planning, even for Olympic figure skater Michelle Kwan.*

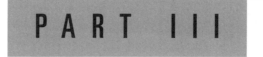

# PART III

# CREATING THE OPTIMAL TRAINING DIET

# CHAPTER SEVEN

# Putting Together
## *your* *Training*
## *Diet*

*"I improved my diet because I needed more energy for practices. Junk food just does not give me that."*
*— Tyler Painter, swimmer*
*member, U.S. national swimming team*

When the body thrives on the proper balance of carbohydrates, protein and fats, it can support a successful training program. But in order to consume a balanced diet, it's essential to practice translating scientifically sound recommendations into everyday food choices. Understanding what the body requires nutritionally is the first step. The next step is to devise your own optimal sports diet.

In Section One, we reviewed the six basic nutrients required for a healthy training diet: water, carbohydrate, fat, protein, vitamins and minerals. In Section Two, chapters 7, 8, and 9 provide guidelines for putting together a personalized diet that suits your training program and athletic goals. This chapter, chapter 7, guides you in choosing a nutrition prescription for carbohydrates and rounding out your diet with the optimal amounts of fat and protein.

Some questions you may have regarding calculation of your sports diet are:

- *How can I translate my carbohydrate, protein, and fat requirements into practical food choices?*
- *What is a food system I can use to plan my meals?*
- *What are some practical food examples?*

Begin at the beginning, and start with your carbohydrate requirements. Carbohydrates are the foundation of a healthy sports diet, with most athletes requiring around 60 percent of their total calories from this fuel in order to replenish depleted glycogen stores. Diets with adequate carbohydrate also have plenty of health benefits. But as stated previously, percentages do not provide the whole story. Consuming enough total grams of carbohydrate, based on your body weight and training intensity and duration, is one of the most important features of an effective sports diet. Athletes in any sport benefit from consuming the carbohydrate servings and portions appropriate for them.

After ensuring that carbohydrates are plentiful, you must meet your protein requirements for rest, repair and recovery. Again, how much protein you require depends on your body weight and training program. Whatever the amount you require, protein needs are easily met in a balanced sports diet.

Finally, fat, which is a part of any healthy diet, will round out your calorie needs. You need some fat at meals and snacks in order to feel full and satisfied. Fat should not be consumed at the expense of valuable carbohydrates.

## CARBOHYDRATES

Let's start with your carbohydrate prescription. Refer back to Table 3.1: Daily Carbohydrate Requirements. Based on your volume and intensity of training, choose the recommended carbohydrate range that best matches your training program. Lowest carbohydrate needs (2.25 to 3.0 grams per pound) are for athletes engaging in exercise of moderate intensity and duration. Athletes following more prolonged training sessions that incorporate some higher intensity exercise have moderate carbohydrate needs (3.0 to 4.5 grams per pound). Athletes completing very high volumes of training require the greatest amounts of carbohydrate (4.5 to 5.5 grams per pound).

### DAILY CARBOHYDRATE REQUIREMENTS

To calculate your total daily carbohydrate requirements, use the following formula: *Weight in pounds multiplied by carbohydrate requirements per pound equals total daily grams carbohydrate.*

For example, let's say an athlete weighs about 150 pounds and follows an endurance training program. Sessions are often greater than 90 minutes long, and there are several high-intensity training sessions weekly, including interval training. Carbohydrate requirements for this athlete would fall in the middle range of 3.0 to 4.5 grams per pound of body weight, or 450 to 675 grams total for the day. This athlete could easily require about 600 grams of carbohydrate daily for near complete muscle glycogen recovery in under twenty-four hours.

Carbohydrates in the diet are obtained from several food groups: the bread, grain, and cereal group, the fruit and fruit juice group, the vegetable group, and the milk and yogurt group. Basically, you need to determine the number of servings from each of these carbohydrate-containing food groups required daily to meet your carbohydrate prescription and satisfy food preferences.

Grains and starches are likely to comprise a good portion of your diet. They are concentrated food sources and provide a decent number of grams of carbohydrate per portion. Try to choose items from this food group which have been lightly processed, like brown rice, whole wheat bread, bran and other whole grain cereals, oat bran and oatmeal, and bagels and muffins made from unprocessed grains.

Items from this food group also include snack choices such as pretzels and crackers. Other concentrated carbohydrate sources are tortillas, rice, dried peas and beans, potatoes, and winter squash.

The fruit group is your next great source of carbohydrates. Choices here include fresh fruit, canned fruit, dried fruit and fruit juices. Fruits are also great sources of fiber, vitamin C, potassium, vitamin A, and carotenoids. Not only do they supply fuel for your performance, but fruits are excellent sources of nutrients for good health.

*Putting together a balanced sports diet, even for in-line skating, begins with carbohydrates.*

Vegetables are sources of carbohydrates, though not as high per portion as breads, cereals, rice, pasta, fruits and fruit juices. However, few foods can match vegetables for their outstanding nutrient content. Like fruits, these foods are filled with vitamins, minerals, and carotenoids and other phytochemicals.

Milk and yogurt are also good sources of carbohydrate. Yogurts can especially reach high carbohydrate amounts when mixed with fruit and other sugars. Calcium, vitamin D, and riboflavin are also plentiful in milk. In addition, these dairy foods provide significant amounts of high quality protein.

Of course, one last source of carbohydrates is sweets and foods high in simple sugars. While these foods should not routinely replace more wholesome choices in your diet, they

113

# TABLE 7.1: CARBOHYDRATE CONTENT OF FOODS PER SERVING

## CEREALS, STARCHES, GRAINS

### 30 GRAMS OF CARBOHYDRATES PER SERVING

**BREADS**
Bagel, 1/2 whole, 2 ounces
Bread sticks, 4, 2 ounces
Bread, 2 slices, 2 ounces
Cornbread, 1 square, 2 ounces
Pita Pocket, 2 ounces, 1 pocket
Dinner Rolls, 2

**CEREALS**
Cooked Cereal, 1 cup
Cold Cereal, ready-to-eat, varies, 1.5 ounces
Shredded Wheat, 3/4 cup, 1.5 ounces
Grapenuts, 1/3 cup, 5 Tbs.

**GRAINS**
Graham crackers, 6 squares, 1.5 ounces
Rye-Krisp, 1.5 large squares, 1.5 ounces
Saltines, 8 crackers, 1.5 ounces
Zwieback, 6 pieces, 1.5 ounces
English Muffin, 1 whole, 2 ounces
Muffin, low fat, 3 ounces
Pancake mix, dry, 1/3 cup
Pancakes, 4 inch, 3
Pasta, cooked, 1 cup
Waffle, 1 large, 2.5 ounces
Rice, cooked, white, brown, 2/3 cup
Tortillas, corn or flour, 2
Pretzels, 1.5 ounces

**STARCHY VEGETABLES**
Baked Beans, 3/4 cup
Black Beans, 3/4 cup
Kidney Beans, 3/4 cup
Corn, cooked, 3/4 cup
Peas, cooked, 1 cup
Potato, baked, 1 medium, 5 ounces
Sweet Potato, baked, 4 ounces
Squash, winter, mashed, 1.5 cups
Popcorn, no oil, 5 cups

## VEGETABLES

### 10 GRAMS OF CARBOHYDRATES PER SERVING

Artichoke, 1 medium
Asparagus, boiled, 1 cup
Beans, green, boiled, 1 cup
Beet greens, cooked, 1.25 cups
Broccoli, boiled, 1 cup
Broccoli, raw, 2 cups
Brussels Sprouts, boiled, 3/4 cup
Cabbage, cooked, 3/4 cup
Carrots, raw, 2 medium
Carrots, cooked, 2/3 cup
Cauliflower, cooked, 3/4 cup
Kale, boiled, 1.25 cups
Mushrooms, cooked, 1 cup
Mustard Greens, cooked, 1.5 cups
Peppers, sweet, raw, 2 cups
Summer Squash, cooked, 1 cup
Spinach, boiled, 1.5 cups
Tomato, red, raw, 2

## FRUITS & JUICES

### 30 GRAMS OF CARBOHYDRATES PER SERVING

**FRUITS**
Apple, 1.5 medium
Applesauce, sweetened, 1/2 cup
Applesauce, unsweetened, 1 cup
Apricots, raw, 8 medium
Banana, 1 large
Blueberries, raw, 1.5 cups
Cantaloupe, raw, 2 cups pieces
Dates, dries, 5
Fruit Salad, 1 cup
Grapefruit, 1 large
Grapes, small, 30, 1 cup
Honeydew, 1/4 melon
Kiwifruit, 3 medium
Mango, 1 medium
Orange, 2 medium
Nectarine, 2
Peach, 2 peaches
Pear, 1 large
Persimmon, raw, 1 medium
Plum, 3 medium
Raisins, 1/3 cup, 3 Tbs.

**FRUIT & VEGETABLE JUICES**
Apple Juice, 8 ounces
Carrot Juice, 10 ounces
Cranberry Juice Cocktail, 8 ounces
Grape or Prune Juice, 6 ounces
Grapefruit/Orange Juice, 8 ounces
Pineapple Juice, 8 ounces
Vegetable Juice Cocktail, 24 ounces

## SWEETS AND BAKED GOODS

### 30 GRAMS OF CARBOHYDRATES PER SERVING

Fruit Juice bar, 2 bars
Angel Food Cake, 1/12 of cake
Gingersnaps, 6 cookies
Cake, 1/12 cake
Granola bar, fat-free, 1 bar
Honey, 2 Tbs.
Jam, 2 Tbs.
Jelly, 2 Tbs.
Ice Cream, 1 cup
Chocolate milk, 1 cup
Sherbet, Sorbet, 1/2 cup
Syrup, regular, 2 Tbs.
Vanilla Wafers, 10
Yogurt, frozen, 1 cup

## MILK, YOGURT

### 10 GRAMS OF CARBOHYDRATES PER SERVING

Milk, buttermilk, 1%, 8 ounces (12 grams)
Milk, skim, 8 ounces (12 grams)
Milk, 2%, 8 ounces (12 grams)
Yogurt, nonfat, 8 ounces (15 grams)
Yogurt, low fat, 8 ounces (15 to 20 grams)
Yogurt, w/fruit, 8 ounces (30 to 45 grams)

are one of life's pleasures, and they do provide fuel. Some choices include frozen yogurts, jams, and various baked goods. Have them in addition to healthy carbohydrate sources, and watch out for hidden fat.

Table 7.1 is provided to help you determine your carbohydrate food sources and portions. They are:

- *Grains, cereals, pasta, rice group at 30 grams per listed portion*
- *Fruits and fruit juices at 30 grams per listed portion*
- *Vegetables at 10 grams per listed portion*
- *Milk and yogurt at 24 grams per listed portion*
- *Sweets and baked goods at 30 grams per listed portion.*

Let's look at how your intake of carbohydrates from various groups could match up to meet your total carbohydrate requirements. We know that the 150-pound athlete requires 600 grams carbohydrate. One possible combination would be:

| | |
|---|---|
| 1 milk serving | 24 grams carbohydrate |
| 1 yogurt with fruit | 45 grams carbohydrate |
| 5 fruit servings | 150 grams carbohydrate |
| 2 vegetable servings | 20 grams carbohydrate |
| 12 grain/starch serving | 360 grams carbohydrate |
| Total: | 599 grams carbohydrate |

In addition to choosing foods from these lists, you also need to be aware of carbohydrates containing large amounts of hidden fat. Try to limit these foods, especially if you are concerned about limiting calories. Check labels of high carbohydrate processed foods, and watch out for fat content.

Some higher fat carbohydrate foods are listed below:

**CARBOHYDRATE FOODS CONTAINING FAT**
donuts
french toast
pancakes
granola
fried rice
muffins
snack crackers
croissants
pastry
potato chips
popcorn popped with oil
creamed vegetables
potatoes, fried, au gratin
deep fried vegetables
milk, 2 percent and whole

*"When I'm more aware of the foods I'm consuming, it usually means I am increasing "good" foods like vegetables and decreasing 'bad' foods like desserts."*
*–Bliss Livingston*

You may also be interested in utilizing carbohydrate supplements in order to reach your high carbohydrate requirements. Some of these choices and their carbohydrate grams are listed in Table 7.2. But mainly

**TABLE 7.2: CARBOHYDRATE CONTENT OF SPORTS NUTRITION SUPPLEMENTS**

Gatorlode, 16 ounces, 94 grams
Carboplex, 16 ounces, 50 grams
Ultra Fuel, 16 ounces, 100 grams
Exceed High Carbohydrate Source, 16 ounces, 118 grams
Metabolol II, 2 scoops, 40 grams
Power Bar, 2.25 ounces, 40 grams
Optimizer, 3 scoops, 91 grams
BioFix, 2 scoops, 59 grams
Cliff Bar, 1 bar, 51 grams
Cliff Shot, 2.24 ounces, 46 grams

focus on choosing natural and nutritious, low-fat carbohydrate food sources.

## PROTEIN

Protein is also an important part of your training diet.
You obtain this nutrient from meats and many other protein-
rich foods, such as poultry, seafood, dried beans and tofu.
Some of these foods should be consumed daily, though large
portions are generally not necessary, even for larger-weight
athletes. Depending on your weight and current training program, you generally require anywhere from 4 to 8 ounces, or
the equivalent protein servings daily.

There are a number of reasons why overdoing your portions from the animal protein food group is unnecessary.
First, many protein foods may contain fat, namely the blood-
cholesterol raising saturated fat. Second, you can obtain protein from foods not in the animal protein group, and not
traditionally thought of as containing protein. Other protein-
containing foods include plant sources such as grains and
vegetables. Milk and yogurt also supply protein. Beans and
legumes also contribute significantly to your protein intake.
By emphasizing these foods for their carbohydrate content,
you'll also reap the benefits of the protein they provide.

Let's take a look at the protein needs of the 150-pound
athlete. Based on Table 5.1, this endurance athlete would
require anywhere from 90 to 100 grams of protein daily. Six
ounces of animal protein alone would provide 48 grams, or
about half the calculated requirements. Some other top pro-

# TABLE 7.3: PROTEIN FOODS GROUPED ACCORDING TO FAT CONTENT

| VERY LOW FAT PROTEINS (<2 gms fat/oz) | LOW FAT PROTEINS (3 –4 gms fat/oz) | MEDIUM FAT PROTEINS (4 -5 gms fat/oz) | HIGH FAT PROTEINS (6 -8 gms fat/oz) | HIGH FAT PROTEINS (7 -8 gms fat/oz) |
|---|---|---|---|---|
| **FISH**<br>White Fish<br>  Grouper<br>  Tuna<br>  Haddock<br>  Sole<br>  Halibut<br>  Bass<br>Shellfish<br>  Crab<br>  Shrimp<br>  Lobster<br>  Clams | Dark Fish<br>  Salmon<br>  Mackerel<br>  Sardines | Tuna and Salmon, packed in oil | | Any fried fish product |
| **CHEESE**<br>Fat-Free Cheese<br>Cottage Cheese, 1%<br>Cottage Cheese, 2% | Low-fat Cheeses | Feta Cheese<br>Mozzarella, part-skim<br>Grated Parmesan | Mozzarella<br>Neufchatel | American,Cream Cheese, Brie, Gjetost, Cheddar, Edam, Monterey, Muenster, Limburger, Swiss |
| **BEEF**<br>Round, choice, 90%  lean | Round, choice, 85% lean<br>Rib-eye, choice<br>Flank Steak, choice<br>Porterhouse, choice | Round, choice, 73% lean<br>Round, choice, 80% lean | Roast Beef<br>Meatloaf | Short Ribs<br>Corned Beef<br>Prime Cuts |
| **PORK**<br>Ham, lean, 95% fat-free<br>Pork Tenderloin<br>Boneless Sirloin Chop<br>Top Loin Chop | Sirloin Roast<br>Center Loin Chop<br>Boneless Rib Roast<br>Center Rib Chop<br>Blade Steak<br>Canadian Bacon | Pork Butt | Italian Sausage | Pate<br>Pastrami<br>Bacon<br>Pork Sausage |
| **LAMB**<br>Leg, top round<br>Leg, shank, half | Loin Chop<br>Loin Roast<br>Rib Chop | Roast Lamb | | Ground Lamb |
| **LEGUMES** (per cup)<br>Black Beans<br>Kidney Beans<br>Lentils<br>Lima Beans<br>Pinto Beans | Chickpeas | Tofu | Soybeans | |
| **POULTRY**<br>Turkey Breast<br>Chicken, white, no skin<br>Turkey, dark, no skin | Chicken, dark, no skin<br>Chicken, dark, w/skin<br>Turkey, dark,  w/skin<br>Duck, roasted, no skin | Ground Turkey, mixed meat/skin | Duck, roasted w/skin | |
| **OTHER**<br>95% Fat-free Luncheon Meat<br>Egg Whites,<br>Egg Substitute | 86% Fat-free luncheon meat<br>Egg Substitute | Eggs<br>wheat germ, whole grain products | Luncheon Meat, Bologna, Turkey or Chicken Hot-dogs, Salami | Knockwurst<br>Bratwurst<br>Beef/Pork Hot-dogs<br>Peanut Butter |

tein choices would include leaner options.

Table 7.3 clearly outlines choices which are very lean, lean, medium fat, and high fat. Make the very lean and lean choices a regular part of your diet. Emphasize choices high in iron regularly as well. You can also include plenty of plant protein sources such as tofu, and dried peas and beans.

In addition to these 48 grams of protein from the animal protein food group, the athlete will obtain 16 grams of protein from milk and yogurt, about 6 to 8 grams from the vegetable choices, and finally, at least 50 grams from grains. Combining all these food groups provides about 120 grams of protein, which meets and even exceeds this particular endurance athlete's high training protein requirements. See how easy it can be to get enough protein in your diet?

## FAT

As discussed in Chapter 4, the type of fat you consume can have a significant impact on your health. Try to emphasize monounsaturated fats like olive and canola oil, and polyunsaturated fats such as safflower oil, in your diet. Table 7.4 list various sources of the three types of fat: saturated, polyunsaturated and monounsaturated. The portions listed provide approximately 5 grams of fat serving.

*"When I take the extra time to consider planning and preparing foods and meals, I invariably perform a lot better. For me, this doesn't mean going overboard or adhering to a strict diet. It just means I think ahead before shopping for food."*

*—Bliss Livingston*

Athletes with very high carbohydrate requirements need to make sure that fat does not take the place of carbohydrate-containing foods. Generally, fat intake should be kept to 20 to 25 percent of total calories. When considering your total fat grams, keep in mind that some of the protein foods you

| TABLE 7.4: SOURCES OF FAT | | |
|---|---|---|
| **SATURATED FAT- 5 GRAMS SERVING** | **POLYUNSATURATED FAT- 5 GRAMS SERVING** | **MONOUNSATURATED FAT- 5 GRAMS SERVING** |
| Bacon, cooked, 1 slice<br>Butter, stick, 1 tsp.<br>whipped, 1 tsp.<br>reduced fat, 1 Tbs.<br>Cream, half and half, 2 Tbs.<br>Shortening or lard, 1 tsp.<br>Sour Cream, regular, 2 Tbs.<br>reduced fat, 3 Tbs. | Margarine, stick, tub, or<br>squeeze, 1 tsp.<br>lower-fat, 1 Tbs.<br>Mayonnaise, regular, 1 tsp.<br>reduced-fat, 1 Tbs.<br>Nuts, walnuts, 4 halves<br>Oil, corn, safflower, soybean,<br>1 tsp.<br>Salad Dressing, regular, 1 Tbs.<br>Sunflower seeds, 1 Tbs.<br>Pumpkin seeds, 1 Tbs. | Avocado, medium, 1/8<br>Oil, canola, olive, peanut,<br>1 tsp.<br>Olives, black, 8 large<br>Nuts<br>almonds, cashews, 6 nuts<br>peanuts, 10 nuts<br>pecans, 4 halves<br>Peanut butter, 2 tsp.<br>Sesame seeds, 1 Tbs.<br>Tahini paste, 2 tsp. |

eat contain fat, as do certain carbohydrate choices. You should balance out your meal plan with anywhere from three to seven servings daily from the fat group.

Planning your diet based on carbohydrates and protein needs allows you to round out your menus with fat. Using this systematic approach should result in the correct amount of calories. Athletes interested in weight loss should refer to Chapter 13.

To plan your training diet, you need to:

- *Calculate your carbohydrate requirements*
- *Determine various combinations of carbohydrate food group servings which meet your calculated needs*
- *Consume 4 to 8 ounces of protein or the equivalent daily*
- *Try to keep fat servings to three to seven daily*
- *Keep fat choices reasonable and emphasize healthy types of fat*

| TABLE 7.5: DAILY CARBOHYDRATE PRESCRIPTION BASED ON WEIGHT AND ACTIVITY | | | |
|---|---|---|---|
|                   | **120 pounds** | **150 pounds** | **180 pounds** |
| 3 grams per pound | 360 grams | 450 grams | 540 grams |
| 4 grams per pound | 480 grams | 600 grams | 720 grams |
| 5 grams per pound | 600 grams | 750 grams | 900 grams |

Once you have determined how many grams of carbohydrate you require daily for your training program (Table 7.5), you can refer to Table 7.6 for some sample meal plans. These carbohydrate-based plans are rounded out with protein and fat requirements. Total calories and percent carbohydrate are also provided. These food groups and number of servings listed are suggestions; tailor your carbohydrate prescription and daily menus to suit your own food tastes.

Finally, Table 7.7 provides a sample menu based on the 350 grams carbohydrate diet. To determine how to reach higher carbohydrate amounts, simply use the sample 350 gram carbohydrate menu as a framework. In the following columns, find the carbohydrate prescription that most closely corresponds to your carbohydrate requirements. Below these numbers are foods which, when added to the 350 gram base menu, reach the recommended totals.

While diet is individual, trying to recover daily with carbohydrates appropriate for a particular training program can facilitate recovery and improve energy levels for most athletes.

## TABLE 7.6: EXCHANGE MENUS FOR CARBOHYDRATE PRESCRIPTIONS

| Carbohydrate prescription Total calories % Carbohydrate | PROTEIN + FAT | CARBOHYDRATE EXCHANGES |
|---|---|---|
| 350 GMS CHO 2400 calories 58-percent carbohydrate | 6 ounces protein 4 fats | 3 FRUIT 2 MILK 3 VEGETABLES 7 GRAIN |
| 450 GMS CHO 2900 calories 62-percent carbohydrate | 6 ounces protein 5 fats | 4 FRUIT 2 MILK 1 YOGURT W/FRUIT 8 GRAIN |
| 550 GMS CHO 3400 calories 65-percent carbohydrate | 7 ounces protein 6 fats | 5 FRUIT 2 MILK 1 YOGURT W/FRUIT 3 VEGETABLES 10 GRAINS |
| 650 GMS CHO 4000 calories 65-percent carbohydrate | 7 ounces protein 6 fats | 6 FRUIT 3 MILK 1 YOGURT W/FRUIT 3 VEGETABLES 12 GRAINS |
| 750 GMS CHO 4550 calories 66-percent carbohydrate | 8 ounces protein 8 fats | 7 FRUIT 3 MILK 1 YOGURT W/FRUIT 3 VEGETABLES 14 GRAINS |

## FINAL THOUGHTS

Following some structured guidelines, as outlined with the various tables and sample menus, can be helpful in understanding how to put foods together to reach your carbohydrate needs. Protein, while important for athletes, is easily obtained in a balanced diet. Only moderate portions are normally required. Fat is also an important part of a balanced meal plan. Like protein, fat portions should be controlled and moderate.

## TABLE 7.7: SAMPLE MENU

| 350 GM CHO | 450 GM CHO | 550 GM CHO | 650 GM CHO | 750 GM CHO |
|---|---|---|---|---|
| | Add to 350 gm CHO menu: | Add to 350 gm CHO menu: | Add to 350 gm CHO menu: | Add to 350 gm CHO menu: |
| **BREAKFAST**<br>8 ounces orange juice<br>1 cup cooked oatmeal<br>8 ounces skim milk<br>2 slices toast<br>1 tsp. margarine<br>1 Tbs. Jelly | 1 large banana | 1 large banana | 1 large banana | 1 large banana |
| | | **SNACK**<br>8 ounces grapefruit juice<br>1 granola bar | **SNACK**<br>8 ounces grapefruit juice<br>1 granola bar | **SNACK**<br>8 ounces grapefruit juice<br>1 granola |
| **LUNCH**<br>3 ounces turkey<br>2 slices bread<br>1 cup raw vegetable salad<br>1.5 ounces pretzels | | | **LUNCH**<br>1 large mango<br>8 ounces milk | **LUNCH**<br>1 large mango<br>8 ounces milk<br>2 Tbs. salad dressing |
| | **SNACK**<br>1 yogurt w/fruit<br>6 graham crackers | **SNACK**<br>1 yogurt w/fruit<br>6 graham crackers | **SNACK**<br>1 yogurt w/fruit<br>6 graham crackers | **SNACK**<br>1 yogurt w/fruit<br>12 graham crackers |
| **DINNER**<br>3 ounces fish<br>1 large potato<br>1 cup cooked peas<br>Salad greens<br>2 Tbs. salad dressing<br>8 ounces skim milk<br>2 tsp. olive oil | | **DINNER**<br>1 ounce fish<br>2 Tbs. sour cream | **DINNER**<br>1 ounce fish<br>2 Tbs. sour cream | **DINNER**<br>2 ounce fish<br>2 Tbs. sour cream<br>1 tsp. olive oil<br>2 slices bread |
| **SNACK**<br>2/3 cup frozen yogurt<br>1 cup strawberries | | | | **SNACK**<br>1 1/3 cup frozen yogurt<br>1 cup strawberries |

*"You need to eat what makes you feel best. For different team members, that means different things."*

—*Tueting*

# CHAPTER EIGHT

# Planning and Preparing
# *A Training Diet*

> *"It takes a lot of effort for me to partake in practical meal planning. But when I do, I am so much happier. I make myself sit down and write out a list of meals that I enjoy such as pasta, vegetable and chicken dishes. Then, I go shopping and actually obtain the required ingredients. Next, I set aside time and cook an overabundance of a dish, so that I have lots of leftovers, store them in containers in the fridge, and then use the microwave, and I'm in heaven."*
>
> *—Bliss Livingston*

You arrive home tired and ravenous after a long day of both work and training. Having exhausted the appeal of restaurants and take-out food earlier that week, you forage through the fridge looking for tasty morsels. After scarfing down nothing too satisfying, all you can find for making a meal is dried pasta and spaghetti sauce out of jar. You have a hard training session scheduled for tomorrow and need to eat enough carbohydrates and protein.

Mealtime does not need to be this frustrating for athletes dedicated to good nutrition, even with a hectic life and demanding training program. Besides, not only is a relaxing dinner one of life's simple pleasures, eating right also supports your best performance. Before protesting that you just don't have the time, read on for tips and techniques to streamline and make the most of meal planning and shopping. This way, your kitchen can become appropriately stocked for a healthy sports diet.

Some questions regarding meal planning are:

- *How can I keep meal planning simple?*
- *What are some effective meal planning techniques?*

Meal planning is not as complicated as it sounds. It isn't necessary to have your own personal chef for quick, easy and tasty lunches and dinners. But like your training program, it does require organization and planning. With practice these new skills become second nature. All you need is about ten favorite dinner recipes, plenty of breakfast and lunch ideas for variety and nutrition, convenient snacks, and a regular grocery-shopping routine.

## MEAL PLANNING MADE EASY

Give yourself about sixty minutes for effective meal planning. Since dinner is probably the most difficult to put together, focus mainly on this meal. Make a list of ten recipes that you really enjoy and that take only twenty to thirty minutes to prepare. You may need to ask friends to volunteer their favorite recipes or peruse cookbooks for some new ideas. Once you have the recipes identified, listing ten or more that you want to work with should only take about ten minutes.

Next, make a list of your favorite breakfast and lunch meals. Try to write items you enjoy or that sound good, but that you don't prepare or haven't made previously. Maybe there is a killer fruit smoothie recipe you have been dying to try. Don't forget to list post-training recovery nutritional items.

Now that you have a recipe list, you can plan dinners for the next one to two weeks. Table 8.1—Weekly Menu Suggestions—provides ideas of how certain types of meals may be incorporated into your diet. This is a general plan that can provide you with a lot of flexibility. Find a variety of recipes in the different meal type categories that you enjoy. Come up with several seafood recipes, several stir-fry meals, and variations on the same old pasta dish. After a while, you can fine-tune this menu and learn to keep all the foods you need on hand. Menu planning will soon become more second nature and less of a chore.

When menu planning, figure plenty of complex carbohydrates into your meals, such as rice, pasta, beans and potatoes. These items may currently be side dishes, but you can eventually plan them as main dishes. If protein portions are larger—about half your plate—try changing the proportions of the meal by emphasizing the vegetables and starches. Table 8.2—Meal Ideas—offers suggestions with which you can experiment. Start with the theme or type of main dish, and build around that dish.

| TABLE 8.1 : WEEKLY DINNER MENU SUGGESTIONS | |
|---|---|
| **DAY OF WEEK** | **TYPES OF FOODS** |
| MONDAY | SOUPS, STEWS, PASTA |
| TUESDAY | POULTRY |
| WEDENSDAY | MAIN MEAL SALADS |
| THURSDAY | SEAFOOD |
| FRIDAY | STIR-FRY, CASSEROLE, CHILI |
| SATURDAY | RESTAURANT, TAKE-OUT |
| SUNDAY | MEAT |

Now you are ready to make a shopping list. Go through all the dinner recipes and make an ingredient list, including amounts required. Consolidate all the items on the list for breakfast, lunch, dinner and snacks. Mark the total minimum amounts required and group them according to types of foods and supermarket sections and aisles.

From this list of ingredients, you will be able to develop a "stock" shopping list. Take another look at the list of ingredients. Determine which items can be stockpiled monthly, biweekly and weekly. These items, which won't go to waste, can make or break your diet on especially stressful and hectic days. Keep an ongoing shopping list in a convenient location, and add to it when items run out or run low.

*"On a hard training day I will plan ahead and try to get extra carbohydrates. You don't have to weigh your foods and read every label, but rather tailor nutrition needs to your own workout schedule."*
*—Dunlap*

## SUPERMARKET SAVVY

Now that you are armed with this great shopping list, make the most of precious time by employing some savvy supermarket strategies. First and foremost, never shop

128

## TABLE 8.2: BUILDING YOUR MENU IDEAS

### SALAD MEAL
Large bowl greens
Suggested accompaniments:
Slivered meats, low-fat cheese
Various colorful vegetables
Tomatoes and sprouts, Homemade low-fat croutons
Salad dressing from healthy oils
Nuts and seeds
Breads, low-fat muffins
Soups, bean and lentil

### CASSEROLE MEAL
Any baked main dish
Suggested accompaniments:
soup, vegetables, salads, fruit, bread

### VEGETABLE MEALS
Vegetable main dish
Suggested accompaniments:
breads, muffins, rolls, soups, fruits, salads

### LEGUME OR GRAIN MEAL
Legume or grain dish
Suggested accompaniment:
Bits of meat
Vegetables, stir-fired or steamed
Nuts and seeds, bread and salad

### BREAD MEAL
Loaves of fresh bread, pocketbread, muffins
Low-fat cheeses, Sandwich fillings
Leafy greens, Tomatoes, sprouts, raw vegetables

### SOUP MEAL
A hearty soup
Suggested accompaniments:
Raw vegetables with low-fat dips
Homemade bread, dinner rolls, muffins
fruits, baked low-fat dessert

while hungry. You are there to obtain what you need, pay for it and leave. Mulling over some items not on the list will only waste time. To avoid crowds, shop only at non-peak hours. Try shopping at one store that meets all of your needs. You will know where all your regular favorites are located and be able to save time.

One major shopping spree, heavy on dry and frozen staples, can be completed every one to two weeks. However, you may have to shop for fresh ingredients such as fruits and vegetables twice weekly. Quick trips for these foods are worth your time because the antioxidants and other nutrients they provide will help keep you healthy. If you just can't make it to the supermarket, try another increasingly popular alternative: use a grocery store that accepts fax or e-mail orders, or provides home delivery.

*"During heavy training weeks, I have lots of meals ready that I prepare on my day off because I know that I won't have time to cook."*
*—Reid*

## SIMPLE SUGGESTIONS

Good nutrition starts with planning, and then goes on to the grocery store. Let's look at what wholesome foods should be stocked in your cupboard, refrigerator and freezer.

• *Grains and starches:* Stock up on pasta, noodles, rice and potatoes. Also, cook batches of pasta and rice ahead and later reheat them instantly in boiling water. Precooked baked potatoes can also be zapped in the microwave. To avoid monotonous spaghetti meals, keep an assortment of pasta shapes—penne, ziti, rigatoni, linguini—in the cupboard and freezer. Some pastas stuffed with vegetables, rather than meat and cheese, are low in fat and can be frozen for quick meals later on.

• ***Fresh bread is best,*** and you can freeze an assortment including pita, bagels and muffins, which quickly thaw in the toaster or microwave. Boxes of whole grain crackers can also be kept on hand, as can tortillas for quick burrito recipes. Varieties of cereals, both hot and cold, and pancake mixes can also be stored.

• ***For important items*** such as fruits and vegetables, fresh is best. Wilting asparagus sitting in the fridge for five days really won't boost nutritional intake very much.

On days when fresh just can't be done, stock up on frozen broccoli, spinach and winter squash. Frozen stir-fry mixes are also a great convenience when you desire a variety of vegetables mixed with shellfish, tofu or chicken. And another crucial vegetable-based staple is spaghetti sauce. Look for seasoned, low-fat varieties.

In the fruit department, you can store those canned in water or their own juices. Frozen orange juice and other juice concentrates help when fresh runs low. Dried fruits, such as raisins, are great snack and cereal toppings. Plain frozen fruit, including blueberries and strawberries, can be used for smoothies.

• ***Protein:*** Stock up on sports-diet favorites such as canned black and kidney beans. Low-fat, vegetarian refried beans—no lard—are an important burrito ingredient. Canned seafood, such as tuna, salmon and clams, also comes in handy for quick fixes.

SIMON CUDBY

*Most athletes, such as professional mountain-bike racer Alison Dunlap, stock up on their favorite foods for training.*

You can individually wrap and freeze chicken breasts, meat chops and patties, lean ground turkey and fresh seafood. Tempeh and tofu also have a relatively long refrigerator life, as does hummus.

• *Dairy products:* Choices include skim milk, low-fat cheeses, low-fat yogurt and grated parmesan cheese. Cheese can lightly top baked potatoes or be rolled in with burrito ingredients. Yogurt makes a great snack, and milk adds protein to various meatless meals.

## BATCH COOKING

Now that you have favorite recipes, food staples and fresh ingredients all lined up, there are a few additional strategies to employ. One of the most effective is batch cooking. One evening or afternoon during the weekend, prepare three dishes to be reheated for lunches and dinners in the upcoming week. Cooking on the weekends when there is more time is often more enjoyable. And knowing that good food is waiting for you when you are tired and hungry is also comforting. Some good items for batch cooking include lasagna, chili, stews, and bean and lentil soups.

## BREAKFAST

Breakfast really is the most important meal of the day. By skipping breakfast, eating a medium-size lunch, and feasting at dinner, you may be cheating your body of important nutrients. Breakfast foods high in carbohydrate can also fuel or refuel your body before or after morning training. Skipping breakfast is a terrible way to diet; it often leads to overeating later in the day due to extreme hunger. Make sure you eat a substantial enough breakfast to tide you over until the next meal or snack. Small breakfasts may keep digestive juices flowing, but not enouth to satisfy your appetite.

Breakfast can also be a great time to include nutritious fruits and fruit juices that provide vitamin C, folacin and betacarotene. Other nutrients that may be obtained from breakfast are calcium, protein and fiber. Try to make breakfast substantial in calories if your energy needs are high. The meal will supply precious carbohydrates that will help to refuel your body following an evening training session the day before.

Depending on your training schedule, you may need to pack convenient foods to munch on for breakfast. Remember that non-traditional choices are fine. Fruit smoothies also work well for quick meals on the run. Some quick-packs include yogurt, bananas, dried fruit, bagels and muffins.

## TABLE 8.3: BREAKFAST IDEAS

- Cooked oatmeal with raisins, cinnamon, and low-fat milk
- Open-face English muffin halves with slice cheese, broiled
- Egg substitute omelet with vegetables
- Low-fat plain or flavored yogurt with fresh fruit and banana bread
- Homemade low-fat bran muffin with peanut butter
- Whole grain cereal with slice banana and low-fat milk
- Pita bread with 2 ounces low-fat cheese
- Fruit smoothie made with yogurt, frozen or fresh fruit
- Low-fat granola with raisins and milk
- Whole grain bread with peanut butter, banana, and honey
- Any leftovers that sound appealing

## LUNCH TO GO

Lunch can fall under one of several meal strategies. You either pack a lunch, purchase one at a restaurant or cafeteria, or eat at home. Like other meals, lunch should also provide some high-carbohydrate choices. Try to eat lunch when you first become hungry. Hunger is a clear signal that your body requires fuel. With the right food choices, lunch can continue to refuel your body after a morning workout.

Packing a lunch takes a little extra time and planning, but is often well worth the effort. You can ensure that higher fat items are appropriately portioned, and include good low-fat proteins and plenty of carbohydrates.

*"Diet is individual. Find what works for you."*
*—Norman Alvis, Saturn cycling team and 1995 professional road cycling champion*

Sandwiches are always a good start when planning a lunch. Try lean beef, turkey, bean spread, hummus, low-fat chicken and tuna salads, and low-fat cottage cheese mixed with fruit. Liven up sandwiches with plenty of add-ons such as lettuce leaves, sliced cucumber and tomato, bean or alfalfa sprouts, and low-fat cheese. Carbohydrate additions to lunch can include fruits, pretzels, raw vegetables, yogurt, low-fat chips, low-fat crackers, and vegetable and bean soups.

## SNACK TO KEEP YOUR TANK TOPPED OFF

Does the idea of snacking provoke guilty thoughts of vending-machine candy bars, or that secret stash of chips in your desk drawer? Forget about the guilt. Snacking is an important part of an athlete's diet. Many professional endurance athletes swear by snacking. If your fuel needs are high, or your schedule hectic, plan some serious snacking into your diet.

When you are in a heavy training mode, you require plenty of one thing, and that's calories. Snacking is sometimes the only way to get the right food at the right time in order to fuel the demands of training and life. Take a look at your training diary. Is there a particular time of day when you experience an energy low? Snacking may make a difference.

*"If you eat too much, it takes too long for your stomach to digest. A lot of meals and snacks provide a steady flow of energy, rather than ups and downs."*

*—Reid*

For early-morning workouts, experiment with early-morning snacks. When you awake, liver-glycogen stores are depleted and training may lower blood-sugar levels. Often fluid-containing carbohydrates such as juices, milk and soy milk work best. Try other easy-to-digest items such as fruit, energy bars and carbohydrate gels, which won't weight your stomach or workout.

| TABLE 8.4: SMART SNACKS |
| --- |
| Dry cereal<br>Hard and soft pretzels<br>Cracker and rice cakes with peanut butter<br>Baked potato with low fat cheese or nonfat refried beans<br>Muffins and bagels with jam or low-fat cream cheese<br>Fresh fruit, dried fruit, fruit juice, frozen fruit bars<br>Sports bars, breakfast bars, low-fat granola bars<br>Fruit smoothies made with various combinations of ingredients<br><br>For chocolate cravings:<br>Cocoa powder in recipes like smoothies<br>Dip fruit in chocolate-flavored syrup<br>Low fat shake with chocolate-flavored syrup<br>Chocolate nonfat yogurt cone<br>Chocolate angel food cake with cocoa powder |

Afternoon noshes may work, as well. Even when making time for a satisfying lunch, immediate fuel supplies may have run low prior to an evening workout. Therefore, pre-exercise eating may enhance your training program.

Snacking is also a great recovery boost. If you don't have the time or inclination for a heavy meal after training, a snack immediately afterward can provide the correct amount of carbohydrates required for recovery and glycogen synthesis. Snacking may also eliminate the need for heavy meals, which often means longer digestion times that can bog down training.

Plan ahead and fill your home, work place and gym bag with the best food choices. Not planning and allowing yourself to get very hungry. are two ways to guarantee yourself snack choices filled with sugar and fat, rather than whole grains, fruits, vegetables and lean proteins.

To minimize reliance on candy bars and cookies—occasional indulgences are fine—monitor your hunger and fullness. Respond by eating when you are comfortably hungry and you should be able to stop eating when you are comfortably full. Most people run low on liver glycogen at a rate that requires food every three to five hours.

Clearly, snacking does support a successful training program. Here are a few snacking tips:

*"I graze a lot and eat many snacks during the day. Snacking works great with my lifestyle. To accomodate my training, it is better to eat smaller snacks more often, rather than eating larger meals less often. This way I am always ready to work out. Basically, I always have some sort of food in my hands.*
*—Fuhr*

- *Keep it simple and keep it handy.*
- *Emphasize carbohydrate fuel. Mix in some protein.*
- *Snack on healthy fruits and vegetables.*
- *Save processed foods for quick consumption and convenience.*
- *Snack when you are comfortably hungry to prevent extreme hunger.*
- *Plan ahead and have snack choices readily available.*

## LABEL LINGO

Nutritional information on labels can help you determine what foods are high in carbohydrate, fat or both. The information may be used to find foods that fit into your carbohydrate prescription. Note the serving sizes on labels carefully; they may not be the portion that you would normally consume. Also, limit the items that will push the fat level in your diet up too high.

On labels, notice the "Daily Values"—a system designed to help consumers put labels into practical use when planning a healthy diet. Based on a diet of 2000 calories—sometimes also 2500 calories—"Daily Values" for carbohydrates are calculated at 60 percent or more of total calories—300 grams—and at 30 percent or less for fat—65 grams. These values may not exactly fit your training nutrition prescription, but they can be adapted to your own carbohydrate needs. Other nutrients listed on the label—fat, cholesterol, sodium, carbohydrate and

| TABLE 8.5: LABEL LINGO | |
|---|---|
| CALORIE FREE | Less than 5 calories per serving |
| LIGHT/LITE | 1/3 fewer calories |
| | 1/3 fat original version |
| FAT-FREE | Less than 0.5 gms / fat serving |
| REDUCED, LESS, FEWER | At least 25-percent less fat than original |
| LEAN | Less than 10 gm fat |
| | Less than 4 gm saturated fat |
| | Less than 95 mg cholesterol |
| | Per 3.5 ounces serving |
| EXTRA LEAN | Less than 5 gm fat |
| | Less than 2 gm saturated fat |
| | Less than 95 mg cholesterol |
| | Per 3.5 ounces serving |
| LOW SATURATED FAT | Less than 1 gm saturated fat |
| | Not more than 15-percent fat calories |
| CHOLESTEROL FREE | Less than 2 mg cholesterol |
| | Less than 2 gm saturated fat |
| LOW CHOLESTEROL | No more than 20 mg cholesterol and 2 gm of fat |
| LOW SODIUM | Less than 140 mg per serving |
| SUGAR FREE | Less than 0.5 gm sugar per serving |
| HIGH FIBER | More than 5 gm per serving |

protein—will be expressed as a percent of "Daily Values" based on 2000 calories. Table 8.5 deciphers label "lingo."

## FINAL THOUGHTS

A successful sports diet takes time and planning. But developing good meal planning, shopping and cooking habits can significantly enhance the success of a training program. In the long term, this will save time, effort and energy.

# CHAPTER NINE

# Dietary Rules for
# *Restaurants*
## *and the* Road

---

*"When I travel for competition, I try to find a restaurant with a lot of selection and different types of food."*
—*Painter*

M any Americans eat out at least four times per week, and chances are that you do too. A busy lifestyle of working and training results in relying even more on restaurant meals than the average consumer, who munches on 44 percent of their food dollars away from home. Lunch is the meal most frequently eaten out, followed by dinner and then breakfast. You may eat out not only in restaurants, but also at your desk or in the car. It is estimated by the National Restaurant Association that half the food purchased at restaurants is actually consumed elsewhere.

## BASIC SKILLS AND STRATEGIES

N o matter which meal is eaten outside the home, or whether the restaurant is a fast food chain or haute cuisine, the basic strategies for healthy restaurant eating are the same.

Some questions you may have regarding eating away from home are:

- *How can I maintain a healthy sports diet when I am away from home?*
- *What are good choices at various ethnic restaurants?*
- *What are good nutritional strategies when I travel to competitions?*

First, give yourself an attitude check on eating out. Do you view restaurant meals as a special time to overindulge? If you do, move beyond this thinking. It may wreak havoc with consuming a healthy sports diet. Take control of what is ordered and what is actually eaten. One of the best ways to manifest this control is becoming a good fat-finder and fat-avoider!

Learn about the choices at your favorite restaurants. Ask questions regarding food preparation and ingredients. Don't be afraid to ask for modifications or changes. You have the right to order foods as you want, and creatively outsmart the menu as well.

One effective means of limiting fat and sticking to a sports diet is to make protein more of a side dish, rather than part of your main meal. Typical protein portions are often enough for the whole day. These and other high-fat items should be balanced in the context of the entire day's menu. Try to emphasize more whole grains, fruits and vegetables. You may also want to control alcohol intake. Alcohol adds calories, few nutrients, and may impair your desire to eat healthfully.

*"If I eat out, I'll eat only half of a big meal, and then save the leftovers."*
*—Bliss Livingston*

Some basic skills to apply at any restaurant are:
- *Develop a healthy frame of mind*
- *Select restaurants carefully and become familiar with the menus*
- *Have a plan regarding how the meal fits into your day's diet*
- *Be an avid fat-finder*
- *Order according to your sports diet prescription*
- *Practice portion control*
- *Be creative with the menu and make special requests*
- *Know when you have had enough*

## DEVELOPING PERSONAL RESTAURANT STRATEGIES

Besides these helpful general suggestions, you should develop a set of personalized strategies. Start by evaluating your current eating-out habits. Below are some questions to consider. You may want to spend the next week tracking these habits.

How many times do you eat out weekly? How many are lunches, dinners and snacks? What types of restaurants do you frequent most often? Some choices are fast food chains, delicatessens, cafeterias, coffee shops and ethnic cuisines.

*"Travel did create some problems with nutrition. When we went out of the country, many of us brought energy bars and other nutritional supplements containing carbohydrate and protein."*
*—Tueting*

When the places you most often frequent have been identified, write down your favorite meals from those establishments. Provide as much detail as possible about how the food is prepared and served. Don't forget side dishes, toppings, sauces and beverages—including alcohol. Estimate serving sizes as best as possible—small, medium or large. Three to four ounces of cooked animal protein is about the size of a cassette tape. One ounce of cheese is the equivalent of four dice.

After recording eating-out patterns for the week, try to evaluate them objectively. Do any of your current habits interfere with choosing a better training diet? Are there some lighter choices that can be substituted? How do restaurant meals fit in with the rest of your meals and snacks?

Next, put together a plan of action. Plan ahead. Think about where you may eat out during the day. Consider what other meals you should prepare to balance out these choices. Understand the menus at restaurants you frequent. Ask questions. What ingredients are used? How is the dish prepared? You should be able to make special requests at just about any restaurant. Some common requests are to have non-ordered items removed from the table, make substitutions, share dishes, have foods specially prepared, and put dressing, condiments and sauces on the side.

Regardless of what foods you choose, portions may still need to be controled. To do this, order an appetizer or half-size portion, split portions, and take home leftovers.

## ETHNIC CUISINES

Chances are that if you eat out frequently, you enjoy many delicious ethnic cuisines. These cultural edibles may fit into a healthy training diet, but approach ethnic establishments with an understanding of how tasty dishes fit on the menu. Let's take a look at some of the more-frequented ethnic cuisines: Italian, Mexican and Chinese.

## ITALIAN CUISINE

Italian food is very popular and can be consumed at a variety of settings—upscale dining, family style restaurant, pizzeria, or fast food chain. With an emphasis on grains and vegetables, Italian meals can be healthy. Some lighter, lower-fat choices are starches such as spaghetti; low-fat risotto and polenta; tomato-based sauces, zucchini and other vegetables prepared without fat; and lean meats such as skinless chicken, veal, shrimp and grilled fish. You can also try condiments such as herbs, cooking wines, vinegar, garlic and crushed red peppers.

There are plenty of heavier choices at Italian restaurants, such as cheese-filled manicotti and ravioli. Starches such as garlic bread and focaccia contain fat, as do fried vegetables and salami, proscuitto and sausage. Watch out for high-fat cheeses and dishes prepared with cream, butter, and even olive oil, which still contains plenty of fat calories.

You can make special requests, including removing the olive oil, having the skin taken off chicken, and serving salad dressing on the side.

## MEXICAN CUISINE

Mexican cuisine may also be an ethnic favorites. Like Italian food, this cuisine contains both light and heavy choices. Many staples of Mexican cuisine can be considered low-fat items, such as whole beans, refried beans and rice prepared without oil, tortillas, grilled vegetables and salsa. Grilled proteins such as shrimp, fish or chicken are good choices, as are whole black beans.

Some heavier choices at Mexican restaurants are tortilla chips, chimichangas and taco shells. Guacamole, olives, chorizo, sour cream and cheese are also high in fat.

## CHINESE CUISINE

Chinese food prepared in regional styles is a frequent favorite at mall eateries and small neighborhood restaurants. While there are light choices in Chinese cooking, there are also many high-fat pitfalls. To keep your meal on the light side, look for stir-fried vegetables. There are a variety to choose from, such as peapods, bamboo shoots, water chestnuts, cabbage, baby corn and broccoli.

*"I try to eat a variety of foods. I often go by how I feel. You need to know your own body."*
*—Tonia Kwiatkowski, figure skater and U.S. silver medalist; World Team member in 1993, '96 and '98*

Proteins that are lean and found in Chinese dishes with these vegetables dishes include shrimp, chicken, tofu, and lean cuts of beef and pork. Dishes may also contain low-fat fruits such as pineapple and orange sections. Mustard, soy sauce, ginger, sweet sauce and garlic will also not increase the fat content of meals.

Likewise, Chinese cuisine contains plenty of high-fat choices. Everyone is familiar with fatty, breaded and fried, sweet and sour dishes. Fried rice has twice the calories as steamed rice, with all the additional calories coming from oil. Fried noodles can also increase fat intake. Stay away from fried seafood, pork, spare ribs, and duck with skin. Stir-fried dishes that contain nuts will also be much higher in fat, as will any dish in which oil is used heavily. Request that your dish be prepared with as little oil as possible, and try to split entrees with somebody else or take some home—portions are often large.

## OTHER RESTAURANT CHOICES
### SALAD BARS

Visits to the salad bar, with visions of colorful vegetables, are often well-intended. However, salad bars can result in surprisingly high-fat meals. Besides those healthy raw vegetables—spinach, tomatoes, broccoli and green peppers—there are plenty of items mixed with fat or sitting in oil. Some of the less healthy choices include pasta salad, potato salad, marinated vegetables, cheeses, and bean salads made with oil. And, of course, there is that final injury, salad dressing.

Salads bars have plenty of carbohydrates and fiber, and can help keep your protein portion low and reasonable. Obviously, fresh greens and plain raw vegetables are the best choices. Starches on the salad bar may include chickpeas, kidney beans, green peas, crackers and pita bread.

Lean protein salad-bar choices include plain tuna, cottage cheese, egg, ham and feta cheese. Avoid most cheeses and pepperoni. Keep marinated vegetable portions small, and especially watch out for tuna, chicken, seafood, macaroni, potato and pasta salads. They are dripping with oil. Other high-fat items include peanuts, sesame and sunflower seeds.

Of course, salad dressings, especially when used liberally, are a considerable source of fat. Try to choose light or fat-free versions, or simply watch portions carefully.

## Fast food

Although fast food can be excessive in protein and fat, and low in calcium, carotenoids and vitamin C, you can still make choices that fit into a sports diet. If you eat hamburgers, try the smaller ones that have two to three ounces of meat. Broiled chicken sandwiches are better, while chicken pieces are generally fried. The same goes for seafood and fish sandwiches—there is plenty of unwanted oil. Emphasize baked potatoes over french fries, and order skim milk whenever possible. Fruit juice is also available in some places, contributing nicely to your carbohydrate intake. Choose vegetables and salads whenever possible—but watch the dressing. Whenever possible, limit sauces and toppings.

## Making changes

Modifying a menu reduce save a significant amount of fat and calories from your daily intake. Even making minor changes over several weeks can result in trimming extra dietary fat. So evaluate your current diet, plan ahead, eat healthy at-home meals. Ask about the menu at favorite restaurants, make lighter choices, ask questions, control portions, and don't be afraid to make special requests. It will keep good health and training on the right track.

*The U.S. women's gold medal hockey team, and most other athletes, pack their favorite sports nutrition products when traveling.*

## SMART TRAVEL CUISINE

It's Friday, the day before a weekend of competition, and you are working late. Fortunately, everything is packed and ready to go. By the time you are on the way, your stomach says it's time to refuel. Of course, by now you know that eating right the night before competition can improve performance. Carefully consider the options. Falling into a trap of greasy-platter predicaments doesn't have to create distress when traveling and racing. Cyclists just need to plan and use a little culinary know-how to create a positive gustatory experience.

Chances are you will be eating out fre-

*"I eat airline food only when the choices appear acceptable. This is where planning comes into play. I always have water and energy bars with me for emergency food, just in case the airline forces a white-bread-and-slab-of-cheese sandwich on me."*

*—Bliss Livingston*

149

*"Generally, when I travel I take the majority of my food with me. I usually have one gym bag that is filled with food. This, along, with a cook pot, and I am set. You never know what type of food will be available when you travel to many different places, so this keeps my diet consistent."*

*—Fuhr*

quently when traveling for competition. Now that you know about restaurant eating, make special requests and choose correct portions. This will help make traveling more manageable.

Regardless of whether traveling by road or air, drink plenty of water. Traveling dehydrates the system. Also, pack plenty sports nutrition supplements, especially if you rely upon them heavily. Road travelers may want to bring a cooler packed with their favorite food stash, while some items may fit into suitcases. Items that travel best are sports nutrition bars, breakfast cereals, dried fruit, and liquid meal supplements.

## FINAL THOUGHTS

Eating away from home is common with today's fast-paced lifestyles. Like a healthy sports diet at home, eating while away takes knowledge and planning. Preparing meals and snacks to be eaten away from home can be extremely helpful. In addition, knowing what low-fat choices are available at various types of eating establishments is also useful for maintaining a balanced and healthy sports diet.

# PART IV

# COMPETITION
# NUTRITION

# CHAPTER TEN

# Nutrition Before
# *Training and*
# *Competition*

---

*"The day before a race, you have done all you can do. At that
point, it's resting and having a well-balanced meal."*

—*Walton*

It's the night before an important competition. You have
been focusing on this particular event all season, and
especially for the past several weeks. At this point, more
training won't make a difference. All you can do is rest and
prepare the best pre-day and pre-race meals possible.

In Section I, you learned that consuming an optimal daily
sports diet supports recovery from a demanding training program. In Section II, you learned how to put together a great
sports diet. Now, in Section III, guidelines are outlined for eating and drinking properly in the hours before and during exercise and competition in order to optimize performance.

This chapter provides specific recommendations for beginning each exercise session well hydrated and with adequate body-fuel stores. Even with a great daily recovery diet, what, when and how much you eat and drink in the day, hours and minutes before training and racing can have a positive effect upon performance.

Some questions that you may ask yourself about pre-exercise eating are:

- *What are the benefits of proper pre-exercise nutrition?*
- *What types of foods and fluids should be consumed? And in what amounts?*
- *How should my meals be timed?*

## PRE-EXERCISE EATING
### MAXIMIZING THE PHYSIOLOGICAL EDGE

Eating properly before training and competition can improve performance in a number of ways. One of the most important results of proper eating before exercise is ensuring that you begin exercise with adequate muscle glycogen stores.

Carbohydrates consumed several hours before exercise can "top off" these muscle glycogen stores. These benefits continue, as carbohydrates consumed in the hour before exercise can directly fuel muscles during activity. Exercise of all types draws upon these energy stores. As discussed previously, just how much glycogen your body requires depends upon the type, intensity and duration of the training session and competition.

Eating correctly before exercise also increases liver glycogen stores—a handy technique for preventing low blood sugar, otherwise known as hypoglycemia. Liver glycogen is broken down

| TABLE 10.1: BENEFITS OF PRE-EXERCISE EATING | |
| --- | --- |
| **Proper fuel before training and competition will:** | |
| Finish filling muscle glycogen stores | Settle your stomach and prevent |
| Top off liver glycogen stores | hunger pains |
| Minimize risk of developing hypoglycemia | Provide a psychological edge |
| Provide fuel during the early part of exercise | Keep you well-hydrated |

during exercise in order to maintain blood glucose levels. Carbohydrates that continue to be absorbed by the intestines early on during exercise, also maintain blood-glucose levels.

Having adequate blood glucose is essential. Glucose fuels the brain and can prevent symptoms of fatigue, light-headiness, and helps maintain concentration and good judgment during exercise. In addition, consuming adequate fluid prior to exercise also ensures proper hydration.

## MAXIMIZING THE PSYCHOLOGICAL EDGE

Besides physiological benefits, eating right before training and competition can provide a distinct psychological boost. You benefit from knowing that you have consumed foods that are tolerable and effective in improving performance. Knowing that you won't experience hunger or a churning stomach during exercise is reassuring. Table 10.1 summarizes some of the benefits of optimal pre-exercise eating.

## TOLERATING FOOD BEFORE EXERCISE

Though eating several hours before exercise can clearly improve performance, you may be concerned about experi-

TOM MORAN

*All types of activities draw upon the body's energy stores.*

encing gastrointestinal (GI) distress. Sports that provide the stomach a more stable position during exercise, such as cycling, swimming and cross-country skiing, seem to result in fewer GI problems. Often, sports such as running—where the body moves more or is jostled—can result in GI problems. But athletes participating in all sports can test and improve tolerance to pre-exercise eating. A body can learn to handle greater amounts of foods or liquids as exercise time approaches. You will have to experiment to find out what foods work best for your sport, tolerance, competition schedule and lifestyle. Before competition, follow what has worked best in training as much as possible.

Easy to moderately hard exercise should not significantly

| TABLE 10.2: EATING BEFORE EXERCISE |
|---|
| **Factors that can increase GI problems are:** |

| | |
|---|---|
| Inexperienced athlete | Excess caffeine |
| Trying new or unusual foods | Nerves of emotional stress |
| Intense exercise | Dehydration |
| High fiber foods | Jostling of stomach during exercise |
| Large amounts of fructose | |

impair digestion. The more intensely the exercise, the more likely GI problems can occur. That's because there is a greater shift of blood away from the stomach and intestinal system and toward the exercising muscles. Keeping a pre-exercise meal low in fiber, and perhaps fructose, can also help prevent GI problems.

Athletes who are tense and nervous prior to exercise, especially before competition, are most likely to experience GI problems. Excess caffeine may also be a problem for some athletes, which causes increased tension and jitters. Beginning a workout when dehydrated can also increase the risk of experiencing GI problems. And of course, trying new and unusual foods prior to exercise may cause problems. Table 10.2 list some potential causes of GI problems.

## GLYCOGEN AND TYPES OF TRAINING

The proportion of carbohydrate and fat burned during exercise depends upon the type, intensity and duration of the activity (see Chapter 1). Long and high-intensity competitive events such as cycling road races, marathons, triathlons and cross-country skiing, place a greater demand on muscle glycogen stores. Exercise in which high-intensity work is repeated often, such as in interval training, can also rapidly deplete glycogen. Non-endurance sports where the intensity is lower, or high for only short periods of time, such as gymnastics, figure skating, football and track and field, do not place as high a demand on carbohydrate stores.

During high-intensity exercise, carbohydrates from glycogen are the predominant fuel. Unfortunately, the amount of stored glycogen is often inadequate to meet energy demands and can quickly become depleted. When carbohydrates are the primary fuel source, muscle and liver glycogen stores can become exhausted within one to one-and-a-half hours.

Regardless of whether or not the competition is an endurance event, training for it may incorporate several types of glycogen-draining sessions—endurance work, sprint training, interval workouts and strength training. All of these forms of training sessions can significantly dip into muscle-glycogen stores. Athletes engaging in these types of training sessions should consume a balanced sports diet as described in Sections One and Two. Paying close attention to what you eat several hours before training can also improve the quality of exercise.

## CARBOHYDRATE AND FLUID BEFORE EXERCISE

You should arrive for any intense training session or competition with carbohydrate stores lasting longer than one to one-and-a-half hours. Muscle glycogen, at up to 1400 calories of stored energy, is the largest carbohydrate supply. Liver glycogen is more limited at about 400 calories. Depletion of liver glycogen can occur within three to five hours when not exercising and fall to low levels overnight, a concern for early-morning exercise. Blood glucose is very limited at 80 calories. Late in a training session, blood glucose may be the only carbohydrate fuel left for your exercising muscles.

Regardless of the size and timing of a pre-training or pre-competition meal, carbohydrates should predominate to top off and maintain muscle- and liver-glycogen stores and blood-glucose levels. Foods that provide these carbohydrates are grains, starchy vegetables, milk and yogurt, fruit and fruit juices. Table 10.3 lists high carbohydrate, low-fiber foods that can be consumed prior to exercise.

Some athletes may need to choose low-fiber, carbohydrate foods to avoid digestion problems prior to exercise. Some high fiber foods that may be best avoided are: bran cereals and muffins, fresh fruit with skins, and most raw vegetables. You may also consider having moderate portions of fruits and juices before exercise. These foods contain fructose that can cause GI problems in

| TABLE 10.3: HIGH CARBOHYDRATE, LOW FIBER FOODS |
|---|
| **30 grams of carbohydrate per serving** |
| bagel, 2 ounces |
| bread, white, 2 slices |
| pita pocket, 1.5 rounds |
| dinner rolls, 2 |
| English muffin, 1 |
| muffin, low fat, low fiber, 3 ounces |
| tortillas, 2 |
| cooked cereal, 1 cup |
| apple, 1.5 medium |
| applesauce, sweetened, 1/2 cup |
| grapefruit, peeled, 1 large |
| canned fruit, 1 cup |
| cold cereal, low fiber, 1.5 ounces |
| graham crackers, 6 |
| saltines, 8 |
| rice, cooked, white, 2/3 cup |
| pasta, cooked, 1 cup |
| pretzels, white flour, 1.5 ounces |
| potato, baked, no skin, 1 medium |
| sweet potato, no skin, 4 ounces |
| apple juice, 8 ounces |
| carrot juice, 10 ounces |
| grape juice, 6 ounces |
| cranberry juice cocktail, 8 ounces |
| milk, skim, 20 ounces |
| yogurt with fruit, 1 cup |

*"It's important to eat right the week before the race, so I can train and recover during that time and improve for the race."*
*—Brian Walton, Saturn cycling team and 1996 Olympic silver medalist*

some athletes. However, when consumed as part of a meal consisting of a variety of carbohydrate sources, they are usually well-tolerated. You may also want to limit gas-producing foods such as broccoli, cauliflower and cabbage. Use your own good judgment regarding personal food tolerances.

| TABLE 10.4: LOW TO MODERATE GLYCEMIC INDEX FOODS | |
| --- | --- |
| **Low glycemic index** | **Moderate glycemic index** |
| peach | orange juice |
| apples | orange |
| yogurt | macaroni |
| ice cream | raisins |
| chickpeas | beets |
| milk | grapes |
| pears | spaghetti |
| lentils | pinto beans |
| grapefruit | sucrose |
| plums | green peas |
| cherries | navy beans |
| soybeans | |
| fructose | |

**THE GLYCEMIC INDEX**

The glycemic index of foods has been the subject of pre-exercise research. While the high-glycemic carbohydrates may facilitate glycogen synthesis (see Chapter 3), low to moderate glycemic index foods may work best prior to exercise. These foods raise blood glucose more slowly, providing sustained energy that makes them ideal for exercise. Table 10.4 lists some low to moderate glycemic index foods.

But keep in mind that you have to consume large amounts of these foods, by themselves, to receive their potential benefits. Also be aware that no one has shown that high-glycemic index foods before exercise are harmful to performance. More research regarding the practical application of glycemic index to pre-exercise meals needs to be conducted. Performance benefits have not been consistently demonstrated with this food-ranking system. Besides, if you follow these low glycemic pre-exercise meals with carbohydrates taken in during exercise, the positive effects may become negated anyway.

## A BALANCED MEAL

While about two-thirds to three-fourths of pre-exercise meals should consist of carbohydrate, it can also contain some protein. Because proteins take longer to digest and absorb, it's good to have moderate, low-fat choices on hand as well. Some choices meeting this criteria are skim milk, skim milk yogurt, lean poultry, fish, and cheeses with less than one gram of fat per serving. Higher fat proteins that are less quickly and less easily digested are regular cheese, eggs, steak, fatty meats, lunch meat and sausages (see Table 7.3).

*"Before a big race, especially a race I know will be long and grueling, I am conscious of getting plenty of complex carbohydrates the night before. I've found that if I eat a good pasta dinner, I have enough energy the next day to last until the end of the race."*
*—Bliss Livingston*

Other hidden fats, which are used in meal preparation or added to foods, also delay stomach emptying and can create a heavy, sluggish feeling. Try to limit portions of butter, margarine, cream cheese, peanut butter, and oils used in salad dressing, grilling or cooking. Experiment and determine the balance that works best for you. Some protein and fat keeps hunger at bay and blood-glucose levels nice and steady.

## TIMING

Carbohydrates should predominate any pre-exercise meal, but the actual amounts required depend upon the time interval between eating and exercise. Anywhere from half-a-gram to just under two grams of carbohydrate for every pound you weigh—1 to 4 grams per kilogram—is needed in the one-to four-hour period before exercise. Some athletes prefer eating several hours prior to exercise, while others eat in the last hour. Also prior to exercise, it is best to consume 8 to 12 ounces of water every thirty minutes.

## THE NIGHT BEFORE

Often training sessions and competitions take place in the early morning, when liver-glycogen stores are at their lowest. Because liver glycogen is the body's main source of blood glucose, exercising in this state can cause an unwanted drop in blood glucose. This situation may lead to fatigue and light-headiness. Having a high-carbohydrate dinner and even a light-carbohydrate evening snack the night before will fill the liver with a good amount of glycogen. Just make sure that any late-night noshes are easy to digest. Go to bed comfortably full, not stuffed. Drink plenty of fluids, especially water.

## THREE TO FOUR HOURS BEFORE EXERCISE

Having a time span of three to four hours to eat before training and racing allows you to consume a large meal or snack, which can top off muscle-glycogen and refill liver-glycogen stores. Research has shown a significant improvement in performance when, four hours prior to an exercise test, cyclists consumed just under two grams of carbohydrate for every pound they weighed. This large meal is the equivalent of 300 grams of carbohydrate and 1200 calories for a 150-pound athlete. Large carbohydrate meals can be extremely filling. Having a significant portion of these carbohydrates in liquid form is helpful.

You can maximize muscle-glycogen stores in this manner for several exercise scenarios. Consider having a large afternoon snack for late-evening training sessions. You can also use this three- to four-hour opportunity to digest a large meal before a mid-morning or early-afternoon training session or race start. Drink at least 24 to 36 ounces of fluid at this meal.

## Two hours before exercise

Here, the same principle as eating three to four hours before exercise applies. Consume as many grams of carbohydrate as is comfortable two hours before exercise. One gram of carbohydrate per pound of weight, about 150 grams for a 150-pound athlete, should be well-tolerated. This "lighter" meal can be consumed as an afternoon snack, or early breakfast for a mid-morning training session or competition. Again, drink at least 24 ounces of fluid.

## An hour before exercise

Early studies triggered much debate over the wisdom of consuming carbohydrates one hour before exercise. This timing was questioned as these studies demonstrated that thirty-minute pre-exercise carbohydrate triggered insulin secretion, resulting in lowered blood-glucose levels and symptoms of hypoglycemia. Researchers speculated that this reaction would adversely affect performance.

However, many more recent studies have reported that such a reaction is not common. If it does occur, it is small in magnitude, and short-lived, lasting only about thirty minutes into exercise, while producing no adverse symptoms and performance effects. However, it is possible that some individuals may be sensitive to carbohydrates this close to exercise. Experiment in training to determine if this hypoglycemia occurs for you, and, if needed, simply avoid carbohydrates for thirty minutes before exercise.

For the majority of athletes who tolerate carbohydrates close to exercise, a performance boost can result. Staying around half-a-gram per pound of weight works best. This is about 75 grams for a 150-pound athlete. Obviously, this close to exercise time you will want to eat only well-tolerated foods. Try your favorite energy bar or two squeeze-bottles-worth of a sports drink. Drink at least 12 ounces of fluid the hour before exercise.

Consuming carbohydrate so close to exercise can be practical in a number of situations. If you had a larger meal three to four hours prior, eating one hour before exercise can provide an added carbohydrate boost. Having a light carbohydrate snack one hour before exercise, rather than nothing, can also be energizing.

## IMMEDIATELY BEFORE EXERCISE

Fluids can be consumed in the final minutes prior to exercise. Drinking a sports drink during this time can boost blood-glucose levels and compensate if you are not able to drink early on in exercise. Carbohydrates, probably in the form of a sport drink, are also safe at this time, as insulin secretion is suppressed by exercise.

## EATING BEFORE COMPETITIVE EVENTS

### SHORT-DURATION EVENTS

All out events lasting up to four minutes are fueled by muscle stores of ATP, CP, and glycogen. If you are competing in this type of event, it is important that you have allowed adequate recovery time and replenishment of these body fuels since your most recent training session or competition. Athletes training for these events should consume a daily diet adequate in carbohydrate for recovery. You should also consume a properly timed morning meal high enough in carbohydrate to fill liver glycogen stores, and which will be well-tolerated and prevent hunger.

### IMMEDIATE-DURATION EVENTS

Some competitive events require intense exercise for four to ten minutes or longer, such as certain swimming or rowing events. Muscle glycogen is the predominant fuel for these events, as the intensity precludes the use of fat for fuel.

If you compete in these types of events, you should ensure that muscle-glycogen stores are adequate when you hit the start line. While the actual competitive event is not of a long enough duration to deplete muscle glycogen, the training sessions leading up to competition can drain this fuel. To ensure that glycogen stores are replenished, it would be prudent to taper training and consume a high-carbohydrate diet several days before competing. Being well-hydrated is also crucial, and consuming a high-carbohydrate pre-competition meal two hours prior to competition would be beneficial. Focus on pre-competition exercise goals for at least twenty-four hours.

## MULTIPLE EVENTS

If your competition schedule includes several events in one day, the repeated all-out efforts of both short- and intermediate-duration events can deplete muscle-glycogen stores. Athletes often required to compete several times in one day include swimmers, inline skaters, track cyclists, track-and-field athletes, and wrestlers. For these types of events, a fueling-up period of twenty-four to thirty-six hours should be sufficient.

Nutritional goals for this scenario would be optimal hydration, adequate liver glycogen and blood-glucose levels, and preventing extreme depletion of muscle-glycogen stores. Throughout the day, schedule food and drink breaks of high-carbohydrate, low-fiber foods in order to restore glycogen levels. Easy-to-digest foods such as bananas, energy bars, fig bars, graham crackers and bagels can be consumed along with liquid carbohydrates from sports drinks and tolerated juices. More filling meals can be consumed when events are separated by several hours. Many athletes prefer using conveniently packaged liquid meals, as they satisfy the body's nutritional demands, leave the stomach rapidly, are low in fiber, and are hydrating.

## ENDURANCE EVENTS

Athletes who compete at high intensities for sixty minutes or longer can significantly deplete specific muscle-glycogen fibers. Longer events that are greater than ninety minutes will also take a toll on muscle-glycogen. Events such as a cycling criterium or road race, triathlons, half or full marathons, and cross-country skiing races require careful nutritional preparation prior to competition.

During longer competitive events, muscle-glycogen stores are progressively depleted. When these stores drop to low enough levels, it is difficult to sustain high-intensity exercise, and you may need to reduce your pace in order to continue. That's why glycogen supercompensation—otherwise known as "carbohydrate-loading"—can be beneficial. This technique can increase muscle-glycogen stores by 50 to 100 percent.

For events of this duration, if your competitive schedule allows, nutritional planning should take place several days prior to the event. That's because rest is a key component to fueling up muscle-glycogen stores. Fuel-depleting or muscle-damaging training sessions should be done at least several days before competition. Then, engage in lighter exercise, and rest the days before.

Aim to eat as close to your recommended carbohydrate amount—up to 5 grams per pound—as much as possible. Utilize the list of high-carbohydrate foods provided, and strategically plan meals and snacks. While an everyday diet should meet these requirements, take extra care the days leading up to competition.

If you compete so frequently that resting for several days is inconceivable, try increasing total carbohydrate intake even a day or two earlier prior to a key competition. Some helpful strategies are:

- *Utilizing commercial carbohydrate supplements*
- *Emphasizing low-fiber, carbohydrate-dense foods such as bagels*
- *Trying more dense, sugar-containing foods such as fruit juice and sports drinks*
- *Making certain that fatty foods do not replace carbohydrates*
- *Limiting protein foods to minimal amounts*
- *Avoiding or limiting filling, but relatively low-carbohydrate foods such as vegetables and salads*
- *Obtaining carbohydrates from liquids for hydration as well as carbohydrate-loading*
- *Following a pre-determined plan*

### CARBOHYDRATE LOADING

Serious carbohydrate loaders probably are familiar with various techniques advised over the past several decades. Supersaturating muscles stores requires a diet of at least 70-percent carbohydrate and adequate calories two or three days before competing. Activities that may benefit from serious carbo' loading are long-distance swimming events and training sessions, cross-country skiing, long-distance cycling, mountain biking, triathlons and soccer. Activities that may not benefit are shorter swimming races, downhill skiing, downhill mountain-bike racing, football games, and shorter track-and-field events.

## TABLE 10.5: HOW TO EAT BEFORE TRAINING AND COMPETITION

| Timing | Carbohydrate/Food Recommendations | Sample foods | Start times | Types of events |
|--------|-----------------------------------|--------------|-------------|-----------------|
| Night before | High carbo meal<br><br>300 grams carbs<br><br>Low in fiber<br><br>Plenty of fluid | Pasta dishes<br>Rice dishes<br>Lean protein<br>Easy on fat<br>Cooked vegetables | Essential for early start time<br><br>Helpful for any start time | Endurance events<br><br>Intermediate distance<br><br>Short duration events |
| 3 to 4 hours prior | Carbohydrates:<br>1.5 to 2 grams per pound weight<br>(3 to 4 grams/kg)<br><br>Low fat protein<br>Low fat and fiber<br>Plenty of fluids | 150-pound athlete:<br>225 to 300 gm of carbohydrate<br><br><br>Cereals, bread, crackers, milk,<br>yogurt, fruit, juices,<br>jelly, muffins, bagels | For mid-morning starts: Eat at 7:00 a.m. for 10:00 a.m. start<br><br>Mid-afternoon starts: Eat at 10:00 a.m. for 2:00 p.m. start | Endurance events<br><br>Intermediate distance |
| 2 hours prior | Carbohydrates:<br>Up to 1.0 grams per pound of weight<br>(2 grams/kg)<br><br>Minimal low fat protein<br>Low fat and fiber<br>Plenty of fluids<br>Carbohydrates:<br>0.5 grams per pound weight<br>(1.0 gms/kg) | 150-pound athlete:<br>130 to 150 gms carbohydrate<br><br><br>Cereals, bread, milk,<br>yogurt, fruit, juices,<br>jelly, crackers | For mid-morning starts: Eat at 8:00 a.m. for 10:00 a.m. start<br><br>For mid-afternoon start: Eat at 12:00 noon for 2:00 p.m. start after a large morning breakfast<br><br>For late starts: Eat at 6:00 p.m. for 8:00 p.m. start after adequate carbohydrate meals throughout the day | Short duration events<br><br>Intermediate distance<br><br>Endurance events<br><br>Multiple events |
| 1 hour prior | Emphasize liquids<br>Easy to digest carbohydrates<br>Avoid protein, fat, and fiber | Sports drinks<br><br>Concentrated carbohydrate supplements<br><br>Sports bars<br><br>Tolerated fruits<br><br>Water | For early starts:<br>Eat at 6:00 a.m. for 8:00 a.m. start<br><br>For mid-morning starts:<br>For 10:00 a.m. start, have snack/liquid at 9:00 a.m. in addition to 6:30 - 7:00 a.m. meal | Short-duration events<br><br>Intermediate-length events<br><br>Endurance events<br><br>Multiple events |
| Immediately prior | Carbohydrates | Sports drinks<br><br>Energy bars if exercise starts at moderate intensity for at least 30 minutes | For any start time | Any event requiring carbohydrates and hydration |

## TABLE 10.6: SAMPLE PRE-COMPETITION MEALS

Meal providing 75 grams of carbohydrate and 340 calories
2 slices toast or a small bagel
1 large banana
1 Tbs. Jelly
*or*
1.5 cups concentrated carbohydrate beverage

Meal providing 150 grams of carbohydrate and 750 calories
2 slices bread
1 cup of yogurt with fruit
1 large banana
2 tsp. peanut butter
2 Tbs. jelly
4 ounces fruit juice
*or*
3 cups concentrated carbohydrate beverage

Meal providing 300 grams of carbohydrate and 1400 calories
2 cups of cooked cereal
12 ounces skim milk
1 large banana
4 Tbs. raisins
2 slices toast
4 Tbs. jelly
1 cup yogurt with fruit
8 ounces of juice
*or*
6 to 7 cups concentrated carbohydrate beverage or liquid replacement meal

Initially, classic carbohydrate loading involved a more extreme regimen that included a "depletion" phase of prolonged, high-intensity exercise and low-carbohydrate eating. Because this method can produce negative side effects and disrupt quality of training close to competition, a modified regimen has been in place since the 1980s.

This modified carbohydrate-loading regimen occurs over a six-day period. For the first three days, consume a diet that is 50-percent carbohydrate, followed by a 70-percent carbohydrate diet over the next three days. On the seventh day, or

| TABLE 10.7: GLYCOGEN SUPERCOMPENSATION REGIMEN* | | |
|---|---|---|
| Day | Diet | Training |
| 1 | 50% carbohydrate or 2 grams CHO/lb wt | 90 minutes 70 to 75% VO$_2$ max |
| 2 | 50% carbohydrate or 2 grams CHO/lb wt | 40 minutes 70 to 75% VO$_2$ max |
| 3 | 50% carbohydrate or 2 gms CHO/lb wt | 40 minutes 70 to 75% VO$_2$ max |
| 4 | 70% carbohydrate or 5 gms CHO/lb wt | 20 minutes 70 to 75% VO$_2$ max |
| 5 | 70% carbohydrate or 5 gms CHO/lb wt | 20 minutes 70 to 75% VO$_2$ max |
| 6 | 70% carbohydrate or 5 gms CHO/lb wt | rest |
| 7 | Competition | Race |

*Adapted with permission from "Eating for Endurance," by Ellen Coleman, RD, Bull Publishing Company, Palo Alto, CA.

competition day, follow the pre-competition guidelines appropriate for your start time and personal tolerances.

During the three days of 50-percent carbohydrate consumption, training should be at 70- to 75-percent VO$_2$ max. On day one, exercise for about ninety minutes, then only for forty minutes on days two and three. Over the next two days, or days four and five, training should be twenty minutes at 70-percent VO$_2$ max. The last day of high-carbohydrate eating, or day six, should be a rest day. Table 10.7 outlines these glycogen supercompensation guidelines.

This gentler regimen has been shown to raise muscle glycogen to levels comparable to the "classic" loading regimen. Because endurance training is the main stimulus for muscle-glycogen synthesis, endurance-trained

## TABLE 10.8: SAMPLE CARBO-LOADING ONE DAY MENU

### BREAKFAST
1 cup orange juice
3/4 cup Grapenuts
1 large banana
1 cup skim milk
2 slices toast
1 tsp. margarine
2 Tbs. jelly
147 gm carbohydrate, 895 calories

### SNACK
1 cup yogurt with fruit
45 gm carbohydrate, 240 calories

### LUNCH
3 ounces of lean turkey
2 slices of bread
1 1/2 ounces of pretzels
1 large pear
12 ounces apple juice
135 gm carbohydrate, 725 calories

### SNACK
Energy bar
12 to 16 ounces liquid supplement
135 gm carbohydrate, 1040 calories

### DINNER
2 cups cooked rice
3 ounces ground turkey
1 cup cooked peas and corn
2 slices bread
160 gm carbohydrate, 961 calories

### SNACK
12 ounces frozen yogurt
2 Fig Newton's
102 gm carbohydrate, 460 calories
TOTAL: 724 GM CARBOHYDRATE, 4321 CALORIES

athletes are the main beneficiaries of carbo' loading. Another requirement is that the exercise utilized to deplete muscle glycogen is the same exercise performed in the upcoming competition. Runners deplete their running muscles, mainly hamstrings, of glycogen. Cyclists deplete their cycling muscles, mainly quadriceps. Also, training must be tapered adequately, or too much glycogen is burned for fuel and supercompensation will not occur.

One possible side effect of even the modified regimen, is a bloated or heavy feeling. For every gram of carbohydrate stored, about 3 to 5 grams of water is also stored. Some athletes have noted a feeling of stiffness or heaviness with super-glycogen storage. This side effect should be relieved with exercise, and the extra water can help cool the body during exercise. To effectively carbohydrate load, follow the tips outlined above to obtain the needed grams of carbohydrate.

> *"When it is done perfectly, there is an advantage to accenting carbohydrates in the diet for the three to four days leading up to a maximum-endurance event."*
> *—Virgin*

## FINAL THOUGHTS

Regardless of your event, the correct pre-exercise meal may serve some benefit to performance. It should consist mainly of carbohydrate, and be lower in protein, fat and fiber. The meal should provide energy, hydration, prevent hunger, and be well tolerated. Determining just how much and what works best for you takes practice, whether it is a small snack, or light to large meal. Just make sure that every pre-event meal has been tested. No one meal works for all athletes.

RICH CRUSE

*Endurance athletes, such as Hawaii Ironman winner Peter Reid, require careful pre-competition eating.*

# CHAPTER ELEVEN

# Eating Right *during* Training and Competition

---

*During long races, if you feel thirsty, it's too late. You need to be well hydrated before a thirty-five-mile race."*
*—Hedrick*

I t's morning. You eagerly anticipate the start of the race. Though your body hits the shock of cold water, the intense physical effort of swimming creates heat. Next, you are on your bike, exposed to sun and wind, and the flow of air created by cycling. The day progresses and becomes hot and humid. Sweat is dripping down your back. You drink in anticipation of the grueling run ahead. The pounding begins. You are thirsty. It's a long, hot triathlon.

While the Ironman World Championship Triathlon and other ultraendurance events can represent the extreme in heat-related fluid and electrolyte losses, staying well hydrated and fueled during training and competition can enhance almost any athlete's performance. The longer and harder your exercise, the greater the risk that nutrient losses can impair your performance. That's why consuming adequate fluid and carbohydrate during training or competition is beneficial. This practice can:

- *prevent dehydration*
- *maintain blood-glucose levels*
- *offset muscle- and liver-glycogen depletion*
- *fuel your brain and prevent central nervous system fatigue*

Some questions you may have regarding nutrition during exercise are:

- *When does performance benefit from fluid and carbohydrate intake?*
- *What and how much should I drink during training and competition?*
- *What are the best sports drinks?*
- *What about electrolyte losses?*

Clearly water is an important nutrient for any athlete, making daily optimal hydration practices essential (see Chapter 2). But paying close attention to certain fluid strategies during exercise also enhances training sessions and competition efforts. Moderate- to high-intensity exercise of longer duration is the type of activity most likely to result in dehydration.

One study found a 34-percent decrease in maximum cycling time at high-intensity levels, with only a 2-percent drop in body weight due to dehydration. Increased muscle temperature also leads to premature glycogen depletion. Why is heat production such an issue during exercise? Exercise increases muscular heat production by one hundred times the resting rate. Obviously this heat must be quickly dispelled. Evaporating 1 liter of sweat dissipates nearly 600 calories of heat.

There are many good reasons for preventing dehydration. The physiological effects of various levels of dehydration include:

- *increased heart rate*
- *increased body temperature*
- *decreased blood volume*
- *increased perception of effort*
- *compromised mental concentration*
- *compromised fine motor skills*
- *increased risk of GI upset*
- *delayed stomach emptying of fluids*

*"Drinking enough in training can make a long ride with bad legs feel reasonable. Not drinking enough in a race can turn great legs knotty."*

*—Alvis*

With a little planning, keeping up with daily fluid losses of eight to ten cups is easy, especially when compared to matching exercise fluid losses. While average sweat losses during exercise are 1 to 1.5 liters per hour, during hot weather, high intensity exercise losses can easily reach 2 to 3 liters per hour. These sweat rates can vary tremendously between athletes. Athletes also need to know that a high level of fitness also promotes a more efficient sweat response, increasing total sweat losses further.

Many athletes struggle with replacing these sweat losses. Studies have shown that endurance athletes typically replace about 50 percent of these losses. Research shows that athletes participating in team sports also experience a fluid deficit. To off-set these losses, you need to devise a drinking strategy. But even with strong efforts at matching sweat losses, your GI system probably can only handle about 1 to 1.2 liters of fluid per hour.

Again, basic fluid requirements are:

*BEFORE*
- *up to 24 ounces, two hours before exercise*
- *8 to 16 ounces, fifteen minutes before exercise*

*DURING*
- *4 to 8 ounces, every fifteen to twenty minutes*

*AFTER*
- *three cups of fluid for every pound of weight loss*

Previously, recommendations have been to replace 100 percent of fluid losses post-exercise. Practice guidelines have been 2 cups of fluids for every pound lost. But a recent study suggests that replacing 150 percent of fluid losses may be best for complete rehydration, basically to compensate for post-exercise urine losses. For every pound of weight loss, you should consume 3 cups of fluid.

Whether you can maintain full hydration status during exercise is much more a matter of practicality than scientific theory. While team sports may incorporate planned or spon-taneous breaks, athletes performing continuous activity such as cycling, must drink while performing exercise. Consuming

the recommended amounts can be challenging and often impossible due to:
- *logistics and the opportunity to drink*
- *the availability of fluids and supplements*
- *taste preferences*
- *GI tolerances and intolerance's*

Clearly you need to assess the situation regarding your own sport, and plan accordingly. Some athletes must carry their own supplies, while others rely on aid stations, or team personnel. You are more likely to consume fluids, which taste good and are the correct temperature. Commercial sports drinks often appeal to hot, sweaty athletes, and manufacturers are continually trying to find just the right blend of flavors. In addition to flavor, sports drinks are a supplementary source of fuel and electrolytes in the form of carbohydrate and sodium chloride.

*"Whereas carbohydrate and protein are more subtle recovery aids, fluid is more directly viable. I can think of many races where I was consciously aware that my effort to take in more fluid helped me win the race. The first time was the national road championship in 1990. It was a hot day and I drank a full water bottle every five miles. I felt better as the race went on, and it was my best performance up to that time."*

*—Bliss Livingston*

## CARBOHYDRATE REPLACEMENT DURING EXERCISE

### ENDURANCE EXERCISE

Research data from dozens of studies has clearly demonstrated that carbohydrate intake during exercise of greater than ninety minutes and at moderate intensity is performance enhancing. Carbohydrate taken during exercise can maintain blood glucose levels, and provide a fuel to glycogen-depleted muscles. Carbohydrate consumption may also provide the opportunity for glucose to be stored in more active muscle fibers. When exercising at low intensity, muscle fibers that fuel high-intensity efforts may be replenished. Carbohydrates consumed during exercise can also spare liver glycogen. This allows the liver to maintain glucose output later in exercise.

## EXERCISE LASTING ONE HOUR

While sports drinks may benefit athletes starting longer duration events with suboptimal carbohydrate stores, recent research has provided a new twist on sports drinks recommendations. Several studies have demonstrated that athletes would be wise to consider consuming a sports drink for certain types of exercise or competition lasting about one hour.

These studies have looked at high-intensity exercise at 80- to 90-percent $VO_2$ max, lasting about one hour. Several showed performance benefits when consuming a sports drinks, though the physiological mechanism for this was not discovered.

In addition, several studies looked at intermittent high-intensity exercise lasting about one hour; again, exercise intensity is key at this one-hour time interval. Consuming a sports drink at rest intervals allowed interval training to continue longer. Researchers speculate that carbohydrate drinks provided the fast-twitch muscle fibers—which operate at higher intensities—some fuel to work with at rest intervals between high-intensity efforts. More research is needed regarding carbohydrate consumption and exercise lasting one hour.

## SPORTS DRINKS
### CONSUMING THE CORRECT AMOUNTS

Before reviewing just what portions of a sports drink are correct for you, let's take a look at the path these beverages must follow through your body. First you must drink it. Then it reaches the stomach. Next, it must empty from the stomach, going to the small intestine. The drink is then absorbed through the small intestine and into the blood. This is how the carbohydrate and electrolytes contained in these drinks reach your bloodstream and fuel your body.

In an effort to provide the most scientifically sound formulation, sports drink research has looked at each one of these steps to see where the flow may actually slow down or speed up. If your sports drink gets bogged down in any one of the steps, that means it takes the fluid and carbohydrate that much longer to reach you. Consequently, it is not as performance enhancing.

Basically, two factors determine how quickly a sports drink leaves your stomach—the volume of fluid in your stomach, and the concentration of the food or fluid.

### CONCENTRATION

The greater the concentration of the fluid, the longer it takes to leave the stomach. Research has determined that carbohydrate solutions of about 4- to 8-percent concentration empty very efficiently. Conveniently, most sports drinks fall into this gastrically acceptable range. Solutions falling into this range provide an optimal balance between carbohydrate and fluid delivery.

This drink concentration allows fluid to reach the bloodstream almost as quickly as water, but still delivers performance-boosting carbohydrates at an acceptable rate. Drinks of these concentrations are also well tolerated by most athletes, and can improve with practice. In contrast, drinks of 10- to 12-percent concentration, such as soft drinks, are emptied more slowly, but do provide carbohydrates and, therefore, energy. Drinks of less than 4-percent concentration would not supply enough carbohydrate to enhance performance, but would still be hydrating.

## VOLUME

Volume, which affects the degree of stomach distention, also affects gastric emptying. Increased stomach distention will result in liquids emptying from your stomach more quickly with about 50 percent of stomach contents being emptied every ten minutes. To maximize emptying, try to start exercise with a comfortably full stomach and drink at regular intervals of about ten to fifteen minutes, if possible. How much fluid an athlete can empty from their stomach is highly variable. However, rates of 800 to 1200 milliliters per hour are commonly seen.

## INTESTINAL ABSORPTION

Studies measuring intestinal absorption rates have determined that sports drink solutions are as readily absorbed as water. Different forms of carbohydrates are absorbed across the intestinal wall, utilizing various transport mechanisms. Again higher concentration drinks should be avoided, as they must draw water into the intestinal tract before being absorbed.

## TYPE OF CARBOHYDRATE

Because of the wide variety of sports drinks products available, there are a wide variety of carbohydrate sources. These include glucose polymers, glucose, sucrose and fructose. Many drinks have a mix, allowing various carbohydrate types to be transported simultaneously. These carbohydrate mixes all appear to have a moderate to high glycemic index, handy for quickly raising blood-glucose levels.

Glucose polymers do not seem to offer any absorption advantages over glucose, but are popular because they have a milder rather than overly sweet taste. Fructose is the only beverage not used in high amounts or solely in a sports beverage. Large amounts of fructose are not well absorbed and can lead to gastrointestinal upset. But drinks that contain some fructose should provide easily tolerated concentrations.

## AMOUNT AND TIMING OF CARBOHYDRATE

Basically the amounts of sports drinks you consume should mimic the water intake guidelines described previously, about 4 to 8 ounces every fifteen to twenty minutes. Performance benefits begin when about 30 grams of carbohydrate per hour are delivered. However, 50 to 60 grams may be optimal to meet fuel needs during exercise after muscle glycogen depletion has occurred.

When using a 6-percent solution, you would have to consume one liter of fluid in an hour to obtain 60 grams of carbohydrate. A 7-percent solution provides 50 grams when 700 milliliters is consumed in one hour. Check labels and instructions of your favorite sports drinks. Then determine how much you would need to consume in an hour to obtain 30 to 60 grams of carbohydrate.

*"Nowadays, even with all the glucose products available, it is still difficult to eat enough during races lasting more than seventy miles. Sometimes you need to eat real food to keep up with what you burn."*
*—Walton*

As far as timing is concerned, large single feedings and smaller, regular intakes are both beneficial. Basically, drink whenever possible given the nature of the training session and competition. Consuming carbohydrate after depletion has set in can help. But consuming the carbohydrates early on in order to prevent fatigue appears prudent.

## FORM OF CARBOHYDRATE

Both liquid, semi-liquid and solid carbohydrates are well tolerated by many athletes during exercise, though these tolerances can vary. Obviously, carbohydrate drinks offer the advantage of hydration.

While sports drinks are practical, many endurance athletes like using some of the more concentrated carbohydrate gels for situations when energy needs outweigh the desire for fluid. These products, however, should be consumed with some fluid. More solid items, such as energy bars, bananas or Fig Newton's are also well tolerated by many endurance athletes, such as cyclists, who experience minimal stomach jostling. Endurance athletes can also learn to tolerate beverages of a more concentrated nature, frequently having liquid meals during competitions such as during cycling stages. These products help offset the very high fuel demands of the exercise.

Basically, fluid and carbohydrate choices can be somewhat individualized. Sometimes it is possible for fluid needs to be of greater significance, as on a hot, humid day, so a 4-percent concentration may be desired. If carbohydrate needs are a greater priority, such as later on

TOM MORAN

*Drinking fluids is a savvy race strategy for world mountain-bike champion Alison Sydor.*

in exercise, gels, bars, and more concentrated carbohydrates fluids may be emphasized.

Usually a range of nutritional choices are ingested over an endurance event, with the athlete fine-tuning a balance between energy and fluid needs and gastrointestinal tolerances. Exercise pace may sometimes need to be adjusted in order to accommodate nutritional intake, or athletes can take advantage of lulls in the pace. Usually these adjustments are

*"The 1997 Ironman was the first time I took sodium supplementation. During the entire race, I took approximately a total of eight to ten tablets, containing 179 milligrams of sodium each. With each of the sodium tablets, I drank at least 8 ounces of water. This seemed to work well, and I never got the cramping or sore muscles I had in the past.*

—*Fuhr*

offset by the performance benefits derived from appropriate nutritional intake.

## THE ELECTROLYTE EDGE

Though sweat is mainly water, it does contain a number of electrolytes. However the concentration of these electrolytes is much lower than that found in body fluids. Composition of sweat can vary among athletes, mostly in regard to electrolytes or salts. But because electrolytes are the major solid component of sweat, research has focused on replacement needs of these nutrients. Sodium and potassium have been most frequently studied, though chloride is also a consideration.

The major electrolytes lost in sweat, and which form salt, are sodium and chloride. You may have noticed dried salt on your body after heavy sweating. Minerals lost in small amounts from sweat include potassium, magnesium, calcium, iron, copper and zinc.

To appreciate if and when electrolyte replacement is required during exercise, you need to know what happens to blood electrolyte concentrations during exercise. During high sweat rates, the concentrations of sodium and potassium increase, chloride and calcium remain constant, and magnesium levels usually fall.

Overall, even during most prolonged exercise, electrolyte deficiencies probably won't occur. However, electrolyte imbalances may occur during ultraendurance events such as ultra-marathons and Ironman triathlons. The recovery period after excessive sweating may also result in electrolyte deficiency. Minor sodium, chloride and potassium losses need to be replaced daily with a balanced diet in order to prevent deficiencies from occurring over time. If losses are not replaced, a deficit may occur over four to seven days of hard training.

Generally, electrolyte replacement for most forms of exercise is not required. But the sodium found in sports drinks does improve taste, and fluid and glucose absorption throughout the intestine. Sodium may also stimulate the thirst and drinking mechanism. The amount of sodium in most sports drinks is relatively low. These small amounts certainly are not detrimental to performance, while excessive intakes of salt may aggravate electrolyte balance.

*"In the summer of 1998, I was in France at the fourth women's World Cup race, where it was one hundred degrees. I drank water and carbo' fluid consistently and when 'crunch-time' came, women who normally out-perform me on the hills were fading back fast. I finished really strong when everyone else complained of chills and the heat."*

*—Bliss Livingston*

However, during ultraendurance activity, cases of hyponatremia or low blood sodium have been identified. The most common cause of this potentially dangerous condition is overhydration that leads to water intoxication. During exercise lasting four to five hours or longer, athletes lose sodium through sweating, then consume large amounts of fluid, especially plain water. This fluid is retained, and body fluids eventually become very diluted, and sodium levels decrease.

Therefore, in ultraendurance events, solutions with sodium are recommended. Aim for 250 to 500 milligrams per

| TABLE 11.1: COMPARISON OF COMMERCIAL SPORTS DRINKS PER 8 OUNCE SERVING | | | | | |
|---|---|---|---|---|---|
| **PRODUCT** | **TYPE OF CARBOHYDRATE** | **CHO CONC.** | **CALORIES** | **CHO GRAMS** | **SODIUM MG** |
| All Sport | Fructose, sucrose | 7% | 70 | 19 | 55 |
| Body Fuel 750 | Maltodextrin, fructose | 7% | 70 | 17 | 70 |
| Coca Cola | Corn syrup, fructose | 12% | 108 | 29 | 9.2 |
| Cytomax | Fructose, maltodex-trin, Polylactate | 8% | 83 | 19 | 10 |
| Endura | Glucose polymers, fructose | 6% | 60 | 15 | 92 |
| Exceed | Glucose polymers, fructose | 7% | 70 | 17 | 50 |
| Gatorade | Sucrose, glucose | 6% | 50 | 14 | 110 |
| Hydra Fuel | Glucose polymers, fructose, glucose | 7% | 66 | 16 | 25 |
| Performance | Maltodextrin, fructose | 10% | 100 | 25 | 58 |
| PowerAde | Fructose, sucrose | 6% | 55 | 14 | 50 |
| 10-K | Sucrose, fructose | 6% | 60 | 15 | 54 |
| Orange Juice | Fructose, sucrose | 11 to 15% | 112 | 26 | 2.7 |
| Water | — | — | — | — | — |
| Warp Aide | Fructose, maltodextrin | 8% | 70 | 19 | 80 mg |

hour. Some sports drinks and gels are higher in sodium than others. Athlete competing in these events should also consume adequate salt several days prior to assure normal sodium levels at start time.

## FINAL THOUGHTS

- *Maintain adequate daily hydration with eight to ten cups of fluid daily.*
- *Drink liberally during the hours before exercise.*
- *Practice fluid-replacement strategies during training.*
- *Experiment with various sports drinks for best flavor and tolerance.*
- *During exercise, aim for an intake of 4 to 8 ounces every fifteen to twenty minutes, 16-40 ounces per hour are possible.*
- *Monitor your fluid losses by post-exercise weight, and replace 150 percent of losses.*
- *Start exercise with a comfortably full stomach, and then drink every ten to fifteen minutes to maximize gastric emptying.*
- *Keep fluid accessible during exercise and competition.*
- *Use a sports drink during high-intensity exercise lasting sixty minutes or longer, and endurance exercise lasting over ninety minutes.*
- *If they stimulate drinking and fluid intake, sports drinks may be beneficial in any situation by promoting hydration.*
- *Begin refueling early on during exercise.*
- *Use sports drinks of 4- to 8-percent concentration, or gels, sports bars, and easily digested carbohydrate foods, which are well tolerated.*
- *Ultraendurance events may require higher sodium nutritional products during exercise.*

# PART V

# BODY WEIGHT, BODY FAT, AND DIET

# CHAPTER TWELVE

# BODY
# *Composition*
# *and*
# *Performance*

*"Obviously there is an ideal percent body fat for each athlete as an individual. Likewise, there is a high level of variability from one athlete to the next. An individual's sport will influence what is ideal for performance. For instance, a runner will function better at a lower percent body fat than a swimmer."*
*—Tiffany Forbes, swimmer and swim coach, and 1998 national master's champion, age 30-34, 1000-yard freestyle, 400-yard IM*

Athletes come in a variety of shapes and sizes, usually demonstrating a physique and body composition suited to successful performance in their sport. Various sports often represent the extremes in body types, from the petite gymnast to the tall pole vaulter, to the bulk of the football player. Body composition is a result of both genetics and sport-specific training. Often, athletes naturally fall at optimal body composition levels, while others may struggle with genetics in attempting to reach the body-fat and muscle-mass levels required for optimal performance in their sport.

In order to determine ideal body weight, much importance has been placed upon standing on the scale. However, this instrument provides only a very rudimentary measure at best, and cannot differentiate between fat pounds and muscle pounds.

If you step on the scale and determine that you are over-weight, it simply indicates that you weigh above the average for your height. Underweight individuals, as determined by the scale, weigh below the average for their height. Stocky, muscular athletes are not favored by the scale, while thin small-boned people are. That's why body composition measurement, which is an attempt to determine the percent of weight that is fat, is considered a more accurate indicator of appropriate weight for optimal performance.

*"Street wisdom says the skinnier the better, but staying healthy becomes a challenge."*
*—Alvis*

Some questions athletes may have regarding body composition are:

- **What body-fat levels are both healthy and optimal for my performance?**
- **What is the best way to test my body fat?**

For an athlete, optimal weight can refer to a number of considerations, which may include optimal performance, health and body image. Most research has focused on finding an ideal body weight for good health. On the other hand, society's standards for ideal weight may not always be the healthiest, or in accord with optimal performance.

194

The four major body components of interest in body composition measurement are: total body fat, fat-free mass, bone mineral and body water. Various techniques may analyze, two, three or four of these body-composition components.

Total body fat consists of both essential and stored fat. The brain, nervous system and other body structures rely upon essential fat for proper functioning. Men require levels of essential fat at 3

TOM MORAN

*Athletes have their own optimal body-fat level–as does Saturn Cycling team member Dede Demet.*

percent, and women 12 to 15 percent, though this can vary considerably among individuals.

Storage fat, the fat that athletes may be concerned about, is simply excess stored energy. Obviously levels of stored fat can vary considerably based on genetics, training and diet. Storage fat surrounds the body organs, but a substantial amount is located under the skin. Fat-free mass is primarily water and protein, with smaller amounts of minerals and glycogen. These fat-free body tissues are often referred to as lean body mass. About 70 percent of your fat-free weight is water.

Bone minerals are also a substantial body tissue. Bone is about 50-percent water and 50-percent solid mass. Bone weight can account for 12 to 15 percent of total body weight. Overall, body water accounts for about 60 percent of total body weight of both fat and fat-free mass. Although amounts can vary widely, a typical young adult male may be 60-per-cent body water, and 40-percent solid matter, which consists of 14-percent fat, 22-percent protein and 4-percent bone minerals.

*"You don't have to be ultra lean or thin to ride well; you have to be healthy."*
*—Dunlap*

For the general population, men are classi-fied as healthy at 15- to 18-percent body fat, overweight at 19- to 24-percent, and obese when 25 percent is exceeded. Women are generally healthy at 20- to 25-percent fat, over-weight at 26- to 29-percent, while greater than 30 percent is obese. Lean levels of body fat are 6- to 10-percent for men and 10- to 15-percent for women. Many athletes, particularly endurance athletes and other types of athletes who would find excess body weight to be a disadvantage, fall at these lower body-fat levels.

## BODY COMPOSITION AND PERFORMANCE

How much body fat can positively affect performance depends upon your chosen sport. Purely skill-based sports such as golf, archery and shooting, are minimally affected by body fat. In contrast, sports where an increased power-to-muscle ratio, or less "dead weight" is optimal, ben-efit from lower body-fat levels.

Athletes who benefit the most from lower body-fat levels are those who move their bodies over long distances, such as endurance runners, road cyclists and triathletes. Athletes who pull their weight up climbs such as mountain bikers, and cyclists participating in stage races also benefit.

But not only endurance athletes benefit from low body-fat levels. Athletes who move vertically against the effects of gravity, spin or rotate like gymnasts, figure skaters, pole vaulters, basketball players and high jumpers are negatively affected by excess body fat. Another type of athlete, one who requires speed and agility such as soccer and certain football positions, probably benefits from lower body-fat levels. Even athletes who need bulk to protect them from body contact would prefer that this weight be lean muscle mass rather than excess fat, in order to maximize speed.

*World champion mountain-bike racer Cecilia Potts takes an opportunity to re-hydrate.*

While excess fat certainly is not desirable for most sports, keep in mind that body-fat percentage is only one of several interconnected factors that influence performance. Yes, studies do demonstrate that body fat is related to performance. But many athletes who do not have "ideal" body-fat levels have performed at the top of their sport, while the leannest do not always win.

It can also be difficult to predict the precise percent body fat an individual athlete requires for optimal performance,

*"I found a 4-percent body-fat level to be too low, and now stay at a healthy 6 percent."*

*—FitzRandolph*

something research studies don't measure. Fighting against a more natural body shape can also wreak havoc physically and psycho-logically. Excessive weight loss can lead to muscle loss, resulting in decreased power and sprinting ability. Weight loss goals should not be based upon some arbitrary body fat number, such as 8-percent body fat. Especially when you consider that all body-fat measurement techniques carry some degree of error.

An ideal body-fat level for an athlete is individual, but it should:

• *not necessarily be based on minimal levels, or that of one successful athlete in a chosen sport.*
• *account for individuality*
• *be in keeping with good health*
• *be associated with good performances*
• *not require an extreme diet or overtraining*

## BODY COMPOSITION ASSESSMENT

Besides athletes who need to weigh-in for weight limits, the only other good use of a scale is to monitor pre-and post exercise hydration-level changes, and daily body-fluid changes. A number of more refined techniques are available to assess body fat and fat-free, or lean, body mass. But these techniques do utilize only indirect body-fat measurement methods.

*"I fight with my weight. I have always tried to be really lean, but at my best Ironman ever I was ten pounds heavier than usual. So, I pushed my ideal weight back up a bit.*

*—Reid*

## Underwater weighing

Underwater weighing, commonly used in research, actually measures body density. Different formulas, depending on the age and sex of the individual, are recommended. But even this "gold standard" has weaknesses. Some assumptions of body density may not be valid for certain athletes, and this technique still carries a standard error of 2 to 2.5 percent. Therefore, an athlete measuring at 15-percent body fat, may actually be 13- to 17-percent body fat.

## Body plethysmography

One commercial product utilizing body plethysmography is the Bod Pod. This technique actually measures air displacement versus water displacement of the technique described above. Measurements appear to correlate with underwater weighing, and it may be a more convenient technique because of equipment considerations.

## Body Impedance Analysis (BIA)

BIA technique is based upon the principle of resistance to an electrical current that is applied to the body. Newer techniques and prediction equations have lowered the margin of error to 3 to 4 percent. BIA may not work well with the very lean athlete.

### Dual Energy X-ray Absorptiometry (DEXA)

DEXA is a computerized X-ray technique that images body tissues and measures bone mineral content, body fat and fat-free mass. While highly desirable for measuring bone mass, it may not be as accurate for body fat, and not any more effective than underwater weighing.

### Infrared interactance

Infrared interactance is based on infrared light's interaction with tissue components as it passes through them. Standard of error is approximately 4 to 5 percent.

### Skinfolds

This technique measures the fat under skin or subcutaneous fat with the use of calibrated skinfold calipers. It is commonly used in non-research settings such as wellness and fitness centers. Values are taken at various sites around the body and then inserted into a specific formula, preferably one for athletes. For best accuracy, a skilled technician should utilize an acceptable pair of skinfold calipers. The standard of error appears to be 3 to 4 percent.

### Anthropometric measurements

Anthropometry is an inexpensive technique that measures skin, muscle, fat and bone. Measurements are taken at thigh, abdomen and arm sites. These measurements are incorporated into various formulas to predict body fat and lean mass.

When utilizing a technique to assess body composition, the following should be considered:

- *It is should be done by a trained technician*
- *It uses an appropriate population-specific formula*
- *The same technique by the same technician should be used over time to monitor changes*
- *Methods that can travel to various competition sites may be useful*
- *Results should be interpreted by an expert*

## FINAL THOUGHTS

Being at an appropriate level of body fat can positively impact performance. However, what is ideal can vary greatly among athletes. While the scale is only a crude measurement of ideal body weight, several body composition techniques are available. These techniques should be kept in perspective, as they all contain some margin of error. Body composition should be measured by a skilled technician and utilized to measure body composition changes over time, rather than determining absolute values.

MICHELLE HAVRATH

*Some athletes, such as figure skater Tonia Kwiatkowski, benefit more than others from lower body-fat levels.*

# CHAPTER THIRTEEN

# Changing *Body Composition*

*"One or two pounds can throw off timing on a jump. So if you can maintain ideal weight and still have enough energy to train, that is best."*

—*Kwiatkowski, figure skater*

Despite their high activity levels and demanding training programs, many athletes are concerned with body-fat levels. There are many valid reasons why athletes would want to lose weight. You may wish to build on your training program and improve performance. Lower body-fat levels may be required in sports such as gymnastics and figure skating. Injury, off-season habits or various lifestyle factors may also have resulted in weight gain. What is important is that you have realistic weight-loss goals, safe weight-loss techniques, and a balanced diet that will allow you to train appropriately. Conversely, you may desire to build muscle mass to increase strength and power. Dietary measures for building mass should also be safe and appropriate.

While body-fat loss means simply consuming less calories than you burn, achieving this can often be much more complex, and even difficult for some athletes.

First, let's consider the various body types. There are three specific body types that are determined by genetics.

• *Endomorph—round and soft, prone to relative fatness*
• *Mesomorph—heavy muscular development*
• *Ectomorph—small bone structure, long limbs*

Often a person gravitates toward a sport that suits their body type. But this may not always be the case. A person may choose a sport simply because they love it, and find themself struggling with body-composition issues.

Some questions you may have regarding body-composition changes and fat loss are:

• *Are there any problems associated with dieting?*
• *What is a healthy way to lose body fat?*
• *What are the dangers of very low body-fat levels?*
• *What is the best type of diet for building lean body mass?*

## HEALTHY BODY-FAT LOSS

First, be realistic about your genetics and body type. Have your body composition determined by a skilled technician. Keep the margin of error inherent in all the techniques in mind, and develop a realistic weight-loss goal. Then, monitor body composition at regular intervals, not just your weight. During heavy training, you may actually gain muscle mass while lowering body-fat levels.

KEVIN ECCLES

*Building muscle for in-line skating requires adequate protein and calories.*

Plan not to exceed a weight loss of 2 pounds weekly, or even only 1 pound weekly during heavy training periods. Greater rates of weight loss may compromise recovery and energy levels. Losing 1 pound weekly requires a deficit of 500 calories per day. Losing 2 pounds weekly requires a 1000 calorie deficit—clearly calling for some intense calorie-cutting and calorie-burning efforts. Try to accomplish these goals in a reasonable amount of time, at an "off-season" time of year.

Trimming no more than 200 to 300 calories daily from your usual intake may be the safest and most effective long-term weight-loss approach. This mild reduction should have no metabolism-lowering effects and will not precipitate feelings of hunger and deprivation. How and

*Swimmer, Tiffany Forbes*

where you cut out these calories should really be tailored to modify your usual diet.

You already know that meeting daily carbohydrate requirements, whether they are moderate or high, is important for recovery. In turn, protein needs are slightly elevated due to training, but easily met with proper food choices. And finally, some fat in your diet is necessary. But where are extra calories coming from? That is contingent upon the composition of your diet. But depending on current caloric intake, eliminating only 200 to 500 daily may not be that difficult.

> *"Exercise in conjunction with a smart eating plan is the best approach for weight loss. Eating healthy and intelligently will lead one to a better balance within the body. Exercise will complement this format. Committing to a schedule is also of paramount importance to successful weight loss.*
> *—Forbes*

Start by keeping an honest and detailed food diary for a week. Try to track the grams of carbohydrate you are consuming. Determine if, overall, you are meeting carbohydrate train-

## TABLE 13.1: WEIGHT LOSS TIPS

GOAL SETTING
Be realistic about your genetics and body type
Check you body composition and keep in perspective
Lose only up to 1 to 2 pounds weekly
Set a reasonable time goal for your weight loss efforts
Keep a food journal for several days
Track grams of carbohydrate
Determine if you eat for reasons other than hunger

NUTRITION TIPS
Determine if you are consuming too much carbohydrate or protein
Identify sources of hidden fat
Make a plan to trim 200 to 300 calories from your diet
Time your meals and snacks to prevent extreme hunger
Eat when you are comfortably hungry
Savor and enjoy your meals, try not to rush
Stop eating when you are comfortably full, not stuffed
Fill up on high-fiber foods like fruits and vegetables
Ride out cravings or satisfy them with small portions
Find non-food substitutes for cravings
Limit exposure to problem food sources
Program healthy foods into your environments
Allow room for favorites
Avoid fad diets and extreme calorie restrictions

ing requirements. Or are you exceeding these requirements? Next look for sources of hidden fat, maybe in snack items or baked goods. Maybe frequent restaurant eating is increasing your fat intake.

Of course, cutting out obvious sources of fat and switching to leaner versions of protein foods will help. You may also want to be moderate regarding alcohol intake, as it provides calories and very little nutritional value. All of these small, simple changes could easily trim 200 to 300

*"If I buy lots of vegetables, I try to chop them up when I get home, so I will be more likely to eat them instead of chips when I get hungry after a ride, or at 3 p.m.*
*—Bliss Livingston*

calories or more from your diet.

Meal timing is also very important. To keep hunger at bay and prevent ravenous overeating, never skip a meal, especially breakfast. In the morning, your body is waking up—and metabolism needs a jump start. Feeding it correctly sets it in motion for the day and prevents ravenous hunger pains. You may also want to plan in snacks, and spread your food choices throughout the day. Every time your body processes a meal or snack, calories are burned and you receive a steady supply of fuel.

*"My coach would always say, 'If you want a hot fudge sundae, eat it.' If someone tells you you can't have something, you want it more. But, you also have to have some self-control."*

*—Kwiatkowski*

Another benefit of small, frequent meals is that you can often prevent the extreme hunger that leads to overeating. Eat when hunger is at a comfortable level. Then pay closer attention to fullness and stop eating when you are comfortably full, rather than stuffed. That stuffed feeling usually means that too many calories have been consumed—and they will likely be stored as fat. In fact, check your food diary to determine if too much time between meals results in high levels of hunger, poor food choices and larger portions. Fiber can also fill up your stomach. Choose high-fiber foods such as fresh fruit, vegetables and whole grains. These foods are also very nutrient dense, and low in calories.

One of the hardest parts to losing weight can be "changing your mind." Ask yourself why you may overeat at times. Is it because you are bored, stressed, tired, or simply because it "tastes so good"? Try to ride out cravings, and for difficult eating times program healthy foods into your home and work environments to automatically produce improved choices. But no matter what you do, you should still allow for favorites. Trying to restrict them too much can lead to overeating later on. Plan them as an occasional, but normal part of your diet.

If you are having problems incorporating or identifying sensible weight-loss strategies, consult a qualified sports nutritionist and dietitian. Fad diets and extreme calorie restrictions have no place in a healthy sports diet. Trying to reach a body-fat level similar to that of a successful competitor can produce negative performance and long-term health implications.

> "A grazing program has been really helpful, and I lost 4 kilograms, thanks to my nutritionist. I have been racing my best for the past two years. I am sure, losing weight has helped my performance."
> —Daucourt

## THE "DIET" TRAP

Food is the body's fuel, and bodies don't like it when fuel runs low. A low fuel gauge sends out a slew of appetite-triggering brain chemicals that drive people to eat. What many dieters perceive as lack of willpower is really the body's drive for self-preservation.

Often the food cravings elicited by these chemicals center on carbohydrates. Regardless of what people may crave and overeat, this mind-body connection clearly illustrates a dieting danger. Restricting foods leads to overeating and even binge-eating, thwarting weight-loss efforts.

Besides triggering overeating, drastically restricting calories can result in breaking down the body's protein stores for energy, as it can more easily be converted to glucose. Eating more protein while on a low-calorie diet won't prevent this structural breakdown, as it, too, is converted to glucose. This muscle loss can compromise your strength and power, and also slow down your metabolism. The more muscle you have, the more calories you burn, and the more you can eat. So avoid dieting to prevent this vicious cycle of lowered metabolism, further food restriction to compensate, decreased energy, and finally, poor performance.

## THE MIND TRAP

Besides playing games with the body, dieting wreaks havoc with the mind. Restrictive eating and avoiding certain foods deemed "bad," leads to feelings of deprivation, and a preoccupation with food. This, in turn, often leads to excessive and binge eating.

Continued cycles of severe dieting and overeating can result in erratic eating patterns; over time, some athletes could develop full-blown eating disorders. Though these disorders have many environmental, genetic and psychological causes, dieting, preoccupation, and distortion of body image increase the risk of developing such a condition.

### PHYSIOLOGICAL CONSEQUENCES

Besides harming your psyche and performance, severe caloric restriction can damage long-term health. Humans carry body fat for a number of reasons: to provide insulation and protection for organs, to preserve body hormone levels, and to provide energy reserves. Times of famine were common in human history and this was a healthy adaptation.

# Disordered Eating

Because athletes may be obsessive by nature, perfectionistic, and can develop tunnel vision in hopes of improving performance, many can set unrealistic body-fat and weight-loss goals. Pressure to set these weight-loss goals may also come from a number of outside sources, including trainers, coaches and athletic peers. Successful athletes may have a certain physique that is helped by genetics, which other athletes in the same sport cannot realistically achieve. Generally, North American women are at the highest risk for setting unhealthy weight goals and being dissatisfied with body image.

What often develops is disordered eating, which represents a full spectrum of behaviors. Poor eating habits may lie at one end with full-blown clinical eating disorders of anorexia nervosa and bulimia lying at the other end. While full-blown eating disorders are not exceptionally high in most sports, studies indicate a high prevalence of disordered eating behavior among athletes—falling at various points along the disordered eating spectrum. Prevalence is higher in women, and especially in sports where weight and body fat is an issue. In general, eating-disordered behavior among athletic people appears to be on the rise.

Clinical eating disorders are characterized by extreme disturbances in eating behavior. Diagnoses include anorexia nervosa and bulimia nervosa. Athletes are also at risk for anorexia athletica. Experts believe that even if athletes exhibit some of the symptoms of these disorders, it should be addressed immediately.

Anorexia nervosa criteria includes refusal to maintain a minimal body weight, presence of a distorted body image, an intense fear of weight gain or fatness. Amenorrhea is also present in these underweight individuals. Bulimia nervosa involves binge eating, at least twice weekly, for three months. Purging and other compensatory behaviors follow. Finally, anorexia athletica is mainly characterized by an intense fear of becoming fat or gaining weight. Reduced calorie intake and compulsive exercise, binge eating, and use of laxatives, vomiting and diuretics are possible.

An athlete with anorexia nervosa, bulimia nervosa, and other eating disorders, requires the professional help of someone skilled and trained in treating this condition. This may include a team of a physician, dietitian and psychologist. Both public and private institutions offer these services. Table 13.1 describes some of the warning signs of anorexia nervosa and bulimia nervousa. Table 13.2 lists some organizations that can offer help.

Women's bodies try especially hard to retain certain levels of fat for healthy pregnancy and lactation.

Athletes may attempt very low body-fat levels, often during the peak of the season when training intensity and volume is high. However, this attempt can be taken too far, and an intense battle between dieting, training and genetics ensues. Achieving the desired body-fat level can require severe calorie restrictions leading to disordered eating and also excessive training. Often, the initial weight loss does result in an improved performance. However, problems develop later, and the athlete may not attribute them to their dieting efforts. In turn, it can be difficult to convince an athlete that attempting too low a body-fat level was truly the source of the problem.

## TABLE 13.2: POSSIBLE INDICATIONS OF EATING DISORDERS

### CHARACTERISTICS OF ANOREXIA
. Dramatic weight loss beyond what is necessary
. Preoccupation with food, calories, weight
. Amennorrhea or oligomenorrhea
. Gastrointestinal problems
. Hair loss and growth of fine body hair
. Sensitivity to cold
. Low pulse rate
. Distorted body image
. Overuse injuries
. Intense fear of becoming fat
. Food rituals
. Stress fractures
. Abnormal fatigue

### CHARACTERISTICS OF BULIMIA
. Frequent weight fluctuations
. Difficulty swallowing and throat damage
. Swollen glands
. Damaged tooth enamel from gastric acid
. Disappearance after meals
. Bloating
. Menstrual irregularities
. Muscle cramps
. Callous or abrasion on back of hand
. Extreme concern about body weight and shape
. Ability to eat enormous meals without weight gain

## SLOW BURNERS

Some individuals feel strongly that they must eat less than others in order to maintain a

| TABLE 13.3: RESOURCES FOR EATING DISORDERS |
| --- |

AMERICAN DIETETIC ASSOCIATION  800/366-1655
REFERAL TO SPORTS NUTRIITONIST SKILLED IN
EATING DISORDER TREATMENT

AMERICAN ANOREXIA/BULIMIA ASSOCIATION INC.  212/575-6200
OFFER WRITTEN MATERIALS, REFERRALS

NATIONAL EATING DISORDERS ORGANIZATION
LAUREATE PSYCHIATRIC HOSPITAL  918/481-4092

THE RENFREW CENTER  800/RENFREW
PROVIDES REFERRALS AND TREATMENT CENTER

THE REMUDA RANCH  800/445-1900
TREATMENT CENTER

specific weight. When examining athletes' diets, researchers and nutritionists have noted that some individuals re-port an energy intake that appears inadequate to meet their daily energy requirements. Yet these athletes often do not lose weight. Often, these athletes are described as being energy efficient—using every calorie consumed efficiently and maintaining weight on less calories than expected.

Energy efficiency in athletes is a difficult and time-consuming thing to measure, and there are few studies researching this theory. Some scientists doubt its existence, believing that many athletes are simply under-reporting the amount of food they eat. Yet, two studies conducted at Arizona State University found otherwise.

Two groups of male endurance runners matched for weight, body composition and energy expenditure were classified as being low or adequate in energy intake through detailed analy-

# Muscle in the right nutrients for resistance training

In contrast to athletes who wish to lose or maintain weight, others desire to increase muscle mass. Just as some individuals struggle to reach body-fat-loss goals, others with thin, slender frames may find it difficult to achieve the ideal muscle-bound body. Often athletes engage in resistance training during their "off-season." Muscle building can increase the strength-to-weight ratio, and ultimately increases strength and power, and therefore performance. Even athletes who benefit from bulk such as football or hockey players, would prefer the majority of this extra mass come from muscle rather than fat.

There are three basic requirements for building mass:

- *An excellent strength-training program*
- *Adequate caloric intake*
- *Adequate protein intake*

Gaining muscle with a well-designed training program requires the support of adequate calories. Just as your body requires calories to make and store fat, it also requires energy to form muscle tissue. Where these additional calories come from should support good health. Often, the perception is that these additional calories should come from protein.

Your protein needs for weight training, especially if you are new to this type of exercise, are elevated above a sedentary individual. As discussed in Chapter 4, strength-training athletes require 0.5 to 0.7 grams of protein per pound weight, with novices requiring 0.8 grams. These requirements are easily obtain in a well-balanced sports diet. But most importantly, the protein consumed will be used for muscle tissue building and repair, rather than energy; but only if you eat an adequate amount of calories.

Most athletes eat plenty of protein, but can fall short of the calories required for muscle building. An additional 400 to 500 calories daily are needed to gain about 1 pound of muscle mass in a week. Because muscle glycogen is a major fuel source during resistance training, it would be prudent to make carbohydrate foods the main focus of recovery and daily diet. Muscle glycogen burned during exercise needs to be replaced. This fuel source is part of any balanced diet, and provides the calories that nutritionists refer to as "protein-sparing."

Because food sources supply adequate amounts of protein, most athletes probably don't require protein supplements to meet requirements for muscle building. However, lifestyle, training programs and convenience may justify using these supplements in place of real food.

In a limited number of research studies, liquid protein-carbohydrate supplements consumed immediately and two hours after resistance training were found to enhance recovery. This form of supplementation increased blood levels of insulin and growth hormone, both of which are tissue-building agents. A more recent study found that a supplement containing about 22-percent protein, 68-percent carbohydrate, and 10-percent fat produced a greater insulin response than a placebo. Muscle-glycogen synthesis also increased.

Besides convenience, protein-containing supplements may provide the advantage of including high-quality sources such as milk, egg and soy protein, without any of the fat and cholesterol. But conversely, these supplements may not supply nutrients found in protein-containing foods. But convenience aside, there is no reason to believe that protein supplements offer an advantage in terms of muscle building and recovery, over the equivalent amount of protein in real foods.

Protein soon after exercise is an option, but not absolutely necessary. Even carbohydrate alone after resistance training may facilitate recovery. One recent study found that one-half-a-gram of carbohydrate per pound of weight—1 gram per kilogram—immediately after resistance training, decreased the amount of body protein breakdown that normally occurs with intense weight training.

In addition to boosting recovery after training, taking carbohydrate during resistance training may also be of benefit. Longer, intense exercise sessions can dip into muscle-glycogen stores and utilize blood glucose for fuel. Sports drinks will not only maintain hydration, but supply needed carbohydrates. This technique may be especially helpful when you are training on a relatively empty stomach and your fuel tank is registering low. Table 13.4 summarizes some muscle-building strategies.

In addition, many ergogenic aids are heavily marketed to athletes for muscle building. Refer to Chapter 15 for an evaluation of chromium, creatine, amino acids and HMB.

There are also athletes who have exceptionally high caloric needs. This may be due to large body mass, heavy training demands and genetics. Consequently, they may only be able to reach these high energy demands from smart meal planning. Several snacks daily may be required to meet energy needs, while foods concentrated in calories are helpful. Higher calorie nutritional supplements may also be beneficial. Table 13.5 lists some calorie boosting strategies.

---

### TABLE 13.4: MUSCLE BUILDING BASICS

. CONSUME ENOUGH CALORIES: ABOUT 400 TO 500 EXTRA DAILY
. MEET PROTEIN NEEDS FOR RESISTANCE TRAINING
. CONSUME CARBOHYDRATE ALONE OR CARBOHYDRATE PLUS PROTEIN AFTER AN INTENSE RESISTANCE TRAINING SESSION
. CONSUME A SPORTS DRINK DURING SESSIONS LASTING OVER AN HOUR
. CONSUME CARBOHYDRATE ONE TO TWO HOURS PRIOR TO TRAINING
. DRINK PLENTY OF FLUID BEFORE, DURING, AND AFTER TRAINING

---

sis. The low-intake group was not dieting and reported no difficulty in maintaining weight. But despite maintaining weight, the low group was measured as having a lower twenty-four-hour energy expenditure, mainly accounted for by burning less calories at rest. Athletes appearing to be energy efficient may also have a lower level of spontaneous physical activity. They simply burn fewer calories in normal, daily life.

Researchers are not sure why these athletes have a lower resting energy expenditure. It may be due to genetics. The low-intake athletes may also be more mechanically efficient when training, meaning their calorie needs were overestimated. More answers are needed in this area of energy efficiency.

## LONG-TERM HEALTH CONSEQUENCES
## OF LOW BODY-FAT LEVELS

Besides harming psyche and performance, severe caloric restriction can damage long-term health. Female athletes who restrict calories and exceed their personal safe threshold of training and body-fat levels experience a decline in hormone levels, including estrogen.

## TABLE 13.5: WEIGHT GAIN STRATEGIES

BOOST YOUR CALORIES BY:

. Choosing higher calories juices such as apple, cranberry, nectars, and various blends
. Choose calorically dense cereals like muesli, granola, Grapenuts
. Cook hot cereal with milk instead of water
. Add wheat germ, dried fruit, sunflower seeds to cereals
. Snack on dried fruit and bananas
. Use denser, higher calorie breads for sandwiches
. Have lentil, bean, and split pea soups
. Have starch vegetables like peas, corn, and winter squash
. Have snacks between meals to boost calories
. Make fruit smoothies with milk, yogurt, frozen fruit

What can result is oligomenorrhea (irregular menstrual cycle) and amenorrhea (absence of menstrual cycle). This disturbance signals that the athlete is at risk for losing bone mineral, as estrogen is a bone-building hormone in women. This syndrome is often referred to as the female athlete triad: disordered eating, amenorrhea and osteopenia—reduced bone density. If this situation continues, greater risk of stress fractures can occur, and premature osteoporosis can even result. Clearly, this problem requires early and effective treatment.

Each of the disorders making up the female athlete triad can exist by itself. Each is complex and can have its own origins, with one not necessarily leading to the other. Each athlete has their own threshold for when these problems may occur. Some female athletes have very low body-fat levels, and amenorrhea does not occur. Gymnasts, who often have low body weights, experience high mechanical loading stress that can compensate for lower suboptimal estrogen levels.

TOM MORAN

*Professional mountain-bike racer Andy Bishop benefits from an optimal strength-to-weight ratio, as do most cyclists.*

Other risk factors for osteoporosis may also exist (see Chapters 6 and 16).

In turn, the situation of hormone irregularities and bone osteopenia may not be restricted to only female athletes. Training may cause hormone suppression in men, including testosterone, which builds bone mass in men. While males would not have a marker, such as amenorrhea, of hormone imbalances, overtraining syndrome and fatigue may be general indicators. Men also have other osteoporotic related risk factors (see Chapter 16).

## FINAL THOUGHTS

Many athletes strive to lose body fat. To do this appropriately, body-fat levels should be determined. Margin of error should be considered, and realistic body-fat-loss goals determined. Weight should be lost slowly, with a mild calorie restriction. It is best to first cut back on excess fat, then protein, and finally carbohydrate, if necessary. Recovery and energy for training should not be compromised. Severe dieting can lead to physiological complications, and there are health and performance risks associated with very low body fat levels.

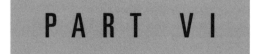

# PART VI

# NUTRITIONAL ERGOGENIC AIDS

# CHAPTER FOURTEEN

# *Evaluating Nutritional Ergogenic Aids*

*"I have always been somewhat skeptical of products that make claims as to 'enhancing performance.' I feel that much more research must be done on these products before I will really take them with much validity."*

—*Fuhr*

It used to be a salesman's pitch from the back of a wagon or maybe a hastily erected tent on the outskirts of town. Now it comes by advertisements, mail, and even e-mail: "How about an exclusive, natural product for increasing endurance and fat loss without dangerous side effects? After nearly twenty-seven years of clinical research and five U.S. patents, our product is now available as a dietary supplement that offers remarkable results. It has been clinically shown to increase metabolic rate, increase fat loss up to 48 percent without exercise, and increase exercise endurance by 20 to 50 percent." Wow!

A lot of promise, a lot of hype.... But athletes are always looking for that extra performance edge. That's why sports nutrition supplements make up a billion-dollar industry worldwide. And while many products such as fluid replacement and recovery drinks are supported by sound research, sales of other products are often fueled by outrageous claims like those above. With new products coming out monthly, athletes need to be discerning when evaluating nutritional ergogenic aids or performance enhancers.

Some questions you may have regarding nutritional ergogenic aids are:

- *How do ergogenic aids work?*
- *How can I evaluate claims regarding ergogenic aids?*
- *Are claims surrounding ergogenic aids legal?*
- *How do I know if a product is safe?*
- *What right do I have to take ergogenic aids?*

Proper training, which increases physical power, is the most effective means for improving athletic performance. An optimal diet is also an effective tool for supporting a great training program. However, as athletes continue to test their limits, or seek relatively easy methods for improving performance, they turn to ergogenic aids.

The term ergogenic means "to produce work." Ergogenic aids have a long use in sporting history and can work in several ways. They are designed to increase physical power or energy production, enhance mental strength, or provide a mechanical edge. Each of these three ergogenic aids categories has several angles that can be exploited. For example, in the case of power output, the rate of a metabolic process that provides energy can be increased. Delivery of energy supplies to the muscles can also be improved.

Sports ergogenics have also been classified into five basic categories: nutritional, pharmacological, physiological, psychological and mechanical. This chapter, and the next, addresses nutritional ergogenic aids.

## NUTRITIONAL ERGOGENIC AIDS

The foods you eat provide a wide variety of nutrients, and they all, one way or another, affect energy production. Some of these nutrients can serve as an energy source, such as carbohydrate. They can regulate energy production in the body, as do B vitamins. Other nutrients, such as protein, provide for growth and development. Basically, nutritional ergogenic aids act upon the body's energy or power systems (see Chapter 1) to increase power output. Some even provide a mechanical edge, by promoting loss of body fat or increasing muscle mass. Caffeine, which can be classified as a dietary component or drug, may provide a mental edge through stimulation of the nervous system.

> *"If you feel that an ergogenic aid may work, then perhaps that is enough."*
> *—Alvis*

### LAWS REGARDING NUTRITIONAL ERGOGENIC AIDS

Athletes are bombarded about the magical effects of nutritional supplements upon sports performance. And studies indicate that they often do use several nutritional supplements concurrently, and in high doses. Increased advertising and strong claims surrounding supplements has occurred since the passing of the Dietary Supplement Health and Education Act (DSHEA) in 1994. DSHEA is affected and significantly changed how these products were marketed, tested, labeled and manufactured.

225

From its inception, this new law generated much debate as to whom it really benefits, the consumer or the supplement industry. But one thing is clear, even with newer legislation and quality control, consumers need to be informed and make thoughtful decisions regarding dietary supplements and ergogenic aids.

Under DSHEA, a broad array of products falls into the category of dietary supplements. This includes vitamins and minerals, herbs or other botanicals, amino acids, substances that supplement the diet by increasing total dietary intake, and a concentrate, metabolite, constituent, extract, or combination of any of the above.

In addition, a somewhat looser category of "nutrition support claims" is permitted for dietary supplements. These claims may relate to the role of dietary supplements regarding "structure and function" of the body and general "well-being." Unlike health claims, nutrition support claims do not require prior approval by the Food and Drug Administration, though a certain set of conditions must be met.

Manufacturers must be able to substantiate that the claim is truthful and not present it in a misleading fashion. Furthermore, the FDA must be notified of the existence of the claim within thirty days. For supplements using a nutritional support claim, the product label must also read: "This statement has not been evaluated by the Food and Drug Administration. This product is not intended to diagnose, treat, cure, or prevent any disease."

Critics of DSHEA, argue that the law is weakened the FDA's authority to enforce laws because the burden of proof was been placed upon the agency. DSHEA also altered the standards of safety, and manufacturers no longer have to prove that their products are safe. Under the old rules, manufacturers were required to provide evidence at the FDA's request. Under the new law, the FDA is required to take the manufacturer to court, if a violation is suspected, requiring FDA enforcement to be selective.

With the burden of proof on the FDA, the burden of responsible choices falls on the consumer. Sifting through all the claims regarding ergogenic aids can be overwhelming. And the placebo effect of these products is very effective. Objectively measuring what is often a very subjective variable can also be difficult. But should you really take a product and assume it is effective based on debatable research?

> *"I believe that ergogenics are largely and ultimately harmful for any human body. I miss the days of good old competition. Whoever gets there first, wins."*
> —*Forbes*

### Improved Quality Control and Labeling

With DSHEA now more than five years old, the concerns raised regarding product safety, quality control and inconsistent labeling resulted in several important legislative changes.

Since March 23, 1999, the new Dietary Supplement Label has been seen on products. This label was designed to identify these products in a similar fashion to conventional foods. "Supplement Facts" now provides information on:

- *Statement of identity (e.g. "ginseng")*
- *Net quantity of ingredients (e.g. "60 capsules")*
- *Structure-function claim statement, "This statement has not been evaluated by the FDA. This product is not*

*intended to diagnose, treat, cure, or prevent any disease."*

- *Directions for use (e.g. "Take one capsule daily")*
- *Supplement Facts panel (lists serving size, amount, and active ingredient)*
- *Other ingredients are listed in descending order of predominance and by common name or proprietary blend.*
- *Name and address of manufacturer, packer or distributor. This is the address to write for more product information.*

Unlike conventional foods, the dosage is not standardized, but determined by the manufacturer. What can occur is a recommended dose provided by the organization trying to sell a product. So consumers should continue to obtain objective information on correct and safe dosing.

In addition to this new label, the dietary supplement industry implemented a self-regulating quality assurance program in January of 1999. This program was based on an FDA proposal, but then was packed by industry organizations with more stringent regulations. Over the next several years it will be interesting to observe the effects of these new programs, and their impact on consumer safety, education and health. For the latest on DSHEA and new legislation, you can access the FDA Web site at http://vm.cfsan.fda.gov./list.html.

## Is it effective?

### Research regarding nutritional ergogenic aids

Valid scientific testing of a nutritional ergogenic aid costs time, money and resources. Tests of a supplement's effect upon performance should be conducted with elite or well-trained athletes. For these and other reasons, much of the supplement industry forgoes testing and relies heavily on testimonials, anecdotes, and untested scientific theories—not research studies—to promote their product.

But, theory is not proof. A theory is a hypothesis or intriguing idea that requires testing. "Scientific breakthroughs" may be new and interesting ideas with little or no basis in fact.

A scientific trial remains the best way in which to examine the effectiveness of ergogenic aids on performance. Here, athletes' experiences can be helpful to researchers, who desire to focus on potentially effective substances. Scientists can use them to determine what products are worth testing and what dosages are appropriate for test protocols. Testing should closely mimic real athletic performance conditions. Researchers should control for age, level of training and nutritional status. Various dosages, supplementation periods, types of exercise and performance testing may need to be incorporated.

Studies should control for the placebo effect as much as possible by incorporating a double-blind design. Subjects receive both the substance being tested and a placebo. To minimize bias, subjects and researchers don't know which product is being administered when. In addition to a placebo trial, there may be a control group—meaning no treatment.

These are only some of the needed features of well-designed testing that satisfy the scientist, but not always the athlete. A large change in performance is required for outcomes to be considered statistically significant. In many cases,

# Placebo Effect

Eliminating the placebo effect in research studies is important. The strong psychological effect of believing that a product can improve your performance should not be discounted. Estimates for the placebo effect to produce positive physical or mental performance results are as high as 40-percent. One study directly tested the placebo effect.

Experienced weight lifters were told that they had qualified to receive anabolic steroids under close supervision in order to increase their lean body mass. They were, however, actually given a simple injection of water. Nonetheless, increases in lean body mass were greater with the placebo than they had been prior to receiving the placebo.

however, changes produced by nutritional supplementation are likely to be smaller. While a 1- to 3-percent change may not be statistically adequate, it may be useful in elite competition where competitions can come down to fractions of seconds.

Researchers also report the overall performance effect within a group. Positive results of individuals within a group may be diluted by the negative or neutral responses of other subjects. Not all subjects respond in the same way to a particular substance.

Unfortunately, even well-designed studies can be quoted out of context. Research findings are extrapolated to inappropriate conclusions. Companies often state that they are in the process of conducting research. Other times they say that research is "in-house"—that is, research that has never been published in reputable peer-reviewed journals. And even well-designed preliminary studies require verification through additional sound research. Unfortunately, even studies published in reputable journals can provoke criticism when placed under close scrutiny.

Patented nutritional ergogenic aids may also look impressive. Yet patents are not granted based on the effectiveness of the product, but rather on its distinguishable differences. Patents can be obtained with a theoretical model rather than objective double-blind research.

Even if companies are accused and fined regarding false claims on dietary supplements, they aren't always deterred from promoting new products. Before their claims are investigated, enough revenue may be generated to render the fine insignificant. One $29 million a year company that promotes bodybuilding and performance supplements was fined only $400,000 for falsely claiming that its product would grow large amounts of muscle.

## IS IT SAFE?

False claim aside, the next step in evaluating ergogenic aids should be determining safety? Some nutritional substance may be toxic or decrease the absorption of other nutrients, especially in high doses, when the "more is better" belief prevails. Some of the negative effects may be acute, mild and temporary. On the other hand, they can also be chronic and serious. Many nutrients, taken in high doses, can impair health. Little research testing the safety of these products is available.

## IS IT LEGAL?

All athletic governing bodies have some regulation regarding the use of ergogenic aids. You should be aware of those within your own sport. Most of these however, pertain to pharmacological ergogenics and medications. Most of this legislation was designed to prevent cheating and to protect the athlete's health.

## MARKETING OF PRODUCTS

Specific nutritional ergogenic aids can benefit athletes under certain conditions. However the supplement industry is an extremely profitable business often relying on testimonials and scientific theories to market its products. Often ergogenic aid theories are extrapolated from clinical research on disease states or nutrient deficiencies. If a product produces a benefit when there is a disease or deficiency state, then some would have you believe that more of that nutrient can produce results, even when a deficiency is not initially present. This thinking represents a leap in logic, not a scientific breakthrough.

Regardless of research support, testimonials from athletes are one of the most effective and popular selling techniques. Anecdotal support is often more than enough for athletes to try a new product because the impression that "everyone is doing it" has been created. Success stories from other athletes are often a powerful incentive for using an ergogenic aid.

## FINAL THOUGHTS

Success in sports is complicated and based upon a variety of factors. It shouldn't naïvely be attributed to a single substance. Genetics, training, equipment, nutrition, mental preparation and motivation all play a role in racing success. And while a specific nutritional ergogenic aid can provide small, but significant, improvements in performance, it is not a substitute for the basics.

Even with proven ergogenic aids, it is important to keep their role in perspective.

# CHAPTER FIFTEEN

# The Latest on *Popular Ergogenic Aids*

*"I tend to believe more in hard work and myself. I think too often ergogenics seem to be an easy way or some get-fast-quick scheme."*

—*Painter*

'Increase lean mass and lose body fat." For serious athletes, these are enticing words. Maybe you are finding it hard to obtain that same lean physique from your usual training program and diet. Perhaps you feel that you are fighting genetics in order to achieve the form ideal for your chosen sport. Or perhaps your current weight loss program just needs a little coaxing along. So taking a legal, performance-enhancing supplement, without investing in more training time or having to cut back on calories is definitely appealing. Compelling claims such as these have led to high sales of many nutritional supplements.

Information on nutritional ergogenic aids is at times overwhelming and confusing. Some questions this chapter will answer regarding popular ergogenic aids are:

- *How is the ergogenic aid supposed to enhance performance?*
- *What is the data on the product's effectiveness?*
- *Is the product safe to take?*
- *Is the product legal?*

Various popular nutritional ergogenic aids are listed in alphabetical order. Ergogenic aids that are most popular and prevalent in recent marketing are reviewed in greater detail.

## ARGININE, LYSINE, ORNITHINE

Arginine and ornithine are nonessential amino acids, while lysine is an essential amino acid. Research has demonstrated that infusing amino acids directly into the bloodstream stimulates release of human growth hormone. HGH is involved in tissue building, including muscle tissue.

However the effects of oral amino acid supplements on HGH is questionable. Four well-controlled studies support that oral supplementation is not comparable to intravenous infusion. All the studies used men who were experienced in resistance training. No effects on blood HGH were observed. One study, which used very high doses of oral ornithine, showed a possible increase in circulating HGH. But side effects make this strategy impractical, as the high dosage used resulted in gastrointestinal distress. Other studies have been criticized for statistical procedure and measurement techniques. Studies with weight lifters have found no significant effect upon body fat, lean mass, or muscular strength, power and endurance with supplementation of these amino acids.

Arginine, lysine and ornithine are available individually or in mixtures in powder or tablet form. Dosages used in research were 2 to 3 grams daily. Consumption of greater than 6 grams may cause gastrointestinal distress. High doses of amino acids may also inhibit absorption of other amino acids. Otherwise, no adverse health effects have been reported, and their use is currently legal. However use of these supplements is unlikely to be beneficial.

## ASPARTATES

Potassium and magnesium are salts of aspartic acid, which is a nonessential amino acid. It has been theorized that these substances improve performance in a number of ways—by enhancing fat metabolism and sparing glycogen, and by minimizing ammonia accumulation. Both these purported mechanisms could enhance prolonged, aerobic exercise.

Because studies have produced conflicting results, research findings are considered inconclusive. While two studies found no improvements, three did demonstrate significant improvements in exercise time to exhaustion. Additional research is required.

Use of these products appears to be safe, though large doses may cause GI distress. And these products are also legal.

## BEE POLLEN

Bee pollen is a mixture of vitamins, minerals, amino acids and other trace minerals. It is advertised as improving output of all three energy systems. Six well-designed studies have found no positive performance effects with bee pollen supplementation. Poorly controlled field research and anecdotal claims are often cited with advertising.

Bee pollen ingestion should be safe for most individuals. However, it may cause serious allergic reactions, such as headache, nausea, abdominal pain, and anaphylaxis, in susceptible individuals. Bee pollen is a legal supplement.

## BETA-HYDROXY-BETA-METHYLBUTYRATE(HMB)

HMB is a byproduct of leucine metabolism in the body, and is marketed primarily as a dietary supplement to strength- and power-trained athletes. It is theorized that HMB may inhibit the breakdown of muscle tissue during hard exercise, thus increasing muscle mass. Your body produces about 0.2 to 0.4 grams of HMB daily. Study supplement doses are anywhere from 1.5 to 3.0 grams per day, divided into multiple doses.

Several animal studies have indicated that HMB supplementation may increase lean muscle mass and decrease body fat. There is less human data. Three studies involving strength training have produced some intriguing results; indicating that more research would be worthwhile. Scientists have also expressed some concern regarding study design and measurement techniques. Though in the best controlled study, 3 grams of HMB resulted in greater gains of lean tissue mass and strength with resistance exercise than supplementing with 1.5 grams HMB or a placebo. Little data on its effect on aerobic endurance athletes is available. HMB appears to be safe, and it is legal.

## BORON

Boron is a trace mineral found mainly in plant foods, and it enhances calcium and magnesium metabolism. Advertising suggests that boron supplementation increases blood testosterone levels, and subsequently increases muscle mass and decreased body fat. This claim highlights misrepresentation of research.

One study looked at the effect of boron supplementation upon bone mineralization in post-menopausal women deprived of boron for four months. Blood testosterone levels doubled during the boron supplementation period. However, studies have clearly shown that boron supplements do not increase testosterone in men and women who consume a normal diet. Research with bodybuilders have shown no beneficial effects. Boron supplements are safe, but most likely not effective.

## BRANCHED-CHAIN AMINO ACIDS

Leucine, isoleucine and valine are the three essential branched chain amino acids, and are natural components of many protein-rich foods. These have been studied for their ability to enhance physical power and prevent mental fatigue.

Most well-controlled field studies and laboratory studies involving acute BCAA supplementation have reported no ergogenic effects on exercise performance tests. Chronic BCAA supplementation studies are not as prevalent, but one study reported an improvement in a 40-kilometer time trial cycling test following fourteen days of BCAA supplementation.

Several other studies, however, reported no significant performance effects, yet subjects in one triathlon study ran faster while on the supplements—though it was not considered statistically significant. However, because of interest and use, more research on chronic BCAA supplementation is needed. They may be especially helpful for high-intensity, endurance exercise over several hours, during which BCAA may become a needed fuel source.

More recent BCAA research focuses on their ability to prevent mental fatigue, which affects the central nervous system or brain and can impair performance. This theory proposes that low blood levels of BCAA along with high levels of free-floating tryptophan causes central fatigue. That's because when free tryptophan enters the brain, increased production of the neurotransmitter called serotonin results. Serotonin can produce symptoms of sleepiness and fatigue. The amount of free tryptophan entering the brain is limited by high levels of BCAA, which normally block its entry. In addition, this tryptophan is normally bound to the blood protein albumin. But during the latter stages of endurance exercise, more tryptophan is freed up and enters the brain. BCAA levels can also fall during endurance exercise. This happens because exercising muscles use them for a fuel source when glycogen stores run low. Eventually a high ratio of free tryptophan to BCAA develops, allowing more tryptophan to enter the brain. More serotonin is produced and fatigue results.

So in theory, BCAA supplementation would keep the amount of free tryptophan to BCAA from getting too high, prevent rapid entry of tryptophan into the brain, and thereby prevent central fatigue. This theory is considered sound, but the research is not conclusive.

In order to significantly affect tryptophan and serotonin levels, you need to consume substantial amounts of BCAA. Study doses range anywhere from 7 to 20 grams, though most packaged products are in the smaller milligram units. Consuming these high doses is inconvenient and there can be negative effects. BCAA can taste bad, have dehydrating effects, and result in a build-up of ammonia in the muscle.

Overall, more conclusive research data supporting this theory is needed regarding the use of BCAA for strength and endurance athletes and for prevention of central fatigue during endurance exercise. In fact, much of the decrease in blood levels of BCAA, which can lead to fatigue, may simply be prevented by adequate ingestion of carbohydrates.

## CAFFEINE

One of the oldest know drugs, caffeine belongs to a group of compounds known as methyl-xanthines. It is found naturally in coffee beans, tea leaves, cocoa beans and cola nuts. Caffeine-containing foods are commonly part of many athletes' diets including coffee, brewed and iced tea, chocolate bars and soft drinks. Many over-the-counter medications also contain caffeine.

Caffeine spares muscle glycogen during exercise, though scientists who have studied the effects of caffeine upon performance are not sure how it does this. The classic theory is that caffeine elevates free fatty acids in the blood, which are used by the muscle as an energy source. There is also another theory that caffeine gets across to the skeletal muscles and directly impacts the enzyme that breaks down glycogen. Regardless of how caffeine spares muscle glycogen, this effect could improve endurance exercise.

Caffeine stimulates the central nervous system, increasing our level of alertness, and stimulating blood circulation and heart function, which could enhance performance in many sports. Epinephrine is also released with caffeine intake, stimulating a variety of performance-related functions. Caffeine also facilitates the release of calcium from its storage site in the muscle, stimulating muscle contraction. This effect could increase muscular strength and power output for short-term, higher-intensity exercise.

Several hundred studies on caffeine have been conducted, and many have shown that caffeine may improve performance for many types of exercise. Recent, well-designed studies utilizing elite athletes, indicate that caffeine is very effective when consumed in legal amounts. Doses as low as 1.5 to 2 milligrams per pound of weight (225 to 300 milligrams for 150-pound athlete) appear effective in improving performance.

This is especially true for aerobic power and endurance events, but may also benefit power-endurance events.

Caffeine is relatively safe, though individual tolerances vary and there may be side effects. Too much caffeine can give some athletes the jitters, muscle tremors and unsteadiness. Caffeine can also increase heat production at rest, raising your body temperature, and impair your performance in hot weather. Some athletes may even experience nausea, upset stomach and gastrointestinal distress with excess caffeine.

Caffeine's diuretic effect has long been debated, but it is likely insignificant. Studies have shown that caffeine does not increase urine output when taken during exercise. And while caffeine-containing products may not be as hydrating as water at rest, some fluid intake effect is still gained.

Amounts of caffeine leading to urine levels of 12 micrograms per millimeter of urine are illegal as determined by the International Olympic Committee. It is estimated that about 800 milligrams of caffeine would be required to reach this level, though this may vary depending on body weight, gender, and hydration status. Eight cups of percolated coffee or sixteen cans of caffeine containing cola could push an athlete to the 800 milligrams limit.

More caffeine-related research is needed to study its effects in actual or simulated sports competition. Caffeine most likely does not enhance performance in exercise lasting eight to twenty minutes, and during sprinting lasting under ninety seconds, though there is not much research in this area.

## CARNITINE

Often promoted as a "metabolic fat burner," carnitine is formed in the liver from the amino acids methionine and lysine. It is not considered an essential nutrient. Carnitine is easily obtained from animal foods in your diet, such as red meat, poultry and dairy products.

After you either produce carnitine or eat carnitine-rich foods, the active form called L-carnitine travels through your bloodstream and is evenly distributed among all your skeletal muscles and your heart. The skeletal muscles, which power and fuel your performance, contain at least 90 percent of all the carnitine in your body. Once it enters these muscles, carnitine is involved in the many metabolic reactions that have led to its reputation as an ergogenic aid.

In carnitine's most talked about role, it is an essential component of several enzymes that carry the fat released from fat stores into the mitochondria of muscle cells to be burned for energy. The theory maintains that carnitine supplementation should increase the level of these enzymes, bring more fat into the mitochondria, enhance fat-burning and spare your most limited fuel supply, muscle glycogen.

In what is a secondary role for carnitine, and described by one researcher as a "far-fetched" theory, carnitine supplementation is proposed to lead to decreased lactic-acid production and enhance the activity of enzymes used in producing energy from carbohydrate.

But some scientists are questioning if enough carnitine even gets into the bloodstream, which is the lifeline for all tissues in the body, and actually make it into the skeletal muscles. If not, the carnitine theory completely falls apart. Studies that have used actual muscle biopsies, have not found increased levels of carnitine with supplementation. Muscle glycogen stores were also not spared in these studies. Researchers concluded that carnitine supplementation often results in blood carnitine concentrations slightly above normal. One study found a slight increase in muscle content after six months supplementation with 2 grams of carnitine daily.

Carnitine supplementation also does not appear to decrease lactic-acid production. This finding has been documented in many well-controlled studies. Other studies have measured carnitine's effect upon performance. Several indicated no positive effects on $VO_2$ max. Two studies, which did note a positive effect, have been criticized for their methodolgy and design.

Other studies measured the effects of carnitine on the respiratory exchange ration. A lower RER would mean more fat and less carbohydrate is being used for energy. Like the studies measuring $VO_2$, there are conflicting results. Three found positive results, while five found no change in RER with carnitine supplementation. Studies evaluating the effect of supplementation on prolonged endurance exercise are needed, as muscle-glycogen sparing would result if carnitine actually exerted an increased fat-burning effect.

Carnitine supplementation appears to be safe. Make certain that you take the L-carnitine form. DL-carnitine can be toxic as it depletes L-carnitine and may lead to a deficiency.

Most recommendations suggest no more than 2 to 4 grams daily for one month, though lower daily doses of 1 to 2 grams have been used for six months. Larger doses may cause diarrhea. There is little data regarding chronic supplementation.

## CHOLINE (LECITHIN)

Choline is found in various foods, particularly as lecithin, in animal and plant foods. Commercial products are available as lecithin or choline salts.

Choline is involved in the formation of acetylcholine, an important neurotransmitter in the central nervous system. Release of acetylcholine initiates the muscle contraction process. Decreased blood levels of choline have been reported following exhaustive exercise, and may be a contributing factor in the development of fatigue. Supplementation is theorized to maintain normal levels required for neural and muscular function.

Choline supplementation actually does appear to increase blood concentrations at rest and during exercise. This is a good start, but overall field and laboratory investigations demonstrated mixed results. It has been suggested that more research is needed, particularly for endurance exercise.

Choline supplementation of 1.5 to 2 grams in research studies appears safe.

## CHROMIUM

Chromium is a trace mineral, often marketed as a legal alternative to anabolic steroids and human growth hormone.

Scientists have long known that chromium enhances the effects of the hormone insulin, which regulates glucose metabolism. Chromium is part of the organic complex known as glucose tolerance factor. In studies, 50 percent of adults with impaired blood glucose regulation improved when taking chromium supplements. Insulin also promotes the uptake of amino acids into muscle cells and regulated protein metabolism. This protein-building function has linked chromium supplementation to an increase in muscle mass.

*"I think that sometimes ergogenics provide a psychological edge. Some athletes notice a benefit, some don't."*
                        —*Reid*

There are two ways in which chromium is proposed to be a useful ergogenic aid for building muscle, and decreasing the rate of muscle breakdown. First, if an athlete is chromium-deficient, a supplement would improve amino acid uptake. Second, if adequate doses produce these results, higher doses of chromium could stimulate a greater-than-normal amino acid uptake providing greater muscle-building benefits. Fat loss is claimed simply to be a side effect of this increased muscle building. But no scientist supports the claim that chromium itself is a direct fat burner.

The first theory regarding a possible chromium deficiency, is dependent on whether athletes consume less than the recommended 50 to 200 micrograms daily. This type of data on athletes is virtually nonexistent. But one review of the general population reported that men consumed only about 33 micrograms and women 28 micrograms. This poor intake may be partly related to a high intake of refined and processed foods, replacing whole grains. These lower-quality carbohydrates may also trigger a higher release of insulin, requiring you to use more chromium. Simple sugars may also trigger chromium excretion.

Training may also negatively affect the adequacy of an athlete's chromium status. Some studies suggest that endurance exercise may cause your body tissues to send chromium into the bloodstream, with chromium eventually being lost in the urine.

As often occurs, various human studies on chromium have produced conflicting results. While a few early studies showed positive results, their designs have been criticized. Many more recent and better-designed studies have shown no positive effects of chromium supplementation. Three early studies, two of which have only been described in a review article and not had full data published, have been used as examples of chromium's positive muscle-building effects. All the studies combined 200 micrograms of chromium with weight-training programs. However, changes in body composition were measured using skinfold calipers, rather than more accurate body composition testing methods. These studies have frequently been criticized for their design.

Two later studies, which did use underwater weighing to measure body-composition changes, also supplemented weight training with 200 micrograms of chromium picolinate. No increases in lean body mass or muscle strength were found. One of these studies also found that subjects receiving chromium excreted more chromium. Researchers speculated that the subjects did not even retain a good portion of the supplemented chromium.

Since then, several more recent studies have been presented. Three used higher doses of chromium picolinate ranging from 400 to 924 micrograms. While subjects were not athletes, they did follow a prescribed weight training program. No additional muscle building was seen when the chromium-supplemented subjects were compared to controls receiving a placebo.

With sales of chromium picolinate high, and large doses often recommended by manufacturers, safety concerns have been raised. Because chromium is sold as a dietary supplement, safety tests are not required under DSHEA, and have not been done. Basically there is not much long-term data on chromium doses of more than 200 micrograms.

Because chromium is a mineral, concern has been raised about large, chronic doses. Various minerals, such as copper, iron and zinc often compete with each other at absorption sites. Excess chromium intake could decrease absorption of other minerals.

Clearly, adequate chromium intake is important. It is found in all the foods you eat, but some especially good sources of chromium are whole-grain breads and cereals, mushrooms, brewer's yeast, asparagus, apples, raisins, cocoa, oysters, peanuts, peanut butter and prunes. Various supplements like sports drinks, recovery drinks and energy bars, frequently used by athlete, may contain chromium. Many regular multivitamin-mineral supplement contain up to 100 micrograms of chromium. Try not to exceed 200 micrograms daily combined from supplemental sources. This amount should prevent any type of chromium deficiency, even with heavy training, and higher amounts have not shown any beneficial muscle-building effects. Overall, chromium's ability to improve muscle mass in athletes with high supplement doses appears doubtful.

## COENZYME Q-10

Coenzyme Q-10 is a dietary supplement with a chemical structure similar to vitamin K. It is involved in several metabolic processes important for optimal functioning of the oxygen system. CoQ-10 is also an antioxidant. Research with cardiac patients has found that CoQ-10 supplementation improved heart function, VO2 max, and exercise performance in cardiac patients. This has prompted the theory that it could be an effective ergogenic aid in healthy aerobic athletes.

Several studies cited as supporting this theory contained a number of methodological flaws, such as no control group or placebo. They also were not published in peer-reviewed journals. Fully published studies do not support that CoQ-10 is an effective ergogenic aid, either as an antioxidant or enhancer of VO2 max or lactate threshold.

Doses of 100 to 150 micrograms of CoQ-10 appear safe for several months. Though one study did raise concerns that regarding muscle tissue damage with 120 micrograms taken for twenty days. Researchers speculated that this may actually be due to a pro-oxidant effect. Overall, CoQ-10 does not appear to be an effective ergogenic aid.

## CREATINE

Creatine is an amine found in animals. It can also be produced by the body from the amino acids arginine, glycine, and methionine. Creatine supplementation is used by athletes to increase the total amount of and resynthesis of creatine phosphate in the muscle. CP is an essential fuel of the ATP-CP energy systems. Theoretically, creatine supplementation would help prevent fatigue in events affected by a rapid decrease in CP. Creatine has also been studied in resistance training and for its possible role in increasing body mass.

It is known that oral intake of supplemental creatine can increase both total and creatine phosphate in the muscles. Numerous studies have assessed what type of effect this can have upon exercise performance. And as with most scientific research, some studies show a benefit, while others do not.

However, the majority of studies involving the ATP-CP energy system suggest that creatine supplementation may be beneficial. This is mainly true for repetitive, short-term, high-intensity exercise. Optimal fuel is available for this exercise, and the rate of CP resynthesis during the recovery phase is increased. On the other hand, several studies involving one all-out sprint showed no benefit with creatine supplementation.

There are fewer studies involving creatine and the anaerobic glycolysis or lactic acid energy system. The results of these studies are equally positive and negative, indicating that more research is required in this area. In some studies creatine did decrease muscle lactic acid accumulation.

It is very unlikely that creatine supplementation is of any benefit to the oxygen energy system, as CP is not a very important energy source for this exercise. Overall, the limited studies are not supportive of creatine use for this type of exercise.

Many researchers studying the effects of creatine supplementation have reported an increase in body weight. In one week-long study subjects have been found to gain 2 to 5 pounds of weight. Clearly there is some fluid retention occurring, while the degree to which muscle mass is increased has not been determined. However, creatine supplementation has been shown to enhance resistance-training efforts. Over time, this could facilitate an increase in lean body mass, with increases in strength and power.

Many creatine studies have provided 20 to 30 grams daily for five to seven days, to effectively load the muscle. Lower doses of 3 grams have loaded the muscle in four weeks. A dose of 10 grams was used for about ninety days in another resistance training study. Vegetarians seem to have the highest creatine uptake, while others are nonresponders. Taking creatine with carbohydrate appears to improve uptake into the muscle.

Creatine use for up to ninety days at low doses appears to be safe. Health risks associated with long-term use have not been determined. There have been anecdotal reports from athletes of bloating and muscle cramping with creatine supplementation. Creatine is currently legal. It may be beneficial for athletes completing repetitive, high-power tasks with brief recovery periods. It may also improve recovery during sprint workouts. Athletes should consider possible fluid gain with creatine, and determine if this weight gain may be harmful to performance.

## DEHYDROEPIANDROSTERONE(DHEA)

Imagine if you had unlimited access to a hormone that builds muscle, burns fat, extends your life, and makes you look and feel younger. Keep in mind that determining the proper dose is your responsibility and that manufactures are not obligated to warn you of potential risks and side effects.

This is exactly how the hormone DHEA, naturally produced by the body, is marketed. Sales of DHEA have easily exceeded millions of dollars. Besides many other proposed uses, DHEA has been marketed as an ergogenic aid. DHEA was actually banned at one time, in 1995, due to potentially harmful side effects. Later, it was available only by prescription, and is now sold as a dietary supplement under DSHEA despite not even being a nutrient.

Every morning, your adrenal glands secrete DHEA into your bloodstream. After entering your body tissues, it produces small amounts of estrogen and testosterone. Levels of DHEA are high at birth. Production peaks at puberty, then steadily decreases after age thirty.

Many health-related claims surround DHEA supplementation. Some include prevention of obesity, cancer, diabetes and heart disease, in addition to increased well being and extended life span. DHEA's primary function as an ergogenic aid is to increase muscle mass and decrease fat, to obtain enhanced power and strength. Unfortunately, only a few randomized, double blind, placebo-controlled studies regarding the effects of DHEA supplementation have been published.

Besides the data being limited, it is not always relevant to athletes. Two studies that found an increase in lean mass and strength (100 milligrams for three to six months) included sedentary individuals, more than fifty years in age. In addition, six other similar studies (50 to 1600 milligrams for three weeks to six months) found no body-composition changes. One study did find subjective improvements in physical and psychological well being, but no type of performance test was done. Supplementation of DHEA on healthy individuals younger than forty years of age is virtually unstudied.

Many concerns have been raised in regard to DHEA supplementation. Because hormones, such as DHEA, can stimulate the growth of precancerous cells, it is feared that supplementation may increase the risk of developing prostate cancer in men, and breast and endometrial cancer in women. Adverse hormonal effects of DHEA may not stop there. In women, supplementation has lowered the protective HDL cholesterol, and produced acne and facial hair growth.

Athletes need to know that supplementation with DHEA could result in a testosterone-epitestosterone ratio exceeding the six to one limit and is banned by the International Olympic Committee and the U.S. Olympic Committee. Individuals able to use DHEA legally, should take it only under a physician's care and with close monitoring. Clinicians recommend not exceeding a 5 to 10 milligram daily dose. But in reality, it is still unknown what dose and dosing period of DHEA is safe in specific groups of people.

## DIHYDROXYACETONE AND PYRUVATE (DHAP)

DHAP is a combination of two metabolic by-products of glycolysis-dihydroxyacetone and pyruvate. The combination of these two products has been shown to increase muscle glycogen stores. Because of this effect on glycogen, DHAP has been studied as an ergogenic aid.

Two well-designed studies used untrained male subjects. They were provided with 100 grams of DHAP (75 grams dihydroxyacetone and 25 grams pyruvate). The DHAP was substituted for a portion of carbohydrate in the study-controlled diet. Results indicated an improvement in an arm ergometer test to exhaustion at 60-percent $VO_2$ peak after a week of supplementation. Endurance increased significantly, primarily due to increased muscle glycogen, and increased glucose extraction by the muscle. An additional study from the same lab also found some performance improvements with a cycle ergometer exercise test to exhaustion at 70-percent VO2 peak. Finally, a third study from another lab, saw a decreased level of perceived exertion with 75 grams of DHAP.

No major side effects have been seen with DHAP, though intestinal distress was seen in a few subjects. The main concern with DHAP, is that studies did not include trained subjects. Performance tests should be relevant to actual performance situations. That's why more research pertinent to athletes needs to be done to determine if pyruvate enhances athletic performance. Also, commercial supplements of pyruvate contain only 500 milligrams to 1 gram doses and may not contain DHA. These products would not mimic those used in the study.

## GINSENG

Ginseng is a popular substance that has been used for thousands of years in Chinese medicine. Gingseng extracts contain several chemicals, the most important being glycosides or ginsenosides. There are various plant species and forms of gingseng.

Ginseng is considered to be an adaptogen, a term used to describe a substance that aids the body's response to stress and increases energy levels. This includes physical stress such as intense exercise. Numerous theories regarding how gingseng exerts this effect have been proposed, though the actual underlying mechanism has not been determined.

Many of the heavily marketed claims regarding gingseng were conducted in the 1960s and '70s. Few of these studies were well controlled and had many research design flaws. Four more recent, well-controlled studies, reported no significant effects on performance measures.

Gingseng appears to be relatively safe when taken in doses recommended by the manufacturer. However, excessive use may result in high blood pressure, nervousness and sleeplessness in some individuals. Gingseng is legal. Be wary of gingseng containing products that may contain other substances such as ephedrine, which is banned.

## GLUTAMINE

Glutamine is an amino acid that is synthesized in the muscle tissue. It is the most abundant amino acid in the blood and is used as a fuel by the cells of the immune system, particularly lymphocytes, macrophages and killer cells. Impaired glutamine status has been associated with the overtrained state in athletes. Overtrained athletes are thought to be more susceptible to upper respiratory infections and other infections.

Blood levels of glutamine increase during intense, prolonged exercise, and significantly decrease for up to several hours after exercise, due to muscle glycogen depletion. This depletion of glutamine may become cumulative if recovery between training sessions is inadequate. Adequate daily carbohydrate consumption may be the most effective means for preventing glutamine depletion. Preliminary research also suggests that glutamine supplementation may reduce the incidence of respiratory infections in athletes. Other studies indicate that glutamine may stimulate glycogen resynthesis in skeletal muscle.

## GLYCEROL

Glycerol is a colorless, liquid alcohol found naturally in fats. Pure glycerol is not a normal dietary component, but is produced commercially from hydrolysis of fats. It may be available as glycerin. Some sports drinks contain glycerol.

Use of glycerol is thought to be an effective means for "hyper-hydration" before training and competition because it holds and attracts water like a sponge. Athletes have been experimenting with it to prevent dehydration and therefore boost performance. Glycerol may also have the added benefit of increasing blood volume.

As with many other ergogenic aids, the research on glycerol is divided. Several studies support that hyper-hydration from glycerol ingestion can maintain lower heart rate and body core temperature during exercise in the heat. This may enhance prolonged aerobic endurance capacity. In turn, other studies found that this hyperhydration exerted no beneficial physiological effect during endurance exercise.

When diluted with fluid and mixed properly, glycerol appears to be relatively safe to use. It is sold in packets that must be mixed with a specified amount of water. However, some athletes have reported headaches, bloating, nausea, vomiting and dizziness with glycerol use. It should not be used by pregnant women or individuals with high blood pressure, diabetes or kidney disease as it may cause serious health problems.

Infusion of glycerol has been banned by the IOC, but oral solutions are legal. Dosages used in research have been about 0.45 grams per pound of body weight, with each gram of solution diluted with about 20 to 25 millimeters of water. Glycerol solutions should be consumed one to two-and-a-half hours before exercise.

## MEDIUM-CHAIN TRIGLYCERIDES (MCT)

MCTs have been available for clinical use for several decades, but have only recently been promoted to athletes.

MCTs are absorbed differently than other fats. They are absorbed as fast as carbohydrate and can be used as a fuel source during exercise. It is speculated that they may conserve muscle stores of carbohydrate.

To date, one well-designed study determined that carbohydrate combined with 86 grams of MCTs given during exercise improved a 40-kilometer time trial cycling performance which followed a two-hour ride at 60-percent $VO_2$ max. MCT alone impaired performance compared to carbohydrate given alone. Researchers speculated that the MCTs improved performance by decreasing oxidation of muscle glycogen during the two-hour ride.

However, several other studies utilizing a similar protocol found no performance improvements with MCTs. They found that performance was impaired when MCTs were taken alone, but also found no benefits with an MCT-carbohydrate combination.

Overall, the research does not support the use of MCTs to spare muscle glycogen and improve performance. But given some positive results, further investigation is worthwhile.

## PHOSPHATE SALTS

Available as sodium, potassium or calcium phosphate, these salts have theorized to enhance all three energy systems. Phosphorous is part of both ATP and CP in the ATP-CP energy system. Phosphates may buffer lactic acid, and play a role in releasing oxygen to the tissues.

There are no scientific data supporting that phosphate salt supplementation enhances functioning of the ATP-CP or lactic acid system. Four well-controlled studies indicate that the oxygen system may be enhanced by phosphate salt supplementation. There was an increase in VO2 max, and three found improvement in exercise tasks. Of course there are studies that have found no ergogenic effect. More research is needed.

Study doses of 4 grams daily, divided in to four, 1-gram doses taken over for three to four days, appear safe. Excessive phosphate salt may produce GI side effects. Chronic use may also adversely affect calcium balance in the body.

## SODIUM BICARBONATE

Sodium bicarbonate is an alkaline salt thought to buffer lactic acid. Baking soda is sodium bicarbonate. Sodium bicarbonate and performance has been studied extensively. Overall, it has been found to be a very effective ergogenic aid in events that primarily use the lactic acid energy system. The majority of both laboratory and field tests demonstrate that sodium bicarbonate supplements improve performance in high-intensity tasks, both continuous and intermittent, lasting from forty-five seconds to six minutes.

Sodium bicarbonate appears safe in the recommended doses of 140 milligrams per pound of body weight. For a 150-pound athlete, this is about 21,000 milligrams or 21 grams. This translates to about five teaspoons of baking soda. It should be mixed with one liter of water and taken one to two hours prior to exercise. Some individuals have reported GI symptoms such as nausea, bloating, abdominal pain and diarrhea with sodium bicarbonate loading.

## Vanadium

Vanadium is a nonessential mineral. Good sources include shellfish and grain products. It is involved in several enzymatic reactions, including the metabolism of carbohydrates and lipids. Vanadium salts have been shown to improve glucose metabolism in noninsulin-dependent diabetes. Therefore vanadium salts are marketed like chromium supplements—as promoting muscle building and inhibiting muscle breakdown.

Very limited research data is available on this supplement. One well-controlled study found no body composition changes. Obviously, more research is required. One adverse side effect of vanadyl sulfate supplements is GI distress.

## FINAL THOUGHTS

Because of strong interest in improving performance, new nutritional ergogenic aids will always be available and heavily marketed. Clearly, the athlete should be aware of the amount of scientific support behind these claims, their effectiveness in actual competition, and any possible health consequences of taking these supplements. It is also helpful to find a qualified, unbiased health professional to assist you in sifting through all these claims.

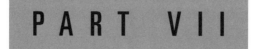

# PART VII

# OTHER NUTRITION CONSIDERATIONS

# CHAPTER SIXTEEN

# Special Nutrient Needs

*"Altitude tears your body down more. You can't train at the intensities that you would at sea level."*

*—Dede Demet,*
*Saturn Cycling Team*

A thletes may encounter unique situations, problems or circumstances that affect their diet and nutritional requirements. Consuming adequate amounts of fluid when training at altitude can be challenging. You may also experience some problems with anemia, injury or muscle cramping. Or perhaps you want to learn more about preventing osteoporosis. You may even be wondering if alcohol can fit into your training diet. In addition, many female athletes continue to follow an exercise program during pregnancy and need to meet their unique nutritional requirements.

Some questions you may have regarding specific situations are:

• *What nutrients do I need more of at altitude?*

- *Can nutritional strategies prevent muscle cramping? What are some nutrients that can facilitate recovery from an injury?*
- *What are some strategies if I become anemic?*
- *What nutritional guidelines do I need to be aware of for pregnancy?*
- *Are men at risk for developing osteoporosis?*

## NUTRITIONAL CONSIDERATIONS OF TRAINING AT ALTITUDE

Altitude presents a challenge to athletes and their bodies. The higher you go, the less dense air becomes. This results in altitude "hypoxia" or a reduction of oxygen in your body's tissues. Fortunately your body adjusts or "acclimatizes" to altitude. And some of the metabolic adaptations of acclimatization do affect nutritional needs. Even moderate elevations of up to five thousand feet change how much you need to eat and drink.

### ENERGY NEEDS INCREASE

When you think about altitude, think about energy. Extra calories at altitude should be a primary nutrition focus. Studies conducted at Pike's Peak (elevation 14,000 feet), in Colorado Springs, Colorado, followed calorie needs closely. Studies indicate that basal metabolic rate increases by as much as 40 percent the first couple of days at altitude. Then the BMR drops and levels off at about 15 to 17 percent above sea level values. Researchers have calculated that basic energy needs at altitude increase by 200 to 300 calories daily.

*Every athlete can benefit from increased fluid intake at altitude.*
*Dede Demet, Saturn Cycling Team.*

Sounds like a simple increase, but it isn't because there is another problem. A real decrease in appetite can set in at high altitudes. Researchers have found that some people undereat by 200 to 300 calories. Individuals may experience various symptoms such as nausea at altitude. What if this nausea or decreased appetite affects you? It is possible that you may fall 500 calories short of your increased energy needs.

*"I really focus on hydration, and always have a water bottle with me at altitude."*

*—Demet*

You may wonder why these extra calories are so important? Undereating and losing weight at altitude does not result in increased leanness. While some body fat may be lost, you will also lose valuable lean body mass. Too much muscle loss will compromise your performance. But there is hope. By meeting your calculated energy needs, weight loss can be slowed or stopped altogether.

Once you know you need to eat more at altitude, where should those extra calories come from? Carbohydrates are your body's first choice at altitude as there is a shift in fuel preference for use of glucose. You may want to add extra calories from grains, bagels, pasta and rice.

This increased use of glucose also occurs during exercise. Many high-living athletes have modified their use of a carbohydrate electrolyte beverage during exercise, using them more frequently, and drinking much more when they train.

## FLUID NEEDS INCREASE

Aside from the increased calorie and training needs, simply taking in more fluid every day at altitude is crucial. Daily hydration should be a heavy focus. Always try to keep some type of fluid source with you. This type of strategy makes sense as the air at altitude is extremely dry; every breath you take results in fluid loss. There is also more fluid loss through skin, which are referred to as "insensible." Normally your insensible fluid losses are about half-a-liter. At altitude, these insensible losses can increase to 2 liters.

But your fluid needs don't stop there. Urinary losses can be from one to 2 liters. You can also lose two liters of fluid per hour while you are exercising. Visualize those fat, plastic soda bottles on the grocer's shelf—that's how much fluid you need to take each hour. Replacing all your fluid needs must be a very conscious effort. You may need to consume up to 8 liters of fluid daily depending on your training schedule.

## VITAMIN AND MINERAL NEEDS

While the research on vitamin and mineral needs at altitude is scarce, it is generally agreed that iron is a nutrient requiring increased attention. To increase the blood's oxygen-carrying capacity at altitude, red blood cell numbers increase. Athletes training at altitude should consider having iron status indicators, such as serum ferritin, hemoglobin and hematocrit checked. Having adequate stores will ensure that you meet the demands of producing more red blood cells.

In addition to good iron food sources, iron supplementation may boost depleted stores. You can appropriately supplement with iron when warranted, but not to excess. Too much iron causes oxidation and free radical production—a reaction that could negatively affect your recovery and health. A physician can advise you on supplement needs and do follow-up testing.

Focusing on foods high in antioxidants, such as vitamins C and E, may also be beneficial. This is because exercising at altitude may increase the "oxidative stress" placed upon your body. Good sources of vitamin C include orange and grapefruit juice, strawberries, kiwi, cantaloupe, green peppers and broccoli. Vitamin E-containing foods are oils made from corn, soybean and safflower, fortified cereals, whole grains and wheat germ. Try to increase your intake of these nutrients at altitude.

Basically higher elevation means higher nutrition. Fill your diet with high quality foods, especially carbohydrates. Keep drinking, both water during the day and a carbohydrate electrolyte replacement beverage while training. And make sure you get enough iron, and vitamins C and E in your diet. Good nutrition can help your body handle the stresses of training at altitude.

## NUTRITION BASICS FOR MUSCLE CRAMPING

Muscle cramps remain a mystery. They can't be induced, are difficult to study, and don't occur consistently in many of the athletes who experience them. But they can be painful and inconvenient, especially if they occur when training, racing and recovering. Muscle cramps are generally associated with long training sessions in high temperatures, and overexertion. The true causes of muscle cramps are not known, but you may be able to help prevent them by following a few basic nutritional steps.

*"You need to have enough fluid so that you don't get cramps or stiffen up."*
*—Kwiatkowski*

### FLUID, ELECTROLYTES AND MINERALS

It has been theorized that muscle cramping is partly caused by dehydration—which, in general, can be prevented by drinking about 8 ounces of water or caffeine-free, non-alcoholic fluid every hour. Urinating frequently and clearly are signs of being well hydrated. Fluid needs during exercise are also high. Make sure you are taking in the recommended 4 to 8 ounces every fifteen to twenty minutes. This is optimal, though not always possible, so it helps to start exercise well hydrated. It's also a good idea to drink plenty of fluid after exercise, especially if you fell short on drinking while training.

Another potential cause of muscle or "heat" cramping is an imbalance of sodium, which is a result of profuse sweating. In particular, salt depletion can occur over the course of several days of heavy training in a hot climate to which you haven't become acclimatized. A sodium imbalance may also be caused by drinking large amounts of plain water, when exercising four hours or more in the heat.

If you anticipate being in this type of hot situation, foods like pretzels, some cereals, cheese, crackers, muffins, spaghetti and yogurt will add sodium to your diet. Most foods contain some sodium, though fruits and juices are virtually sodium free. You don't need to be overly restrictive of sodium in your diet during hot weather. If you find yourself craving salty items, your body may be telling you that it needs more sodium. Then as you adjust to the heat, you will sweat and crave less salt.

So far, it's purely speculative to say that lack of the mineral potassium plays a role in muscle cramping. Exercise-related deficiencies from sweat loss are unlikely. But potassium has many important functions, including neuromuscular activity and a role in glycogen storage. Overall, it's a good idea to eat foods rich in potassium for reasons beyond the possibility of preventing cramps. Fruits and vegetables are good potassium sources, and provide beta-carotene and vitamin C. High amounts of this mineral can be found in melon, bananas, tomatoes, raisins, potatoes, orange juice, and dried peas and beans. You may want to eat generous portions of these foods anyway because they provide carbohydrates.

## SPORTS DRINKS

Besides eating the appropriate foods in your daily diet, you may want to use a carbohydrate electrolyte beverage for extensive exercise in hot weather. The flavors of these beverages may also make drinking easier, helping to prevent dehydration, while the sodium enhances fluid absorption in your small intestine. To really boost your potassium and sodium intake, it also makes sense to bring along munchies like dried fruit for potassium and salted crackers for sodium sources.

## CALCIUM

Another culprit of muscle cramping may be calcium—although this is not conclusive. Calcium is the most abundant mineral in your body and has many functions, including a role in muscle contraction. In theory, the huge calcium stores in your bones should release calcium into your blood to compensate for any deficiencies. But making sure to consume enough calcium can't hurt. It will also help preserve bone mass. Low fat sources of milk and yogurt are easy to add to your diet and absorb well. Plant sources include tofu, broccoli and kale. You may want to try calcium-fortified products as well.

## MAGNESIUM

Another theory is that lack of magnesium, a mineral that plays a role in muscle relaxation, may be related to muscle cramping. To explore this theory, among other things, researchers did various blood chemistries on cyclists during the Hotter 'N Hell Hundred bicycle ride, in which forty-six of its ninety-nine riders studied experienced muscle cramping. Of the various parameters tested—including sodium, potassium, phosphorous and glucose—only magnesium was found to be significantly lower in the cyclists experiencing muscle cramps. If you are interested in increasing your own supply of magnesium, seeds, nuts, legumes, green leafy vegetables and unmilled cereal grain are good sources.

However, finding the causes of muscle cramping may not be as simple as testing blood levels of various minerals and electrolytes. One study conducted during the Ironman Triathlon world championship, in Hawaii, found that pre- and post-competition changes in these parameters were similar in athletes with muscle cramps as those without cramps. So, researchers feel that changes within the muscle fiber, which are difficult to measure, may explain cramping better.

It's also true that muscle cramps may not be solely related to nutrition. In fact, modifying training techniques and better stretching may be the solutions you are looking for. But adding extra fluids, using beverages containing electrolytes during exercise, eating good sources of potassium, calcium, magnesium, and small amounts of sodium could do you some good anyway—and may very well help with your own problem of muscle cramping.

## NUTRITION CONSIDERATIONS WHEN RECOVERING FROM AN INJURY

At some point in your athletic career, it is possible that you may experience some type of injury, from strain, abrasions, bruising and fractures. Likely, the speed with which you recover may become a major concern. Most of you are aware of the physical things you have to think about at such a time, but you should also know that the correct nutritional strategies could also contribute to the healing process.

### WEIGHT CONTROL

During rehabilitation there is a natural fear of putting on fat, and injured athletes often require and seek out a specific nutrition plan. Depending on the extent of your injury and usual training program, caloric expenditure can decrease by several thousand calories per week. For instance, an athlete weighing 150 pounds, who is suddenly forced to train four hours less per week could experience a weekly one-pound weight gain if they kept up with their usual eating habits.

Depending on their rehabilitation program, injured athletes should keep a food record for several days and determine their usual caloric intake. Based on the number of calories you are burning per week in exercise, trim anywhere from 200 to 500 calories daily to prevent weight gain. Often protein and carbohydrate amounts need to decrease slightly from high training levels to prevent body fat gain.

This would also be a good time to trim any excess fat from your diet that was being burned off due to high training needs. Avoid drastic dietary restrictions in order to avoid missing out on needed nutrients. Just shave portions slightly throughout the day, keeping your diet high in carbohydrate, moderate in protein and low in fat. Refer back to the weight control guidelines discussed in Chapter 12.

## RESISTANCE TRAINING

A good resistance rehabilitation training program provides a big calorie advantage. Making muscle takes work and energy, allowing more calories to be consumed and somewhat offsetting your otherwise limited training. Resistance training sessions—and long aerobic workouts—should be followed by recovery carbohydrates to facilitate muscle repair. Consuming carbohydrates a few hours before and during workouts can also boost energy and prevent further drain on a weakened body.

## NUTRIENTS FOR HEALING

When you are injured, consider taking calcium for injury recovery. Besides the obvious function of building bone tissue, calcium is a vital mineral for muscle contraction, regulating blood clotting, and activating a number of enzymes for forming and breaking down muscle and liver glycogen. High doses will not accelerate these processes, but an adequate intake of 1000 to 1200 milligrams daily is needed. For well-absorbed calcium, try two to three servings of low fat dairy products like one cup of skim milk (300 milligrams), low fat yogurt (415 milligrams), and nonfat cheese (200 milligrams).

Good plant sources include dark green leafy vegetables and dried peas and beans.

Your diet should also contain adequate amounts of well-absorbed iron. Iron is part of many enzymes that oxygenate muscle tissue. Heme iron, found in animal foods, is about 10 to 30 percent absorbed. Try lower fat sources such as lean red meat and dark poultry. For athletes who are cautious about overdoing red meats, keep portions to 3 ounces. You can use small amounts in soups, stews and casseroles. Non-heme iron found in plant foods is about 2 to 10 percent absorbed. Good sources include dried fruits, beans and whole grain products. Eating vitamin C or heme source foods will increase the iron absorption in the plant foods—drink orange juice with your iron-fortified cereal.

Zinc is a component of several enzymes involved in energy metabolism, and is used for protein synthesis and wound healing. Good sources include red meat (3 ounces provides 33 percent of the recommended daily allowance), turkey, milk, yogurt and seafood—especially oysters. Zinc from animal protein is best absorbed.

Vitamin C can also enhance the healing process. One of its principal functions is collagen synthesis. Collagen is needed for the formation and maintenance of connective tissue such as cartilage, tendon and bone. Vitamin C also plays a role in red blood cell synthesis. Load up on good food sources like oranges, grapefruit, broccoli, peppers and salad greens. They are low fat, low calorie, and several servings will easily exceed the recommended daily allowance of 60 milligrams. Increasing your intake of fruits and vegetables is important as they also provide the antioxidant beta-carotene and other carotenoids. Antioxidants may protect against further muscle damage during exercise.

Fruits and vegetables also provide bioflavinoids, which perform a variety of functions that may be beneficial to healing. Plant foods of any kind, whole grains and seeds are good sources, with green tea being especially high. And don't forget good sources of the antioxidant vitamin E: wheat germ and whole grains.

Future research may provide more advice on nutritional supplementation for injury repair. Some supplements currently being used or studied in varying combinations are glucosamine salts, chondroitin, cucumerin and antioxidants. More human data is needed for specific recommendations to be made.

Paying close attention to your diet for healing is just as important as eating well for training and racing. Stick with a well balanced diet with a variety of foods, pay special attention to recovery carbohydrates, and eat good sources of calcium, iron, zinc and vitamin C. And if fat gain is a concern, work with a registered dietitian and sports nutritionist. It may just make a difference in how you recover and perform.

## TIRED? YOU MAY BE LACKING IN IRON

You can't see fatigue, but you know when it's there—especially when it puts a halt to your training and competition. While there are many causes of fatigue, if symptoms persist you should see a physician and be checked for iron-deficiency anemia.

## IRON STORES IN YOUR BODY

The trace element iron is present in several forms, all of which have their own functions. In your body, iron combines with a specific protein called transferrin, which then transports iron to the blood and tissues, and finally releases it. When released, iron combines with the protein ferritin, producing the storage form of iron. When erythrocytes or red blood cells are formed, iron binds with another protein, protoporphyrin, to form the heme component of hemoglobin.

*"I actually went through a bout of anemia this past summer, so I take iron supplements. It was due to a combination of hard training and not eating a lot of red meat."*
*—Reid*

## ROLE OF IRON

Hemoglobin carries oxygen to red blood cells. Iron is also a component of myoglobin that carries oxygen to muscle cells and many enzymes involved in metabolism. Iron-containing compounds perform a number of functions that can positively impact oxygen. That's why anemia resulting from inadequate iron stores can impair performance and is best prevented.

## ASSESSING IRON STORES

Before panicking, keep in mind that iron deficiency doesn't just happen overnight, but can occur in three distinct stages. Iron depletion, or a reduced level of serum ferritin, is the first stage. If this iron depletion continues, the second stage, known as iron deficient erythropoiesis or an impairment in red blood cell formation, occurs. When iron is not available to bind with free erythrocyte protoporphyrin. FEP blood levels increase, reflecting an impairment in red blood cell formation. Finally hemoglobin concentrations fall, reflecting that iron deficiency anemia is present.

Normal and healthy hemoglobin levels for men are 14 to 16 grams per deciliter, with anemia classified at less than 13 grams per deciliter. The normal hemoglobin level for women is 12 to 14 grams per deciliter, with anemia at less than 11 to 12 grams. Also, if iron is in short supply, blood transferrin levels will increase.

Some blood test results indicating possible iron deficiency are: low serum ferritin levels, increased levels of FEP, reduced hemoglobin levels, and increased levels of transferrin. Transferrin, however, can also be affected by infection and inflammation. Your blood work must be interpreted to determine if you have iron deficiency, iron deficiency anemia, or sports anemia that is not a true anemia.

Endurance training can cause sports anemia or pseudoanemia. Training increases your blood volume diluting your red blood cells, hemoglobin, and perhaps serum ferritin. Hard endurance training session of 2 hours daily, over one week, can expand your blood volume by more than 13 ounces. While this might sound like a negative aspect of training, red blood cell mass is not actually decreased, so oxygen capacity is truly not impaired. And the larger blood volume means that your heart can pump more blood to your working muscles, enhancing oxygen delivery.

In the early phases of training or when training greatly increases, a short-term sports anemia may develop, though some highly trained endurance athletes may experience a more long-term sports anemia. To determine if true anemia exists, an athlete can be given an iron supplement for one to two months. If hemoglobin rises 1 gram per deciliter, the anemia was probably due in part to iron deficiency.

## IRON DEFICIENCY, PERFORMANCE, AND IRON SUPPLEMENTATION

While transient sports anemia is common and relatively harmless, true iron deficiency is a bit more serious. Prevalence of this condition in athletes, is about the same as in the general population. Data indicates that iron-deficiency anemia is detrimental to performance. This has been determined by giving anemic subjects iron supplements.

When iron levels improve with supplementation, so does performance. However, there is conflicting data regarding the iron depletion that occurs before full anemia sets in. Most well-controlled studies indicate that giving supplements to subjects with iron deficiency, but not full-blown anemia, does improve iron stores, but not performance. However, athletes with iron-deficiency should be treated before the more serious anemia can develop. Additionally, most performance studies only test a single exercise effort, rather than repeated daily efforts. Athletes may experience symptoms even with only iron deficiency, not just full-blown anemia.

Iron supplementation should be used only when warranted. There are dangers associated with taking in too much iron. Two to three out of one thousand Americans have a genetic predisposition that results in iron accumulation in the liver. This condition, known as hemochromatosis, can result in liver destruction. Iron supplements range from 30 to 265 milligrams daily, and can cause uncomfortable gastrointestinal symptoms.

Excess iron can produce other negative side effects. Even doses as low as 25 milligrams per day can inhibit absorption of zinc. Zinc also plays a role in oxygen metabolism and may be marginal in an athlete's diet. High iron stores have also been linked to cancer and heart disease—though no definite link between iron in the diet and risk has been established. Excessively high iron stores may also worsen oxidative injury or free-radical production.

Once an anemia situation has been corrected, athletes, especially women athletes at high risk for anemia, can take a low maintenance dose providing 100 percent of the recommended daily allowance. Large doses should not be taken casually and without follow-up monitoring of iron stores.

## YOU CAN'T GO WRONG WITH FOOD

A common cause of iron deficiency anemia is poor dietary iron intake. Analysis of athletes' diets often reveals an intake below the recommended daily allowance of 10 milligrams for men and 15 milligrams for women. It's especially common in women who may consume lower amounts of calories, follow a modified vegetarian diet, or in athletes who have a poor quality diet. There are several ways to modify your diet to increase iron intake and absorption. Refer to Chapter 6 for suggestions on increasing iron intake and improving iron absorption.

If you suffer from fatigue, it is worth it to have your iron stores checked. If an iron deficiency is identified, plan good food sources of iron into your diet. Take iron supplements appropriately, in the right amounts, and with follow-up testing—all under the guidance of a physician.

## EATING FOR TWO
### CALORIE NEEDS

Eating for two can be easy. After all, building a healthy baby requires a welcome additional 58,000 or so extra calories, starting in the second semester of pregnancy. But what if you are pregnant and want to stay fit and active? It requires knowledge and balance to meet your body's, the baby's, and your exercise energy needs.

Just how much weight should all those calories result in for a healthy weight baby? Your physician will advise you, but generally 25 to 35 pounds is recommended. Underweight or lean women may be advised to gain more—about 28 to 40 pounds.

It all comes down to finding the input and output balance that works best for you and your baby. About 20 pounds of this weight gain reflect changes in your own body weight. Most babies now weigh from 7 to 8 pounds at birth. Fluid, placenta, and other tissues account for the remainder of the weight gain. Your physician will not only monitor your total weight gain, but also the pattern of weight gain to make sure that it is appropriate. Pregnancy is not a time to restrict food or go on a reducing diet. This would put you at risk for developing a low-birth-weight baby. Some fat gain in pregnancy is necessary and healthy.

Total calorie needs for the day are individual and based on your weight and training program. Women who will remain very active should eat 20 calories for every pound of weight. Moderately active women need 15 calories per pound. These calorie levels meet your basic requirements and exercise needs, but what do you need to make a healthy baby?

Pregnancy requires only an additional 300 calories daily, starting in the second trimester in order to build tissues for both you and the baby, and to meet your higher metabolic needs. Protein needs also increase slightly by 10 to 12 grams daily; an amount easily met with food. While eating extra may be easy, it's important that these calories should come from high nutrient foods. After all, your vitamin and mineral needs are elevated, too.

## FOLATE AND IRON

Folate or folic acid deserves serious attention from women even contemplating pregnancy. An adequate folate intake, both prior to conception and during the first several weeks of pregnancy, helps prevent birth defects, particularly spina bifida. Folate is used for synthesis of DNA, the building block of all cells. During the first twenty-eight days of pregnancy, cells divide rapidly and form the neural tubes that become the baby's brain and spine. Like many Americans, you may only consume 236 micrograms of folate daily, falling short of the pregnancy recommended daily allowance of 400 micrograms. Good sources of folate include asparagus, lentils, spinach, kidney beans and orange juice.

Folate is also needed for normal red blood cell development during pregnancy. Since a pregnant women's blood volume increases by 50 percent, any blood-building nutrients are important. Another such nutrient is the mineral iron, with requirements doubling from 15 to 30 milligrams daily during pregnancy. Most pregnant women require an iron supplement, otherwise anemia can develop. Anemia can result in fatigue and shortness of breath, and increase delivery risks. The baby also runs the risk of anemia if iron levels run too low.

## CALCIUM

Aside from iron, calcium is the most important mineral required during pregnancy. It is crucial for building the baby's bones, especially during the last trimester. Your baby will take 300 milligrams of calcium from you daily. You need about 1200 milligrams daily to offset this demand.

Other vitamin and mineral needs increase slightly. This includes the B vitamins involved in processing energy—niacin, riboflavin and thiamin. Vitamin C, E, D, B6 and B12 requirements also go up to amounts still easily met with food. The same goes for your higher need for magnesium and zinc. But what about supplementation?

Stick with the prenatal vitamin prescribed by your physician. Avoid excessive doses. High amounts of vitamin A can cause birth defects, while megadoses of vitamin C can alter the baby's metabolism.

## FLUID

And finally, for pregnant women who exercise strenuously, water remains a very important nutrient, so it is critical to maintain proper hydration. You basic fluid needs are about ten cups daily, plus what you sweat during exercise.

For a healthy baby, certain products should be avoided or limited in your diet. Avoid alcohol because of the severe negative effects it can produce such as fetal alcohol syndrome. Caffeine should be avoided or limited. High intakes have been linked to increase risk of miscarriage. Avoid saccharin, and limit other artificial sweeteners as much as possible. High levels of pesticides and PCBs from fish should be avoided. Large fish like swordfish or shark can be contaminated with mercury, and tuna should be limited to one-half-pound weekly. PCBs may be high in bluefish, mackerel and striped bass. Eat low-fat fish and trim the fat as much as possible.

During pregnancy, build on already good eating habits. A qualified nutritionist can review your diet, help you balance exercise, pregnancy and nutrition, and advise you on the food sources and various nutrients you may be lacking.

## OSTEOPOROSIS CAN AFFECT MEN TOO

Advertising and educational brochures regarding bone health and the prevention and treatment of osteoporosis have long targeted women. Osteoporosis does affect mainly women and as one supplement label describes, "government studies have found that eight of ten women have diets deficient in calcium."

## MEN AND OSTEOPOROSIS

Men can develop osteoporosis, too, and this fact is often ignored. According to the National Osteoporosis Foundation, one-fifth of osteoporotic hip fractures and one-seventh of vertebral fractures occur in men. This year alone one hundred thousand men will suffer related painful hip fractures. Experts project that by the year 2015 up to three-and-a-half million men will have low bone mass, including two-and-a-half million men with osteoporosis.

This statistic is unfortunate when you consider that osteoporosis is a preventable disease. Balancing diet with specific vitamins and minerals, combined with exercise, can leave your bones healthy fifteen years from now. It has long been known that the proper exercise for stimulating osteoblasts, the cells which build bone, is weight-bearing activity and weight-training. So now you may be wondering just how much athletic training can help in building stronger bones and preventing osteoporosis. It may just depend on the sport. But one non-weight bearing sport that appears to put not only women, but men at risk is cycling.

## RESEARCH

One study looked at elite male cyclists and measured their

bone-mineral density. Previously, most men studied had been weight lifters and runners. The study included highly trained cyclists—fourteen of which were U.S. Cycling Federation-licensed cyclists (Categories I to III) and sixteen National Off-Road Bicycle Association riders (expert and professional categories). These cyclists averaged twenty-nine years of age and eleven hours of training weekly, and had been training an average of eight years. None of the cyclists participated in weight training or cross-trained. Twenty-four recreationally active men or "weekend warriors" served as the control group.

Using dual energy X-ray absorptiometry (DEXA), researchers measured total body mineral bone density and bone density at several sites in both the spine and femur. No significant differences in bone-mineral density between the cyclists and controls at any of the measured sites was found. Despite hours and years of training, the cyclists had not benefited by developing greater bone mass.

Researchers were not surprised at these results as cycling is not an impact or weight-bearing exercise, and therefore does not provide an osteogenic stimulus. Loading is what causes the muscles to adapt—the combination of muscles pulling at the bone and the jarring stress of impact. It was hypothesized that there may be enough muscle activity in the hip joint during cycling to benefit bones. But because highly trained cyclists tend to pedal at higher revolutions per minute, the force generated may not be great enough.

Incidentally, the mountain-bike racers had slightly greater bone mass in the femur than the road cyclists, possibly because they train at a lower cadence. However, since much of mountain-bike training is now on the road, this effect may not be significant in the long term.

None of the cyclists studied had bone mass levels placing them at high risk for osteoporosis. Approaching thirty years, they have reached the highest level of bone mass possible. Men generally maintain this bone mass until muscle mass and activity levels tend to decline in their fifties.

### HORMONE LEVELS

Hormone levels in all the men, including testosterone and sex-hormone-binding globulin were also tested. These hormones build bone in men, and can be depleted by overtraining. Bone is constantly being turned over, broken down and rebuilt. With insufficient testosterone, bone may be broken down more rapidly. Hormone levels were found to be within normal in both cyclists and controls indicating hormones did not affect the bone mass readings obtained.

Other studies incorporating male athletes from various sports besides cycling have produced mixed results. Generally, blood testosterone levels seem to fall during long-term exercise and resting levels tend to be low in highly trained endurance athletes.

It's possible that there may be a male counterpart to female athletic amenorrhea, in which there is a blunting of the reproductive system in response to endurance training. The most significant marker of this in men would be a decreased sex drive. Regardless of whether or not this occurs with your training, testosterone levels do decline gradually as men age.

So how can male cyclists, and other men involved in non-weight bearing sports such as swimming, ensure that they have healthy bones? While osteoporosis is underdiagnosed and inadequately researched in men, its risk factors are generally the same in men and women. Men have the advantage of developing bones that are 25 to 30 percent denser than women and do not suffer the accelerated bone loss that menopause triggers in women. But after age sixty-five years, men and women experience the same rate of bone loss. Furthermore, calcium absorption decreases in both sexes as they advance in age.

## PREVENTING OSTEOPOROSIS

To help build greater bone mass, start with incorporating the correct types of exercise into your training. Based on the data available so far, it would be wise for cyclists and athletes in other non-weight bearing sports such as swimming to weight-train and cross-train. But more studies need to be done. For instance, training weekend warriors over the course of a year and see what changes in bone mass occur with cycling would be beneficial.

Like exercise, nutrition plays a large role in osteoporosis prevention. Men's diets seem to become calcium deficient around age twenty-five, with two-thirds of men not meeting the recommended amount of 1200 milligrams daily of dairy foods, which are very concentrated sources of calcium. Skim milk and yogurt are excellent low-fat sources, while cheese is high in saturated fat. Good calcium sources also include frozen yogurt, dried peas and beans, refried beans, and tofu processed with calcium. Vegetables—which are good sources of calcium—include bok choy, broccoli, kale, mustard greens and turnip greens. Figs and corn tortillas also contain some calcium.

Vitamin D is an important nutrient that aids in calcium absorption. You need about 400 IU daily. Ten to fifteen minutes of sunlight daily will allow your body to absorb adequate vitamin D. Milk is also an excellent source, though other dairy foods are not. Magnesium is a mineral that helps maintain the bone matrix. Good sources of magnesium include green, leafy vegetables, nuts and seeds, legumes, and whole grains such as whole wheat bread, whole wheat pasta and brown rice.

As with dietary deficiencies, dietary excesses can contribute to development of osteoporosis. Excess sodium results in increased calcium excretion in the urine, as does excess protein consumption. Every time you double the amount of protein you eat, calcium urine losses increase by 50 percent. Excessive caffeine—from coffee, tea and cola—and excessive phosphate intake—mainly from carbonated beverages—combined with a low calcium intake can also increase osteoporosis risk. Finally, excessive alcohol intake is associated with this disease. Drinking alcohol may even harm the osteoblasts themselves and decrease absorption of bone building minerals.

Osteoporosis may seem an unlikely or remote possibility for all athletes. Like many other steps taken in disease prevention, proper exercise and the right diet, the pay-offs are far from immediate. But taking the guidelines described above seriously may result in more years of training and competition.

## MIXING ALCOHOL WITH TRAINING

Perhaps during various times of the year, such as the holiday season, you put aside strict training rules and drink a little more alcohol than usual. While alcohol is not something you need to avoid entirely, you should know what effect even moderate alcohol consumption has on training performance and health.

### THE "FOOD" DRUG

Though it is a drug, at 7 calories per gram, alcohol provides only slightly less energy than fat (9 calories per gram), and about twice as much as carbohydrate and protein (4 calories per gram). One-half an ounce of pure ethyl alcohol is considered one drink and is the amount found in 12 ounces of beer (150 calories), 4 ounces of wine (100 calories) and 1.25 ounces of liquor (100 calories).

Though you may value alcohol as a social beverage, to your body it is merely a bunch of empty calories that has little food value and few nutrients. While beer and wine contain small amounts of carbohydrate and only trace amounts of protein, vitamins and minerals, they certainly don't offer any immediate and tangible dietary benefits. You would have to consume about twelve cans of beer to meet the recommended daily allowance for riboflavin. Heavy alcohol consumption can even drain your body of vitamins such as thiamin.

## BREAKING IT DOWN

Your body can absorb alcohol quite rapidly, especially if you haven't eaten for several hours. Twenty percent of consumed alcohol is absorbed into the bloodstream through the stomach, with the remainder absorbed through the intestines. The alcohol is then distributed throughout the body. Alcohol dehydrogenate, the enzyme that breaks down alcohol, first attacks it in the stomach and then in the liver.

Alcohol is distributed all over your body, and is diluted by its water content. A small amount, about 3 to 10 percent, is excreted by your kidneys, and in breath and sweat, but the majority is metabolized by the liver. As the blood circulates, the liver of an average adult male will metabolize somewhat less than the amount of alcohol found in "one drink." Smaller athletes will take longer to metabolize alcohol, as will women who make less of the enzyme alcohol dehydrogenate.

Despite originating from fermented carbohydrates, alcohol is actually metabolized like a fat. The liver converts alcohol metabolic by-products into fatty acids, which are then stored in the liver or sent to the bloodstream. So it may come as no surprise that research indicates excess alcohol may truly result in developing a "beer belly."

Much has been made in recent years of moderate alcohol consumption offering protection from heart disease. While alcohol may slightly raise the protective high-density lipoprotein circulating in your bloodstream, overconsumption of alcohol may increase your risk of developing obesity and related health risks. Depositing extra fat in your abdominal area increases a measurement known as the waist to hip ratio. This elevated ratio is often associated with a lipid profile of a high triglyceride combined with a low high-density lipoprotien—indicating an increased risk of heart disease.

Wine, especially red wine, has also received much attention in preventing heart disease. However, much of wine's antioxidant properties can also be obtained by eating a wide variety of fruits and vegetables. But all this doesn't mean that alcohol can't be part of a healthy training diet.

## ALCOHOL AND PERFORMANCE

Most theories surrounding alcohol as an ergogenic aid have focused on its psychological effects. Athletes may use alcohol to unwind and calm frayed nerves from intense competition or to celebrate. But too much alcohol too soon after training or racing will impede recovery, when other fluids should take priority.

Though you may rehydrate well after training, alcohol is a diuretic and causes your body to lose at least as much fluid as it takes in. That's why you need to replace losses after drinking even moderate amounts of alcohol. While moderate social drinking can be part of a healthy training diet for some athletes, consuming alcohol above personal tolerance or too close to training and racing could be detrimental to performance. Alcohol exerts this negative effect through a number of adverse psychomotor and physiological effects.

Excessive alcohol consumed the night before a day of training or racing can impair fine motor ability and coordination. Reaction time could be delayed as would the brain's ability to process information and react to it. Obviously, these effects could hurt performance, as well as compromise the safety of yourself and other athletes. Knowing your personal tolerance and how it can change is important.

Though alcohol can increase fat stores, there is no evidence that it can be used as fuel during training. Because of alcohol's detour to the liver, it would take too much time for its metabolic by-products to reach exercising muscles. Even if the energy from alcohol could be used, it would be inefficient. Burning alcohol for energy takes more oxygen than burning carbohydrate and fat. And finally, because only a certain amount of alcohol can be metabolized by the liver each hour, it would be a limited energy source, especially when training at high intensities.

Alcohol may also interfere with glucose metabolism during exercise. One study reported a significant decrease in aerobic endurance when alcohol was consumed before and during a treadmill run at 80 to 85 percent $VO_2$ max. The liver's ability to make glucose, which is sent to your bloodstream, is also impaired, making it more likely that your blood sugar level could decrease.

Consuming alcohol during cold weather is also not advisable. Alcohol does increase blood flow to your skin, bringing about a feeling of warmth, but this effect can result in considerable heat loss, drain heat from the central part of your body, and lower body temperature. Safer and more warming beverages would be hot cider, hot cocoa, and hot tea with honey.

TOM MORAN

*Adequate iron intake and monitoring bodily iron levels to prevent anemia are important during Olympic speed skating races (here showing Chris Witty).*

Besides the obvious safety concerns regarding excessive alcohol intake, there are also long-term health effects. The most obvious is liver failure, and alcohol has also been linked to certain cancers, heart disease, high blood pressure and stroke.

If alcohol is normally part of your diet during the competition season, keep it moderate. Know your personal tolerance so you don't experience any ill effects the next day for competition and training. And, this should go without saying, don't drive when you drink.

## FINAL THOUGHTS

There are specific nutritional considerations for situations such as muscle cramping, injury rehabilitation, iron deficiency anemia, pregnancy and training, osteoporosis prevention, and incorporating alcohol into a training diet. It may be beneficial to consult with a registered dietitian and sports nutritionist to address some of these unique nutritional concerns.

# CHAPTER SEVENTEEN

# The Vegetarian Athlete

*"We did have a vegetarian on our team, so she was very careful about taking a vitamin and mineral supplement."*

*—Tueting*

In recent years, many nutritionally aware athletes have decreased their intake of fatty meats. Some have even gone a step further and replaced animal proteins with plant proteins. Whether these changes are for health, environmental, animal-rights or taste issues, athletes should strive to make sure that vegetarian eating is wholesome and balanced. Presently, vegetarians make up about 7 to 10 percent of the U.S. population.

Vegetarian is a term that actually incorporates a range of dietary restrictions. Individuals who refer to themselves as vegetarian consume mainly a plant-based diet and may follow any one of the guidelines below:

- *Semi- or near-vegetarians: eat small amounts of fish, poultry, eggs, and dairy, but avoid red meat*
- *Pesco-vegetarians: eat fish, dairy and eggs*
- *Lacto-ovo-vegetarian: eat dairy food and eggs*
- *Ovo-vegetarians: eat eggs*
- *Total vegetarians or vegans: eat no animal foods whatsoever*

Depending on what type of vegetarian diet you currently follow or desire to adopt, pay close attention to specific nutrients food sources. When certain foods are eliminated from your diet, so are their vitamins and minerals, making it necessary to include alternative sources or take an appropriate supplement.

Some possible questions regarding a vegetarian diet are:

- *How can I obtain enough protein from a vegetarian diet?*
- *What are some good sources of calcium, iron and zinc?*
- *How do I obtain enough $B_{12}$ and vitamin D in my diet?*

## PROTEIN

Protein is formed from the building blocks called amino acids. There are twenty amino acids that combine to form an endless variety of proteins. Eleven of these amino acids are produced by our bodies; the other nine are called "essential" because we must obtain them from food. Vegetarians of all types must choose the proper foods in the correct amounts in order to obtain enough of these essential amino acids.

Poultry, fish, milk, yogurt and eggs, all provide adequate amounts of these nine essential amino acids. Soybeans, soy products and quinoa—a grain product—are also considered high-quality protein. Plant proteins or non-animal proteins usually contain all of the nine essential amino acids. However, levels of one or two of these amino acids may be low in plant foods. For example, the levels of the amino acid lysine is lower in grains, as are the levels of methionine lower in beans, than levels found in animal protein.

Years ago, vegetarians were advised to combine a food low in one amino acid with another food containing large amounts of that particular amino acid. Actually, we now know that this strict protein "complementing" at meals is not necessary. Even vegans, who completely avoid all animal products, can obtain plenty of protein. But in order to do so, the diet must be balanced, filled with variety, and most importantly, contain enough calories to meet energy requirements.

How much you need to be conscious of incorporating good quality plant proteins, depends on the type of vegetarian diet you follow. Semi-vegetarians who limit red meat and may have smaller portions of poultry, really should have no problems intaking enough protein. Even lacto-ovo-vegetarians receive a complete amino acid profile from eggs, cheese and milk. It's with a stricter vegan diet that a heavy focus on quality plant proteins becomes important.

But chances are that any type of vegetarian desires to incorporate more plant-based meals into their diet. And one of the best steps for doing this is by incorporating more beans, peas and lentils—otherwise known as legumes—into your diet. A half-cup serving of beans provides 110 to 140

### TABLE 17.1: PROTEIN CONTENT OF SELECTED PLANT FOODS

| FOOD | PORTION | PROTEIN IN GMS |
|---|---|---|
| TEMPEH | 1 CUP | 31 |
| SOYBEANS, COOKED | 1 CUP | 29 |
| SEITAN | 4 OUNCES | 21 |
| TOFU, FIRM | 4 OUNCES | 20 |
| LENTILS, COOKED | 1 CUP | 18 |
| KIDNEY BEANS, COOKED | 1 CUP | 15 |
| LIMA BEANS, COOKED | 1 CUP | 15 |
| CHICKPEAS, COOKED | 1 CUP | 15 |
| BLACK BEANS, COOKED | 1 CUP | 15 |
| PINTO BEANS, COOKED | 1 CUP | 14 |
| QUINOA, COOKED | 1 CUP | 11 |
| SOY YOGURT | 1 CUP | 10 |
| SOY MILK | 1 CUP | 10 |
| TOFU, REGULAR | 4 OUNCES | 10 |
| PEANUT BUTTER | 2 TBS | 8 |
| SUNFLOWER SEEDS | 1/4 CUP | 8 |
| PEAS, COOKED | 1 CUP | 8 |
| BULGAR, COOKED | 1 CUP | 6 |
| BAGEL | 1 MEDIUM | 6 |
| ALMONDS | 1/4 CUP | 5.5 |
| BROWN RICE, COOKED | 1 CUP | 5 |
| WHOLE WHEAT BREAD | 2 SLICES | 5 |
| POTATO | 1 MEDIUM | 4.5 |

calories and 6 to 9 grams of protein. Table 17.1 lists some excellent plant sources of protein.

Besides being a good source of protein, beans are loaded with B vitamins, especially folacin. Minerals supplied by beans include potassium, iron and calcium. Needless to say beans are very low in fat—soybeans are slightly higher—and besides their good protein content, are high in complex carbohydrate, which fuels sports performance. And if that isn't enough, beans are also a great source of fiber.

## ENERGY NEEDS

Vegetarian athletes should take great care to meet energy requirements. First, obtaining adequate energy means that the protein or amino acids consumed will be used for tissue building and repair. If calories fall short, these amino acids may be converted and used for more immediate energy requirements. While your intentions may be the best, obtaining enough energy on a vegetarian diet may be tricky for an athlete in training.

With all the plant foods and fiber they provide, vegetarian diets can be quite filling. You should probably keep a food record to determine that you are reaching a daily carbohydrate prescription. Try to fill up on more concentrated carbohydrates such as beans, peas, corn, potatoes, yams, rice, dried fruit, fruit juice, Grapenuts and pasta. There may also be some room for fat in your diet. More nutritious sources include nuts, seeds and peanut butter. Remember too, that cooked vegetables will provide more calories and less bulk than a raw salad.

## VITAMIN AND MINERAL NEEDS
### CALCIUM

Milk, yogurt and cheese are excellent sources of calcium, though low fat choices should be emphasized for heart health. However, many plant foods are also excellent sources of calcium. Table 17.2 shows selected sources of calcium. Tofu is often recommended as a good source of calcium, but actual calcium content depends on the coagulating protein used in the process of making tofu. Tofu prepared with calcium sul-

| TABLE 17.2: CALCIUM CONTENT OF SELECTED PLANT FOODS | | |
|---|---|---|
| **FOOD** | **PORTION** | **CALCIUM MGS** |
| TOFU, FIRM, PROCESSED WITH CALCIUM SULFATE | 4 OUNCES | 250 MGS |
| TOFU, REGULAR, PROCESSED WITH CALCIUM SULFATE | 4 OUNCES | 120 MGS |
| COLLARD GREENS, COOKED | 1 CUP | 357 |
| RHUBARB, COOKED | 1 CUP | 348 |
| SOY OR RICE MILK, PLAIN, CALCIUM FORTIFIED | 8 OUNCES | 200 |
| SPINACH, COOKED | 1 CUP | 278 |
| BLACKSTRAP, MOLASSES | 2 TBS | 274 |
| TURNIP GREENS, COOKED | 1 CUP | 249 |
| KALE, COOKED | 1 CUP | 179 |
| SESAME SEEDS | 2 TBS | 176 |
| OKRA, COOKED | 1 CUP | 176 |
| SOYBEANS, COOKED | 1 CUP | 175 |
| BEET GREENS, COOKED | 1 CUP | 165 |
| BOK CHOY, COOKED | 1 CUP | 158 |
| TEMPEH | 1 CUP | 154 |
| MUSTARD GREENS, COOKED | 1 CUP | 150 |
| FIGS, DRIED OR FRESH | 5 MEDIUM | 135 |
| TAHINI | 2 TBS | 128 |
| SWISS CHARD, COOKED | 1 CUP | 102 |

fate will be highest in calcium, though this will vary among brands. Generally, firm tofu will contain more calcium.

Overall, plant sources of calcium, such as kale and collard greens, are well absorbed. However, oxalic acid found in spinach, rhubarb, chard and beet greens binds with calcium and reduces absorption of this mineral. Therefore, these foods should not be depended upon for their calcium content. Vegetarians may want to supplement low fat sources of dairy foods with these plant sources, while vegans should aim for three servings daily of the foods listed in Table 17.2.

## IRON

Though heme iron from animal sources is well absorbed, vegetarians can emphasize high iron plant foods such as many varieties of beans, spinach and greens. Including plenty of high vitamin C sources in the diet, which many vegetarians do, will improve the amount of non-heme iron absorbed from these foods. Beans mixed with some type of tomato sauce are a great example, as is tofu mixed with broccoli. Some food items may reduce iron absorption, such as the tannins found in regular tea. Herbal teas do not contain these tannins.

## ZINC

Meats are good sources of zinc, but pesco-vegetarians can benefit from the zinc found in fish, especially shellfish. Zinc is an important mineral involved in many enzyme functions. Good plant sources include black-eyed peas, garbanzo beans, lentils, lima beans, brown rice and wheat germ.

## VITAMIN D

Vitamins D is essential for optimal calcium absorption. Only egg yolks and fatty fish are naturally occurring sources of vitamin D. Milk and butter, which contain vitamin D, have actually been fortified with this nutrient.

Humans, however, can make vitamin D from sunlight. Ten to fifteen minutes of sun exposure on the hands and face several times a week is adequate in summertime. But sun exposure may not be adequate in certain climates during October through April. Older individuals may not make vitamin D as easily from sunlight. Sunsceen will also reduce the amount of vitamin D produced. Vegans should consider a vitamin D supplement.

## VITAMIN B12

Plant foods only contain vitamin $B_{12}$ when they are contaminated by microorganisms. The human intestinal tract does make some vitamin $B_{12}$, but this is generally not well absorbed. While $B_{12}$ vitamin requirements are low, deficiencies can have serious complications and could even lead to irreversible nerve damage.

Milk products provide $B_{12}$, but vegans need to look for alternative sources. Tempeh and miso may be labeled as having $B_{12}$, but are not always reliable sources. $B_{12}$ fortified foods, such as fortified soymilk, would be better choices. A supplement containing 100 percent of the recommended daily allowance may also be beneficial for vegans.

Another B vitamin that vegans should pay close attention to is riboflavin. While milk, meat and eggs are good sources, plant sources include brewer's yeast, wheat germ, soybeans, avocados, green leafy vegetables, and enriched breads and cereals.

## VEGETARIAN MEAL PLANNING

Depending on the type of vegetarian diet you follow, focus on obtaining enough servings daily from various food groups. Semi-vegetarians and pesco-vegetarians may only consume small amounts of animal proteins and fish, and should probably supplement their diet with plenty of low-fat dairy foods, and bean, lentils and tofu.

Of course, lacto-ovo-vegetarians also obtain plenty of quality protein from dairy foods, but should have up to three servings daily, as this will be their only animal source of protein. Additionally, they also require amino acids from beans, legumes, lentils and tofu. Higher-fat nuts and seeds will also supply some quality protein.

Vegans need to be certain to obtain larger servings of beans, lentils and peas, as well as nuts and seeds. All types of vegetarians should consume adequate servings of whole grains as they supply both amino acids and carbohydrates.

## FINAL THOUGHTS

Balanced vegetarian eating and athletic training are compatible. However, in the typical American food environment, this requires knowledge and planning to achieve a diet adequate in protein and calories. Vegetarians should pay close attention to consuming food sources of calcium, vitamin D, iron, zinc and certain B vitamins.

Well-planned vegetarian diets also promote good health and disease prevention.

# REFERENCES

CHAPTER 1: ENERGY AND YOUR TRAINING DIET

McArdle, W.D., Katch, F., and Katch, V., Exercise Physiology: Energy, Nutrition, and Human Performance. Williams and Wilkins, Baltimore, MD, 1996.

Williams, M., *Nutrition for Health, Fitness, and Sport*. WCB/McGraw-Hill, Madison, WI, 1999.

Hawley, J. and Burke, L., *Peak Performance: Training and Nutritional Strategies for Sport*. Allen and Unwin, NSW, Australia, 1998.


CHAPTER 2: FLUID FIRST

Maughan, R., *Rehydration and Recovery After Exercise*. Gatorade Sports Science Institute, Vol. 9, No.3, Chicago, 1996.

Fluids 2000. *Gatorade Sports Science Institute*. Chicago, 1998.


CHAPTER 3: CARBOHYDRATES TO FUEL YOUR FIRE

Akermark, C. et al. 1996. "Diet and muscle glycogen concentration in relation to physical performance in Swedish elite ice hockey players." *International Journal of Sport Nutrition* 6: 272-284.

Blom, T. et al. 1987. "The effects of different post-exercise sugar diets on the rate of muscle glycogen resynthesis." *Medicine and Science in Sports and Exercise* 19: 491-496.

Burke, L., et al. 1993. "Muscle glycogen storage after prolonged exercise: Effect of the glycemic index of carbohydrate feedings." *Journal of Applied Physiology* 75: 1019-1023.

Burke, L., et al. 1996. "Muscle glycogen storage after prolonged exercise: Effect of frequency of the frequency of carbohydrate feedings." *American Journal of Clinical Nutrition* 64: 115-119.

Costill, D.L., et al. 1981. "The role of dietary carbohydrates in muscle glycogen resynthesis after strenuous running." *American Journal of Clinical Nutrition* 34: 1831-1836.

Fallowfield, J., et al. 1995. "The influence of ingesting a carbohydrate-electrolyte beverage during 4 hrs of recovery on subsequent endurance capacity." *International Journal of Sport Nutrition* 5: 285-299.

Foster-Powell, K., and Brand-Miller, J. 1995. "International tables of glycemic index." *American Journal of Clinical Nutrition* 62 (supplement): 871-893.

Ivy, J.L., et al. 1988. "Muscle glycogen storage after different amounts of carbohydrate ingestion." *Journal of Applied Physiology* 64 (5): 2018-2023.

Ivy, J.L., et al, 1988. "Muscle glycogen synthesis after exercise: effect of time of carbohydrate ingestion," 64 (4): 1480-1485.

Kirwan, J.P., et al. 1988. "Carbohydrate balance in competitive runners during successive days of intense training," 65 (6): 2601-2606.

Lamb, D., et al. 1990. "Dietary carbohydrate and intensity of interval swim training." *American Journal of Clinical Nutrition* 52: 1058-1063.

Nicholas, C.W., et al. 1997. "Carbohydrate intake and recovery of intermittent running capacity." *International Journal of Sport Nutrition* 7: 251-260.

Parkin, J., et al. 1997. "Muscle glycogen storage following prolonged exercise: effect of timing of ingestion of high glycemic index food." *Medicine and Science in Sport and Exercise* 29: 220-224.

Pizza, F., et al. 1995. "A carbohydrate loading regimen improves high intensity, short duration exercise performance." *International Journal of Sport Nutrition* 5: 110-116.

Reed, M.J., et al. 1989. "Muscle glycogen storage postexercise: effect of mode of carbohydrate administration." *Journal of Applied Physiology* 66 (2): 720-726.

Sherman, W.M., et al. 1993. "Dietary carbohydrate, muscle glycogen, and exercise performance during 7 d of successive training." *American Journal of Clinical Nutrition* 57: 27-31.

Sherman, W.M., and Wimer, G. 1991. "Insufficient dietary carbohydrate during training: Does it impair athletic performance?" *International Journal of Sport Nutrition* 1: 28-44.

Simonsen, J. C., et al. 1991. "Dietary carbohydrate, muscle glycogen, and power output during rowing training." *Journal of Applied Physiology* 70: 1500-1505.

Tarnopolsky, M.A., et al. 1997. "Postexercise protein-carbohydrate and carbohydrate supplements increase -1883. muscle glycogen in men and women." *Journal of Applied Physiology* 83 (6): 1877

Walberg-Rankin, J. 1995. "Dietary carbohydrate as an ergogenic aid for prolonged and brief competitions in sport." *International Journal of Sport Nutrition* 5: S13-S28.

Williams, M. *Nutrition for Health, Fitness, and Sport, 5th Edition.* WCB/McGraw-Hill, Madison, WI, 1999.


CHAPTER 4: THAT MATTER OF FAT

AHA Medical/Scientific Statement. 1996. "Dietary Guidelines for Healthy American Adults: A Statement for Health Professionals From the Nutrition Committee." *Circulation* 94 (7).

*AHA Recommendation of Fat Intake.* 1997. American Heart Association.

Coyle, E. 1995. "Fat Metabolism During Exercise." *Gatorade Sports Science Exchange* 8 (6).

Lambert, E., et al. 1994. "Enhanced endurance performance during moderate intensity exercise following 2 week adaptation to a high-fat diet in trained cyclist." *European Journal of Applied Physiology* 69: 287-293.

Muoio, D., et al. 1994. "Effect of dietary fat on metabolic adjustments to maximal VO2 max and endurance in runners." *Medicine and Science in Sport and Exercise* 26: 81-88.

Phinney, S., et al. 1983. "The human metabolic response to chronic ketosis without caloric restriction: preservation of submaximal exercise capability with reduced carbohydrate oxidation." *Metabolism* 32: 769-776.


CHAPTER 5: THE POWER OF PROTEIN

Butterfield, G. 1991. "Amino Acid and High Protein Diets. In Perspectives in Exercise Science and Sports Medicine. Ergogenics: Enhancement of Sports Performance," eds. D. Lamb and M. Williams. Benchmark Press, Indianapolis, IN.

Lemon, P., et al. 1992. "Protein requirements and muscle mass/strength changes during intensive training in novice bodybuilders." *Journal of Applied Physiology* 73: 767-775.

Lemon, P., et al. 1995. "Do Athletes Need More Dietary Protein and Amino Acids." *International Journal of Sport Nutrition* 5: S39-61.

Kreider, R., et al. 1993. "Amino Acid supplementation and exercise performance: Analysis of the proposed ergogenic value." *Sports Medicine* 16: 190-209.

Tarnopolsky, M., et al. 1992. "Evaluation of protein requirements for strength trained athletes." *Journal of Applied Physiology* 73: 1986-1995.


CHAPTER 6: VITAMINS AND MINERALS FOR YOUR ACTIVE LIFE

Alpha-tocopherol, Beta-carotene, Cancer Prevention Study Group. 1994. "The effect of vitamin E and beta-carotene on the incidence of lung cancer and other cancers in male smokers." *New England Journal of Medicine* 330: 1029-1035.

American Dietetic Association. 1996. "Position of the American Dietetic Association: Vitamin and Mineral Supplementation." *Journal of the American Dietetic Association* 96: 73-77.

American Dietetic Association. 1998. "Translating the Science Behind the Dietary Reference Intakes." *Journal of the American Dietetic Association* 98: 756.

Chandra, R. 1992. "Effect of vitamin and trace element supplementation on immune responses and infection in elderly subjects." *Lancet* 340: 1124-1127.

Clarkson, P. 1995. "Antioxidants and physical performance. Critical Reviews in Food Science and Nutrition" 35: 131-141.

Clarkson, P. and Haymes, E. 1994. "Trace mineral requirements for athletes." *International Journal of Sport Nutrition* 4: 104-119.

*Environmental Nutrition.* 1997. "As Beta-carotene Promise Fades, Focus Turns to Other Carotenoids." 20 (8).

*Environmental Nutrition.* 1998. "Folic Acid: Once Overlooked, Now a Nutrient on the Brink of Stardom." 21 (1).

*Environmental Nutrition.* 1996. "Beyond Calcium: Nutrition Strategies to Protect Your Bones." 19 (12).

*Environmental Nutrition.* 1998. "Vitamin C Earns and 'A' for Health Benefits; Do You Get Enough?" 21 (6).

*Environmental Nutrition.* 1996. "Vitamin E: Does Evidence Defy Usual Advice to Rely on Foods, not Pills?" 19 (9).

Fogelholm , M. 1995. "Indicators of vitamin and mineral status in athlete's blood: A review." *International Journal of Sport Nutrition* 5 (267-284).

Gatorade Sports Science Institute. 1992. "Exercise, Nutrition, and Free Radicals: What's the Connection? Sports Science Exchange Roundtable" 5 (94): 1-4.

Goldfarb, A. 1993. "Antioxidants: Role of supplementation to prevent exercise-induced oxidative stress. Medicine and Science in Sports and Exercise" 25: 232-236.

Lukaski, H., 1995. "Micronutrients (magnesium, zinc, and copper): Are mineral supplements needed for athletes?" *International Journal of Sport Nutrition* 5: S74-S83.

Pennington, J. et al. 1997. "Derivation of Daily Values used for nutrition labeling." *Journal of the American Dietetic Association* 97: 1407-1412.

Peters, E., et al. 1993. "Vitamin C supplementation reduces the incidence of postrace symptoms of upper-respiratory-tract infection in ultramarathon runners." *American Journal of Clinical Nutrition* 57: 170-174.

Telford, R., et al. 1992. "The effect of 7 to 7 months of vitamin-mineral supplementation on athletic performance." *International Journal of Sport Nutrition* 4: 104-109.

Yates, A., et al. 1998. "Dietary reference intakes: The new basis for recommendations for calcium and related nutrients, B vitamins, and choline." *Journal of the American Dietetic Association* 98: 699-706.

## CHAPTER 7: PUTTING TOGETHER YOUR TRAINING DIET

Pennington, J. Food Values of Portions Commonly Used. Perennial Library-Harper & Row, New York, NY, 1991

American Diabetes Association, Inc. and American Dietetic Association, 1995. *Exchange Lists for Weight Management.*

## CHAPTER 8 : PLANNING AND PREPARING YOUR TRAINING DIET

Brody, J., 1985, *Jane Brody's Good Food Book*, Bantam Books, New York, NY.

FDA, 1993. "Focus on Food Labeling." *FDA Consumer: An FDA Special Report*

Tribole, E. 1992. *Eating on the Run*, 2nd Edtion, Leisure Press, Champaign, IL.

Tufts University Health and Nutrition Letter. 1998. "It's 6 p.m. Do you know where your kitchen is?" 16 (6).

CHAPTER 9: DIETARY RULES FOR RESTAURANTS AND THE ROAD

Warshaw, H. 1995. *The Restaurant Companion: A guide to healthier eating out*, 2nd edtion. Surrey Books, Chicago, IL


CHAPTER 10: NUTRITION BEFORE TRAINING AND COMPETITION

Anderson, M., et al. 1994. "Prelacies meal affects ride time to fatigue in trained cyclists." *Journal of the American Dietetic Association* 94 (10): 1152-1153.

Coyle, E., et al. 1985. "Substrate usage during prolonged exercise following a preexercise meal." *Journal of Applied Physiology* 59 (2): 429-433.

Fabbraio, M.A., et al. 1996. "Carbohydrate feedings before prolonged exercise: Effect of glycemic index on muscle glycogenolysis and exercise performance." *Journal of Applied Physiology* 81: 1115-1120.

Goforth, H., et al. 1997. "Persistence of supercompensated muscle glycogen in trained subjects after carbohydrate loading." *Journal of Applied Physiology* 82: 342-347.

Hawley, J., et al. 1997. "Carbohydrate loading and exercise performance." An update. Sports Medicine 24: 73-81.

Siefert, J., et al. 1994. "Glycemic and insulinemic response to preexercise carbohydrate feeding." *International Journal of Sport Nutrition.* 4: 46-53.

Sherman, W.M. 1989. Pre-event nutrition. *Sports Science Exchange* 12 (2).

Sherman, W.M., et al. 1989. "Effects of 4 h preexercise carbohydrate feedings on cycling performance." *Medicine and Science in Sports and Exercise* 21 (5): 598-604.

Sherman, W.M., et al. 1991. "Carbohydrate feedings 1 h before exercise improves cycling performance." *American Journal of Clinical Nutrition* 54: 866-870.

Siefert, J., et al. 1994. "Glycemic and insulinemic response to preexercise carbohydrate feedings." *International Journal of Sport Nutrition* 4: 46-53.

Thomas, D., et al. 1991. "Carbohydrate feeding before exercise: Effect of glycemic index." *International Journal of Sports Medicine* 12: 180-186.

CHAPTER 11: EATING RIGHT DURING TRAINING AND COMPETITION

Ball, T., et al. 1995. "Periodic carbohydrate replacement during 50 min of high intensity cycling improves subsequent sprint performance." *International Journal of Sport Nutrition* 5; 151-158.

Below, P., et al. 1995. "Fluid and carbohydrate ingestion independently improve performance during 1 h intense exercise." *Medicine and Science in Sports and Exercise* 27: 200-210.

Coleman, E. 1994. "Update on carbohydrate: Solid versus liquid." *International Journal of Sport Nutrition* 4; 80-88.

Coyle, E., and Montain, S. 1992. Carbohydrate and fluid ingestion during exercise: Are there trade-offs? *Medicine and Science in Sports and Exercise* 24: 671-678.

El-Sayed, M., et al. "Effects of carbohydrate feeding before and during prolonged exercise and subsequent maximal exercise performance capacity." *International Journal of Sport Nutrition* 5: 215-224.

Gatorade Sports Science Institute. 1993. Hyponatremia in Sport: Symptoms and Prevention. *Sports Science Roundtable* 8 (2).

Horswill, C., et al. 1998. "Effective Fluid Replacement." *International Journal of sport Nutrition* 8 (2): 175-195.

Jendendrup, A., et al. 1997. "Carbohydrate-electrolyte feeding improve 1 h time trial cycling performance." *International Journal of Sports Medicine* 18: 125-129.

Kang, J., et al. 1995. "Effect of carbohydrate ingestion subsequent to carbohydrate supercompensation on endurance performance." *International Journal of Sport Nutrition* 5: 329-343.

Mason, W., et al. 1993. Carbohydrate ingestion during exercise: Liquid versus solid feedings. *Medicine and Science in Sport and Exercise* 25: 966-969.

McConnell, G., et al. Effect of timing of carbohydrate ingestion during exercise performance. *Medicine and Science in Sport and Exercise* 28: 1300-1304.

Millard-Stafford, M., et al. 1992. Carbohydrate-electrolyte replacement improves distance running performance in the heat. *Medicine and Science in Sports and Exercise* 24: 943-940.

Shirreffs, S., et al. 1996. Post-exercise rehydration in man: effect of volume consumed and drink sodium content. *Medicine and Science in Sports and Exercise* 28 (10): 1260-1271.

Yaspelkis, B., et al. 1993. "Carbohydrate supplementation spares muscle glycogen during variable-intensity exercise." *Journal of Applied Physiology* 75: 1477-1485.

CHAPTER 12: BODY COMPOSITION AND PERFORMANCE

Heyward, V. 1998. "Practical body composition assessment for children, adults, and older adults." *International Journal of Sport Nutrition* 8: 285-307.

Williams, M. 1999. *Nutrition for Health, Fitness, and Sport,* 4th edition. WCB/McGraw-Hill, Madison, WI.


CHAPTER 13: CHANGING BODY COMPOSITION

American College of Sports Medicine. 1996. ACSM Position Stand: The Female Athlete Triad. *Medicine and Science in Sports and Exercise* 29 (5):i-ix.

American Dietetic Association. 1997. "Position of the ADA: Weight Management." *Journal of the American Dietetic Association* 97: 71-74.

Beal, K. and Manore, M. 1994. "The prevalence and consequences of subclinical eating disorders in female athletes." *International Journal of Sports Nutrition* 4: 175-195.

Benson, J., et al. "Nutritional aspects of amennorrhea in the female athlete triad." *International Journal of Sport Nutrition* 6: 134-145.

Brownell, K., Rodin, J., and Wilmore, J., editors. 1992. *Eating, Body Weight, and Performance in Athletes: Disorders of Modern Society.* Lea and Febiger, Philadelphia, PA.

Conley, M. and Stone, M. 1996. Carbohydrate ingestion-supplementation for resistance exercise and training. *Sports Medicine* 21: 7-17.

Gatorade Sports Science Institute. 1995. Methods of weight gain in athletes. *Sports Science Exchange* 6 (3): 1-4.

Hill, J., and Commerford. R. 1996. "Physical activity, fat balance, and energy balance." *International Journal of Sport Nutrition* 6: 80-92.

Pascoe, D. and Gladden, L. 1996. Muscle glycogen resynthesis after short term, high intensity exercise and resistance exercise. *Sports Medicine* 21: 98-118.

Peters, P., et al. "Questionable dieting behaviors are used by young adults regardless of sex or student status." *Journal of the American Dietetic*

*Association* 96: 709-711.

Roy, B. and Tarnopolsky, M., et al. 1998. "Influence of differing macronutrient intakes on muscle glycogen resynthesis after resistance exercise." *Journal of Applied Physiology* 84 (3): 890-896.

Roy, R., et al. 1997. "Effect of glucose supplement timing on protein metabolism after resistance training." *Journal of Applied Physiology* 82 (6): 1882-1888.

Thompson, J., et al. 1995. Daily energy expenditure in male endurance athletes with differing energy intakes. *Medicine and Science in Sports and Exercise* 27: 347-354.

Thompson, J., et al. 1996. "Effects of diet and diet-plus-exercise programs on resting metabolic rate: a meta-analysis." *International Journal of Sport Nutrition* 6: 41-61.

Tribole, E. and Resch, E. 1995. *Intuitive Eating: A Recovery Book for the Chronic Dieter.* St. Martin's Press, New York, NY.

## CHAPTER 14: EVALUATING NUTRITIONAL ERGOGENIC AIDS

Burke, L., and Heeley, P. 1994. Dietary supplements and nutritional ergogenic aids in sport, from *Clinical Sports Nutrition,* McGraw-Hill, Sydney, Australia. 227-284.

Council for Responsible Nutrition. 1994. *The Dietary Supplement Health and Education Act of 1994: Summary and Analysis.* Washington, DC.

Food and Drug Administration. 1994. *Dietary Supplement Health and Education Act of 1994.* FDA: Center for Food Safety and Applied Nutrition.

William, M. 1998. *The Ergogenics Edge.* Human Kinetics, Champaign, IL.

## CHAPTER 15: THE LATEST ON SOME POPULAR ERGOGENIC AIDS

Berning, J. and nelson Steen, S, editors. 1998. *Nutrition for Sport and Exercise.* Aspen Publishers, Gaithersburg, MD.

Berning, J. 1996. "The role of medium chain triglycerides in exercise." *International Journal of Sport Nutrition* 6: 121-133.

Boden, G. , et al. 1996. Effects of vanadyl sulfate on carbohydrate and lipid metabolism in patients with non-insulin dependent diabetes mellitus. *Metabolism* 45: 1130-1135.

Campbell, W., et al. 1997, Effects of chromium picolinate and resistance training on body composition in older men. *Medicine and Science in Sports and Exercise* 29 (5) S277.

Clancy, S., et al. 1994. "Effects of chromium picolinate supplementation on body composition, strength and urinary chromium loss in football players." *International Journal of Sport Nutrition* 4: 142-153.

Clarkson, P. 1991. "Nutritional ergogenic aids: Chromium, exercise, and muscle mass." *International Journal of Sport Nutrition.* 1: 289-293.

Clarkson, P. 1992. "Nutritional ergogenic aids: Carnitine." *International Journal of Sport Nutrition* 2: 185-190.

Davis, J., 1996. Carbohydrates, branched chain amino acids and endurance: The Central Fatigue Hypothesis. *Gatorade Sports Science Exchange* 9 (2).

Decombaz, J., et al. 1993. Effect of l-carnitine on submaximal exercise metabolism after depletion of muscle glycogen. *Medicine and Science in Sports and Exercise* 25: 733-740.

Graham, T., and Spriet, L. 1996. Caffeine and exercise performance. *Gatorade Sports Science Exchange* 9 (1).

Kreider, R., et al. 1998. "Creatine supplement: analysis of ergogenic value, medical safety, and concerns." *Journal of Exercise Physiology-* online 1 (1): 1-11.

Madsen, K., et al. 1996. "Effects of glucose, glucose plus branched-chain amino acids, or placebo on bike performance over 100 km." *Journal of Applied Physiology* 81: 2644-2650.

Nissen, S., et al. 1996. "Effect of leucine metabolite B-hydroxy-B-methylbutarate on muscle metabolism during resistance training exercise." *Journal of Applied Physiology* 81: 2095-2104.

Nutrition Action Healthletter. 1997. DHEA: Not ready for prime time.

Stanko, R., et al. 1990. "Enhanced leg exercise endurance with a high-carbohydrate diet and dihydroxyacetone and pyruvate." *Journal of Applied Physiology* 68: 1651-1656.

Stanko, R., et al. 1990. "Enhancement of arm exercise endurance capacity with dihydrxyacetone and pyruvate." *Journal of Applied Physiology* 68: 119-124.

Volek, J. and Kramer, W. 1996. "Creatine supplementation: It's effect on human and muscular performance and body composition." National

Strength and Conditioning Association, *Journal of Strength and Conditioning Research* 10 (3): 200-210.

Walker, L., et al. 1997. Effect of chromium picolinate on body composition and muscular performance in collegiate wrestlers. *Medicine and Science in Sports and Exercise* 29 (5): S278.

Williams, M. 1998. *The Ergogenics Edge.* Human Kinetics, Champaign, IL.

Williams, M. 1992. Bicarbonate loading. *Gatorade Sports Science Exchange* 4(36).


## CHAPTER 16: SPECIAL NUTRIENT NEEDS

Brooks, G., et al. 1991. "Increased dependence on blood glucose after acclimatization to 4300 meters" *Journal of Applied Physiology* 70 (2): 919-927.

Butterfield, G., et al., "Increased energy intake minimizes weight loss in men at high altitude." *Journal of Applied Physiology* 72 (50: 1741-1748.

Clarkson, P. 1990. Tired Blood: Iron Deficiency in Athletes and Effects of Iron Supplementation. *Gatorade Sports Science Exchange* 3 (28).

Green, H., et al. 1992. "Altitude acclimatization and energy metabolic adaptation in skeletal muscle during exercise." *Journal of Applied Physiology* 73 (6): 2701-2708.

Nieman, D. 1997. "Moderate Exercise Boosts the Immune System." *American College of Sports Medicine's Health and Fitness Journal.* 1 (5).

Worthington-Roberts, B. and Williams, Sue. 1996. *Nutrition and Pregnancy and Lactation, 5th Edition.* Mosby-year Book, Inc., St. Louis, MO.

Warner. S. and Dalsky, G. 1997. Bone mineral density of elite male cyclists. *Medicine and Science in Sports and Exercise* 29 (5): S35.

Williams, M. 1992. Alcohol and sport performance. *Gatorade Sports Science Institute* 4 (40).


## CHAPTER 17: THE VEGETARIAN ATHLETE

Wasserman, D. and Mangels, R. 1995. "Simply Vegan." Vegetarian Resource Group, Baltimore, MD.

# SOURCES FOR FOOD AND NUTRIENT TABLES

United States Department of Agriculture Database.

USDA. *Nutritition Value of American Foods in Common Units*. Agricultural Handbooks No. 456 and No. 8.

Pennington, J. *Food Values of Portions Commonly Used*. Perennial Library — Harper & Row, New York, NY, 1991.

# INDEX

320

# ABOUT THE AUTHOR

Monique Ryan, RD, LD, is founder of Personal Nutrition Designs, a nutrition consulting company based in the Chicago area. Started in 1992, Personal Nutrition Designs provides nutrition assessment, education, and counseling to diverse groups of people with an emphasis on long-term follow-up and support programming. Ryan has more than fifteen years of experience in the specialties of sports nutrition, weight management, injury rehabilitation, maternal nutrition, eating-disorder recovery, and disease prevention and wellness. Her clients are provided with practical cutting edge nutrition information based on current scientific research.

Ryan has been the nutritionist for the Saturn Cycling Team since 1994. She has also been a nutrition consultant for the Volvo-Cannondale mountain-bike team, Rollerblade Racing Team, USA Cycling, and the Trek-Volkswagen and Gary Fisher mountain-bike teams. She spoke about her work with professional athletes at the 1997 "International Sport Nutrition Conference," as well as at the First International Congress On Sports Nutrition in São Paolo, Brazil, in 1998. Ryan has also been quoted frequently in the Chicago Tribune's "Training Table." And she has also lectured extensively on sports nutrition to coaches, trainers, and amateur athletes who train at all levels.

Ryan has also contributed chapters to "Sports Nutrition: A Guide for the Professional Working with Active People." She has appeared on CLTV, FOX TV, and the ABC and CBS news. She is actively involved in the Sports, Cardiovascular, and Wellness Nutritionists (SCAN) practice group and for 12 years had been reviews editor of SCAN's quarterly publication, the PULSE.

Ryan is a registered dietitian and licensed in the state of Illinois. She is a member of the American College of Sports Medicine and is an ACSM Certified Health Fitness Instructor.

# OTHER BOOKS IN THE VELOPRESS ULTIMATE TRAINING SERIES

### *The Female Cyclist: Gearing Up a Level*
*by Gale Bernhardt*

Perfect for the woman cyclist who enjoys cycling for fitness and wants to improve her riding skills and achieve higher goals. Includes special chapter on bike fit, as well as detailed programs for blending cycling and training, women's health and nutrition, and tips for making cycling more comfortable. Great information for male cyclists, too!
6" x 9"
352 pp
Paperback
**P-FEM $16.95**

### *Off-Season Training for Cyclists*
*by Edmund R. Burke, Ph.D.*

Get a jump on the competition with this VeloPress Ultimate Training Series book from Ed Burke. Burke takes you through everything you need to know about winter training — indoor workouts, weight training, cross-training, periodization and more. The best cyclists in the world are doing it; you can't afford not to.
6" x 9"
200 pp
Paperback
**P-OFF $14.95**

### *Weight Training for Cyclists*
*by Eric Schmitz and Ken Doyle*

Written from the premise that optimum cycling performance demands total body strength, this book informs the serious cyclist on how to increase strength with weight training, as cycling alone cannot completely develop the muscle groups used while riding.
6" x 9"
200 pp
Paperback
**P-WTC $14.95**

## COMING SOON

**Sports Psychology for Cyclists,** *by Dr. Saul Miller and Peggy Maass Hill*

## TO ORDER, CALL 800/234-8356
## OR VISIT US ON THE WEB AT WWW.VELOGEAR.COM